Muslim Sects and Divisions

Muslim Sects and Divisions

The Section on Muslim Sects in Kitāb al-Milal wa 'l-Niḥal

by

Muḥammad b. 'Abd al-Karīm Shahrastānī
(d. 1153)

translated by
A. K. Kazi and J. G. Flynn

Kegan Paul International
London, Boston, Melbourne and Henley

First published in 1984
by Kegan Paul International

39 Store Street, London WC1E 7DD, England

9 Park Street, Boston, Mass. 02108, USA

464 St Kilda Road, Melbourne,
Victoria 3004, Australia and

Broadway House, Newtown Road,
Henley-on-Thames, Oxon RG9 1EN, England

Set in IBM Press Roman
and printed in Great Britain by
T. J. Press (Padstow) Ltd, Padstow, Cornwall

Library of Congress Cataloging in Publication Data

Shahrastānī, Muḥammad ibn ʻAbd al-Karīm, 1086?-1153.

Muslim sects and divisions.
Translation of: al-Milal wa-al-niḥal.
Bibliography: p.
Includes index.
1. Islamic sects – Early works to 1800. I. Title.
BP191.S51613 1984 297′.8 83-19995

ISBN 0-7103-0063-8 (U.S.)

Contents

Preface ix

Introduction 1

Translation 8

General Introduction 9

Prelude 31

Part I 33

Introduction 33

Section I Muslims 35

Introduction 37

Chapter 1 The Mu‘tazilites 41

- Introduction 41
- 1 The Wāṣilīya 43
- 2 The Hudhailīya 46
- 3 The Naẓẓāmīya 48
- 4 The Khābiṭīya and the Ḥadathīya 53
- 5 The Bishrīya 56
- 6 The Mu‘ammarīya 57
- 7 The Murdārīya 59

8 The Thumāmīya 61
9 The Hishāmīya 62
10 The Jāḥiẓīya 63
11 The Khayyāṭīya and the Ka'bīya 64
12 The Jubbā'īya and the Bahshamīya 65
Conclusion 70

Chapter 2 The Jabrīya 72

Introduction 72
1 The Jahmīya 72
2 The Najjārīya 74
3 The Ḍirārīya 76

Chapter 3 The Ṣifātīya 77

Introduction 77
1 The Ash'arites 78
2 The Mushabbiha 88
3 The Karrāmites 92
Conclusion 97

Chapter 4 The Khārijites 98

Introduction 98
1 The Early Muḥakkima 99
2 The Azāriqa 102
3 The Najdāt al-'Ādhirīya 104
4 The Baihasīya 106
5 The 'Ajārida 108
(a) The Ṣaltīya 109
(b) The Maimūnīya 109
(c) The Ḥamzīya 110
(d) The Khalafīya 110
(e) The Aṭrāfīya 110
(f) The Shu'aibīya 110
(g) The Ḥāzimīya 111
6 The Tha'āliba 111
(a) The Akhnasīya 112
(b) The Ma'badīya 112
(c) The Rushaidīya 112
(d) The Shaibānīya 112

(e) The Mukramīya 113
(f) The Ma'lūmīya and the Majhūlīya 114
(g) The Bid'īya 114
7 The Ibāḍīya 114
(a) The Ḥafṣīya 116
(b) The Ḥārithīya 116
(c) The Yazīdīya 116
8 The Ṣufrīya Ziyādīya 116
Conclusion 117

Chapter 5 The Murji'ites 119

Introduction 119
1 The Yūnusīya 119
2 The 'Ubaidīya 120
3 The Ghassānīya 120
4 The Thaubānīya 121
5 The Taumanīya 122
6 The Ṣāliḥīya 123
Conclusion 124

Chapter 6 The Shī'ites 125

Introduction 125
1 The Kaisānīya 126
(a) The Mukhtārīya 126
(b) The Hāshimīya 128
(c) The Bayānīya 130
(d) The Rizāmīya 131
2 The Zaidīya 132
(a) The Jārūdīya 135
(b) The Sulaimānīya 136
(c) The Ṣāliḥīya and Batrīya 137
3 The Imāmīya 139
(a) The Wāqifa of the Bāqirīya and the Ja'farīya 142
(b) The Nāwūsīya 143
(c) The Afṭaḥīya 143
(d) The Shumaiṭīya 144
(e) The Ismā'īlīya al-Wāqifa 144
(f) The Mūsawīya and al-Mufaḍḍalīya 144
(g) The Twelvers 145

4 The Ghālīya 149
(a) The Saba'īya 150
(b) The Kāmilīya 151
(c) The 'Albā'īya 151
(d) The Mughīrīya 152
(e) The Manṣūrīya 153
(f) The Khaṭṭābīya 154
(g) The Kayyālīya 156
(h) The Hishāmīya 158
(i) The Nu'mānīya 160
(j) The Yūnusīya 161
(k) The Nuṣairīya and the Isḥāqīya 161
Conclusion 163
5 The Ismā'īlīya 163

Notes 171

Bibliography 177

Glossary 179

Index of personal names 181

Index of sects 188

Index of subjects 191

Preface

When engaged in research in Muslim theology we found that, though there were a number of works in the English language on the subject which quoted original sources, apart from Seelye's translation of Baghdādī's *al-Farq bain al-Firaq*, there were no other translations in English of any other of the main sources for the theological thought of the Muslim sects. The need for further translation was apparent, especially as we found that Seelye's translation, which first appeared in 1910, was in need of revision. Because it was indispensable as a service-book, it appeared to us that there was no more useful work that could be translated than Shahrastani's *Kitāb al-Milal wa 'l-Niḥal.* We accordingly translated that part of *al-Milal* which deals with Muslim sects.

The greater part of our translation first appeared in a number of issues of *Abr-Nahrain*. This translation revised and improved, together with a translation of Shahrastani's long introduction, forms the present work. We express our thanks to E. J. Brill for their courtesy in giving permission to make use of the material already published in *Abr-Nahrain.*

Introduction

The majority of sources on the life of Muḥammad b. ‘Abd al-Karīm Aḥmad al-Shahrastānī,[1] amongst them the *Wafayāt al-a‘yān* of Ibn Khallikān, quote earlier sources that are no longer extant, particularly the *Kitāb al-Dhail* and *al-Taḥbīr* of al-Ḥāfiẓ Abū Sa‘īd b. al-Sam‘ānī, a contemporary of Shahrastānī. The sources all agree that Shahrastānī was born at Shahrastān, a city in the Persian province of Khurāsān, where also he died; but there is no general agreement about the date of his birth. Ibn Khallikān says that according to his own notes on Shahrastānī he was born in AH 469 (AD 1076) and died in AH 548 (AD 1153). He adds, however, that Ibn al-Sam‘ānī says that Shahrastānī himself when asked told him that he was born in AH 479 (AD 1086).[2]

Shahrastānī, according to Ibn Khallikān, was a prominent imām. He excelled in the knowledge of law and was a distinguished theologian. He had also studied *ḥadīth* literature. He taught for a time in the Niẓāmīya at Baghdad, where he spent three years, and where he also gained popularity as a preacher.[3] He wrote a number of books, seventeen of which, apart from the disputed *Mafātīḥ al-asrār wa maṣābīḥ al-abrār fī tafsīr al-Qur'ān* are known to us from various sources; among these is the *Kitāb al-Milal wa 'l-Niḥal*.[4]

Shahrastānī's school of thought

The earliest available source on the life of Shahrastānī, the *Tārīkh ḥukamā' al-Islām* by al-Baihaqī, who like al-Sam‘ānī was Shahrastānī's contemporary and acquaintance, is a work of biographies of Muslim philosophers. Although Shahrastānī is included among them, it is clear that Baihaqī regarded him as a theologian as well as a philosopher.

Baihaqī tells us of a commentary on the Qur'ān on which Shahrastānī was engaged in writing, and in which he interpreted the Qur'ānic verses in the light of philosophy as well as the *sharī'a*.[5] Much to Shahrastānī's annoyance it was an enterprise of which Baihaqī disapproved on the grounds that ḥadīth and not philosophy can explain the Qur'ān. It appears that Baihaqī has some rather heated discussions with Shahrastānī, and pointed out that no one had combined *sharī'a* and philosophy better than al-Ghazālī.[6]

Baihaqī in fact criticized Shahrastānī from a traditionalist point of view; but, nevertheless, he recognized him both as a philosopher and a theologian. Indeed as a philosopher his merits are considerable. Guillaume in his introduction to his edition of Shahrastānī's *Kitāb Nihāyat al-Iqdām* regards him as 'the last great philosopher of Islam before Averroes':[7] an Ash'arite, it is true, though one who 'gave a general, but by no means blind allegiance to the Ash'arite school.'[8]

Serious doubts, however, were raised in the past, and have been more recently revived, as to whether Shahrastānī was in reality an Ash'arite. Al-Subkī, for example, in his *Ṭabaqāt*, says that, according to Dhahabī (AH 673/AD 1274-AH 748/AD 1348) in his *History*, al-Sam'ānī stated that Shahrastānī was suspected of supporting Ismā'īlī views. Nothing of this kind, he tells us, is said by Sam'ānī in his *Dhail*, though in his *Taḥbīr* he accuses Shahrastānī of heresy and of extreme Shī'ite tendencies. Subkī finds the accusation difficult to believe, as there is nothing in Shahrastānī's writings to support it, and thinks that as Sam'ānī does not mention it in his *Dhail* it was added to the *Taḥbīr* by someone else. But even if this were so the difficulty would still remain; for Subkī himself quotes 'the author of *al-Kāfī*', as saying, 'But for the confusion noticeable in his beliefs and his leanings towards the heretics, Shahrastānī would be the Imām in Islām.'[9]

It is possible that neither Sam'ānī nor the author of *al-Kāfī* wished to say more than that Shahrastānī was sympathetic to the Ismā'īlī faction; for *mayl*, which is perhaps the key word in their statements, may be understood in this way. Subkī at all events, regardless of the allegations made against Shahrastānī, includes him among the Shāfi'ite scholars. Al-Ṣafadī too in *Al-Wāfī* says that Shahrastānī having been a disciple of Shāfi'ite-Ash'arite teachers, himself became a theologian of the Ash'arite (Sunnite) school, and was an outstanding imām and *faqīh*.[10] As time passed it seems that Shahrastānī's sunnism was accepted without question. Thus the text of *Kitāb Nihāyat al-Iqdām fī 'ilm al-kalām*, edited by A. Guillaume, is presented by the copyist as الصدق مشائخ اهل السنة تاج الدين برهان الحق ترجمان

عـضـد الشـريـعـة من تـصـنيف امام الائـمة سـيد (a work of the Imām of the Imāms, Prince of the Sunnite *Shaikhs*, the Crown of Religion, the Proof of Certainty, Spokesman of Truth and Pillar of Sharī'a).

There is nothing moreover in the text of the two published works of Shahrastānī which would suggest Ismā'īlī tendencies, but rather the contrary. The phrase 'the view of our Shaikh al-Ash'arī' occurs frequently in the *Kitāb al-Iqdām*,[11] a work obviously in defence of Ash'arite theology. Even in the *Kitāb al-Milal*, where he attempts to be fair to all sects, his sympathies for the orthodox are unmistakeable.[12] Moreover in the *Milal* Shahrastānī clearly dissociates himself from the Shī'ites. Thus in his exposition of Ismā'īlīya beliefs he gives a translation in summary form of the 'new teaching'[13] as it appears in a treatise by Ḥasan al-Ṣabbāḥ, and says, 'We shall reproduce in Arabic what he has written in Persian, but the translator must not be censured.'[14] At the conclusion of the chapter he remarks, 'I have had many a debate with these people but they only say, "Is it you we need? Is it you we must listen to? Is it from you we must learn?"' He adds that he would often for the sake of argument grant that there was need, as they claimed, for a teacher, but would ask in vain where the teacher was and what he would teach. 'You have in reality,' he told them at last, 'closed the gate of knowledge, and opened instead the door of unquestioning submission and blind obedience.'[15]

From all this it would appear that Shahrastānī's orthodoxy was beyond doubt, but that, in the prevailing atmosphere of his day, his frequent contact and discussions with the Ismā'īlī *du'āt* (missionaries) aroused suspicion as to his orthodoxy.

The question of Shahrastānī's orthodoxy has today, however, once again been raised. In the library of the Iran National Assembly there is a manuscript of a *tafsīr* work, called *Mafātīḥ al-asrār wa maṣābīḥ al-abrār*, which bears Shahrastānī's name with the title 'Chief Missionary', and which begins with the famous opening of the *Kitāb al-Milal wa'l-Niḥal* cited almost entirely: 'Praise be to God that is due from all the grateful, a fullness of praise for all his favours; a praise that is abundant, sincere and blessed.'[16] None of the sources on Shahrastānī's biography mentions this work, though, as has been said, al-Baihaqī says that Shahrastānī was engaged in writing a *tafsīr*.

Dr Sayyid Nā'īnī in his introduction to the Persian translation of this work has no doubt that it is the *tafsīr* of which al-Baihaqī speaks. As the *tafsīr* contains a considerable amount of Shī'ite esoteric interpretation, Dr Sayyid Nā'īnī suggests that living quietly in his home town in the last years of his life, and feeling that there was now nothing to prevent him revealing his real thoughts and beliefs, Shahrastānī in this *tafsīr* expressed his true views.[17] No convincing reasons, however, are given by Dr Nā'īnī for this opinion; and in view of what has already been said above of Shahrastānī's published and unpublished works, it is more probable that the *tafsīr* is the work of some unknown author who attributed it to Shahrastānī, and cited the opening of the *Kitāb al-Milal* in an attempt to show that it was by the same author.

Sources of *Kitāb al-Milal wa'l-Niḥal*

Of the *Kitāb al-Milal* Professor A. J. Arberry says, 'It is little more than a farrago of quotations from older writers, loosely arranged and inconsequently strung together without the slightest acknowledgment.'[18] Though this harsh judgment is not justified, it is nevertheless true that, with the exception of al-Ka'bī whose name occurs quite frequently, Shahrastānī rarely mentions his sources. Ka'bī, whose full name as given in the *Ṭabaqāt al-Mu'tazila* of al-Murtaḍā was Abu 'l-Qāsim 'Abdullāh b. Maḥmūd al-Ka'bī, (d. AH 319/AD 931)[19] was a Mu'tazilite, and is mentioned at the very beginning of *al-Farq bain al-Firaq* of al-Baghdādī. He is the author of a work on sects known as the 'Maqālāt',[20] which seems to have been a commonly used source of information on the sects, particularly on the Mu'tazila. Unfortunately this work has not survived, and it is not possible to tell to what extent Shahrastānī used it directly as a source. However, as Ka'bī's name occurs far more often in the *Kitāb al-Milal* than any other author, it is likely that his *Maqālāt* was in fact extensively used by Shahrastānī.

As Shahrastānī is a professed Ash'arite one would naturally expect that he would consult Ash'ari's *Maqālāt al-Islāmīyīn*. In his notes to his edition of the text of the *Maqālāt al-Islāmīyīn*, Ritter shows by cross-references that not only Shahrastānī but also Baghdādī made considerable use of it as a source.[21] A close examination of the texts, however, shows that Shahrastānī's borrowing from the *Maqālāt* was greater on the Shī'ites and the Khārijites than on other sects.

Apart from the section on the Ismā'īlīya, where he seems to be quite independent, Shahrastānī draws heavily on the *Maqālāt* of Ash'arī in his exposition of Shī'ite views. Word by word quotation is frequent. Nevertheless he makes use of other sources at the same time, and often differs considerably from Ash'arī. The difference is most noticeable in the arrangement of the material. Ash'arī, for example, begins with the

Ghulāt (Extremists), whereas for Shahrastānī these form the fourth group.[22] The sub-sects also do not fully correspond. Thus Ash'arī includes the Bayānīya amongst the Ghulāt, but Shahrastānī on the other hand places them among the Kaisānīya. Shahrastānī, moreover, obviously making use of another source, gives a different and fuller account of them. Yet, though classifying them as Kaisanīya, he regards them as also being Ghulāt; for he says of Bayān, the leader of the sect, that 'He was an extremist who believed in the divinity of 'Alī.'[23]

Occasionally in his borrowing Shahrastānī alters Ash'arī's expression so as to give a slight change of meaning. Sometimes indeed the change of meaning is significant. Thus, for example, Ash'arī says, 'The Mufaḍḍalīya not only believed in the divinity of Ja'far but also claimed prophethood and apostleship for him.' Shahrastānī, on the other hand, says, 'He (Mufaḍḍal) believed in the Lordship of Ja'far, but not in his prophethood and apostleship.'[24] Often, however, as we have said, the exact wording of Ash'arī is reproduced. Shahrastānī's account, for example, of the Mughīrīya (except for the introduction which is not found in the *Maqālāt*, and the conclusion of the *Maqālāt* which does not appear in the *Kitāb al-Milal*), is in entire verbal agreement with that of Ash'arī. There is much verbal similarity, too, with the *Maqālāt* in Shahrastānī's accounts of the Manṣūrīya and the Khaṭṭābīya.

The same can also be said of the section on the Khārijites. Thus apart from minor variations whole passages on the Yazīdīya and the Baihasīya are literal quotations from the *Maqālāt* of al-Ash'arī.

An actual Shī'ite source which Shahrastānī does not appear to have used is the *Kitāb al-Maqālāt wa 'l-firaq* by Sa'd b. 'Abdullāh al-Ash'arī al-Qummī. There is no disagreement, however, between his account of the Shī'ites and that of al-Qummī, though on the extremist groups al-Qummī is, if anything, rather more severe than Shahrastānī.

In his treatment of the Mu'tazila Shahrastānī, in addition to Ka'bī, sometimes cites the *Faḍīḥa al-Mu'tazila* of Ibn al-Rāwandī. This is an anti-Mu'tazilite work, which, like the *Maqālāt* of al-Ka'bī, has not survived. Quotations from it, however, are found in the *Kitāb al-Intiṣār wa 'l-radd 'alā Ibn al-Rāwandī* by Abu 'l-Ḥusain al-Khayyāṭ al-Mu'tazilī, and from these it is possible to verify some direct quotations by Shahrastānī from Ibn al-Rāwandī, including some not acknowledged by him. Thus, for example, the statement, 'God created all existing things at one time', attributed to al-Naẓẓām, appears to be quoted directly from Ibn al-Rāwandī without acknowledgment; for al-Khayyāṭ criticizes Ibn al-Rāwandī for reporting it, though untrue, of al-Naẓẓām.[25] Similarly the section on the Murdārīya has a statement which is found attributed by al-Khayyāṭ to Ibn al-Rāwandī and criticized by him.[26] It is probable, indeed, that, while use is possibly made also of al-Ka'bī, the whole section on the Murdārīya is a reconstruction of Ibn al-Rāwandī.

The other major sources of the Mu'tazila are *al-Farq bain al-firaq* of Baghdādī and *al-Tabṣīr fī 'l-dīn wa tamyīz al-firqa al-nājiya* of al-Isfarā'īnī. It is difficult to tell the full extent to which they are used; for as both Baghdādī and Isfarā'īnī occasionally acknowledge al-Ka'bī and Ibn al-Rāwandī as sources, one cannot always be sure whether Shahrastānī in quoting these latter is doing so directly, or indirectly through Baghdādī and Isfarā'īnī.

From both Baghdādī and Isfarā'īnī there is a considerable amount of word by word quotation, especially from Isfarā'īnī; as, for example, the following comment on Wāṣil: 'These are the views of Wāṣil, the head of the Mu'tazila, about the leading Companions and the Imāms of the Family.'[27] Often too the same or similar passage in Shahrastānī is found in both Baghdādī and Isfarā'īnī; but it is likely that in these instances Shahrasānī is following Isfarā'īnī, who in turn is quoting from Baghdādī or paraphrasing him.

An interesting example of a similarity but with a difference between Baghdādī and Shahrastānī is their account of the genesis of Muslim sects. Baghdādī tells us that the first difference in the Muslim community was the one that occurred at Muḥammad's death, when 'Umar protested that Muḥammad had not died.[28] This was followed by the dispute on Muḥammad's place of burial. Afterwards came the disputes on the imāmate, on Fidak, and on the *zakāt*. Shahrastānī in his introduction, though he mentions all these disputes given by Baghdādī, says that the first one was the dispute of the hypocrites with the Prophet.[29]

Shahrastānī differs also from Baghdādī in his treatment of the Khābiṭīya and Ḥadathīya. These sects, which al-Khayyāṭ does not even mention, are not included among the Mu'tazila sub-sects by Baghdādī, and though he gives an exposition of their views he does not regard them as belonging to the fold of Islam.[30] Isfarā'īnī, on the other hand, as does Shahrastānī, treats them as Mu'tazila. In the first part of his account of them Shahrastānī follows Isfarā'īnī, but the last part is based on Baghdādī.

There is, however, as much as a third of that part of the *Kitāb al-Milal* which treats of the sects, for which it was not possible to trace sources. Thus, for instance, no source could be found for Naẓẓām's well-known illustration of his theory of leaps with the example of ropes.[31]

Generally speaking, Shahrastānī reports the views of the sects without elaboration and without comments. Sometimes, however, he offers a brief criticism. Thus, for example, he criticizes Naẓẓām's theory of leaps by remarking that the difference between walking and leaping amounts to no more than a difference between corresponding lengths of time.[32] He also finds fault with Mu'ammar's idea that *ḥudūth* (occurrence) and *'adam* (non-existence) are accidents, and that God only created bodies, on the grounds that it would follow that God did not act at all.[33] Again of Abu 'l-Hudhail's theory of rest to avoid infinity he simply says that the problem still remains.[34]

Shahrastānī's expression in *al-Milal wa 'l-Nihal* is at times very difficult and obscure, due mainly to his compressing a great amount of material in short statements. We have succeeded in 'unlocking the mysteries' in most cases in our translation of the book. It is undoubtedly a major work in medieval Arabic literature on religions and heresies, better organized in its material than most of the other works. One can accept without difficulty al-Subkī's judgment on *Kitāb al-Milal wa 'l-Niḥal*: 'It is in my view the best book in this field.'[35]

It is with great pleasure, therefore, that we present our rendition in English of the major portion of Part 1 of the work, which deals with Muslims, their sects and schools of thought. The Arabic text from which the translation was made is that edited by Muḥammad b. Fatḥullāh Badrān.[36] Manuscripts in the library of 'Ārif Ḥikmat in Medīna were also consulted; but they were not notably different from Badrān's text, and of no help in solving the difficulties of certain passages.

Translation

Kitāb al-Milal wa 'l-Nihal

Praise be to God that is due from all the grateful, a fullness of praise for all his favours: a praise that is abundant, sincere and blessed. May the blessing of God be upon Muḥammad, the chosen one, the apostle of mercy and the seal of the prophets; and upon his descendants who are good and pure: a blessing lasting to the day of judgment, like the blessing bestowed upon Abraham and his descendants. Indeed, God is most worthy to be praised and glorified.

When God enabled me to study the religious beliefs of different peoples (both those belonging to various religions and communities, as well as those following other beliefs and creeds), to investigate also their sources and to seek out both the familiar and the unfamiliar, I decided to gather all this information into a brief compendium containing all the religious beliefs and creeds of different peoples, so as to provide a lesson to one who can reflect and a means of reflection for one who can draw a lesson.

Before proceeding with my main purpose it will be necessary for me to write five introductory chapters. The aim of the first will be to give an enumeration of the different divisions of mankind; of the second to specify the principles on which the numbering of Islamic sects is based; of the third to explain the first questioning that arose in the universe: who caused it and in whom it manifested itself; of the fourth to explain the first questioning that arose in the Muslim community: how it arose, who caused it and in whom it manifested itself; of the fifth to explain the reason which made it necessary to arrange this book according to a mathematical system.

General Introduction

1 General explanation of divisions of mankind

Some divide mankind according to seven regions, ascribing to the inhabitants of each region their natures and psychological dispositions, as indicated by their different colours and languages. Others make a division according to four zonal regions east, west, south and north, describing each region by its particular characteristics, namely, by its different natures and laws. Others, again, base their division on peoples. According to them, the major peoples are four: Arabs, Persians, Greeks and Indians. These people they divide into two groups. Thus they say that the Arabs and Indians so closely resemble one another as almost to share the one outlook. Both seek to determine the particular properties of things, to look for the laws of essences and ultimate realities, and to pursue spiritual things. The Greeks and Persians, too, so closely resemble one another as almost to share the one outlook. They seek to determine the nature of things, to look for their qualitative and quantitative properties, and to pursue material things.

Others divide men according to their ideas and beliefs. That also is what we intend to do in this book. The first and most correct division is into those who belong to certain religions and religious communities, and those who follow other beliefs and creeds. In general those who follow religions are: Magians, Jews, Christians and Muslims. Those following other beliefs and creeds are: philosophers, atheists, Sabaeans, worshippers of stars and idols, and Brahmins. Each in turn is divided into various groups. Those following philosophical and other beliefs do not appear to be restricted in number. However the sects following a religion are definite in number, as tradition tells us, the Magians being divided into seventy sects, the Jews into seventy-one, the Christians into seventy-two and the Muslims into seventy-three. Salvation belongs to only one sect. The reason is that where there are two opposite propositions the truth is in one only. Where there are contradictory propositions wholly opposed to one another, one is necessarily true and the other necessarily false. The truth, therefore, is in one and not in the other. It is impossible to hold of two disputants, who are wholly in conflict on rational principles, that both are right and in possession of the truth. Since the truth in every rational question is one, then the truth in all questions can be found in one sect alone. This we know on the authority of revelation. The Qur'ān tells us in the words of God: 'Of those we created are a nation who guide by the truth and by it act with justice.'[1]

The Prophet also said, 'My community will be divided into seventy-three sects but only one of these will be saved, the others will perish.' When asked which was the one that would attain salvation he replied, 'Those who follow the *sunna* and the congregation.' He was further asked, 'What is the *sunna* and the congregation?' He replied, 'That which I and my companions practice.' The Prophet is also reported to have said, 'In my community there will always be some who till the day of judgment will possess the truth.' Again, he said, 'My community will never agree on an error.'

2 Specification of the principles on which the division of Islamic sects is based

Writers on Islamic sects have different ways of dividing them without following any rule based on a principle or a text, nor any definite and clearly manifested method. Therefore I have not found any two authors in agreement on a system by which the sects are divided.

It is commonly known and accepted that not every one differing from another in holding certain views on one question or another is to be regarded as the founder of a doctrine. The doctrines otherwise could hardly be numbered; for anyone who was alone in holding certain views on, for example, the question of substances, would have to be included among the founders of doctrines. There must, therefore, be some principle determining which questions are basic and fundamental, differences in which are sectarian differences; one proposing such differences, therefore, must be regarded as the founder of a doctrine. Nevertheless, I have not found any of the writers on doctrines attempting to establish such a principle; they simply introduce the views of the different sects of the community in a haphazard manner as they happen to find them, their treatment not being based on any firm rule or fixed principle. Accordingly, doing as well as I could, I restricted the differences to four fundamental points or major principles.

The first fundamental point concerns the attributes and the unity of God in relation to the attributes. This point includes the question of the existence of eternal attributes, which are affirmed by some and denied by others. It also involves an exposition of the essential attributes and attributes of action; of what is obligatory on God; of what is possible for him and what is impossible. There is a difference in these questions between the Ash'arites, the Karrāmites, the Mujassima and the Mu'tazilites.

The second fundamental point is concerned with *qadar* and justice. This includes such questions as divine decree and predestination, predetermination and acquisition, the willing of good and evil, that which is within one's power and that which is within one's knowledge. On all these there are varying opinions, as, for example, between the Qadarites, Najjārites, Jabrites, Ash'arites and Karrāmites.

The third fundamental point concerns 'promise and warning', names and judgments, *al-asmā' wa 'l-aḥkām*. It includes such questions as *īmān* (faith), repentance, warning, postponement, 'declaring someone an unbeliever' and 'leading astray'. On all these questions, too, some say one thing, some say another, as, for example, the Murji'ites, the Wa'īdīya, the Mu'tazilites, the Ash'arites and the Karrāmites.

The fourth fundamental point concerns relevation and reason, apostleship and imāmate. It includes such questions as the goodness of the good and the evil of the evil; [God's doing of] the good or the best; grace; sinlessness in prophets; the conditions required for the imāmate: whether it is based on appointment by decree, as some hold, or on the agreement of the community, as others maintain; the manner of the transmission of the imāmate according to those who believe in imāmate by decree, or its determination according to those believing in agreement. In this question there is a difference between the Shī'a, the Khawārij, the Mu'tazila, the Karrāmites and the Ash'arites.

Whenever one of the leading individuals of the community was found holding an independent viewpoint on one of these fundamental aspects, we considered his view as forming a school of thought, and his followers as constituting a sect. If, however, we found someone holding an independent view on a secondary question we did not consider his view as forming a school of thought, nor his followers as constituting a sect; instead, we included him in one or other of the schools to which his views most corresponded, giving his views the status of a branch rather than a school on its own. In this way the schools have not become too many in number.

When fundamental points which were questions of dispute were thus determined, the basic divisions of Islamic sects were clearly seen; and the major sects, after some of the others were assimilated to them, were reduced to four. These principal Islamic sects are: the Qadarites, the Ṣifātīya, the Khawārij and the Shī'a. These four become intermingled, and at the same time various sub-sects are derived from each, numbering in all seventy-three.

Writers on sects follow two different methods of procedure. The first is to adopt questions as headings, and under each question give the views of all the groups and sects. The second is to use the names of individuals and founders of sects as headings, and to give their views on every question. This brief compendium is arranged according to the second method; for we have found that this method is more accurate, and also more in accord with the principles given in our chapter on calculations.

I impose upon myself the obligation of giving the views of each sect as I find them in their works without favour or prejudice, without declaring which are correct and which are incorrect, which are true and which are false; though, indeed, the glimpses of the truth and the odour of lies will not remain undetected by minds versed in intellectual matters. And God will be our help.

3 An Explanation of the first doubt that arose in the world: from whom it first arose and in whom it was finally manifested

The first doubt that arose in the world was the doubt of Iblīs: may the curse of God be on him! Its source was his assumption of independence in opposition to a clear instruction; his preference for his own inclination over a command; his pride in the matter out of which he was created, that is, fire, in contrast to the matter out of which Adam was created, that is, dust. From this doubt seven other doubts arose which spread amongst men and permeated their thinking till they became sources of erroneous and false beliefs. These doubts are found mentioned in commentaries on the four gospels, namely, Luke, Mark, John and Matthew; they are also mentioned in the Torah in various places in the form of dialogues between Iblīs and the angels after the command given him to make obeisance, and his refusal to do so.

Iblīs is reported to have said:

> I admit that God is my God and the God of creation, knowing and powerful; that his power and will cannot be questioned, and that whenever he wills a thing he says to it 'Be,' and it becomes. I also admit that he is wise, but concerning his wisdom a number of questions can be raised.

The angels asked, 'What are these questions and how many are they?' Iblīs replied: 'Seven.' He continued:

> The first question is, that as God knew before he created me what I would do and how I would act, why did he create me? And what is his wisdom in creating me?
>
> Secondly, if he created me in accordance with his will and pleasure, why did he command me to know and obey him? Moreover, since he does not derive any benefit from obedience, nor is he harmed by disobedience, what is the wisdom in this command?
>
> Thirdly, when he created me and commanded me to acknowledge and obey him, I adhered to his command, and acknowledged and obeyed him. Why, then, did he command me to obey Adam and make obeisance to him? What is his wisdom in this particular command, since it does not add to my knowledge of him, nor increase my obedience to him?
>
> Fourthly, when he created me and not only commanded me in general, but gave me also this particular command, then, when I did not make obeisance to Adam, why did he curse me and cast me out of paradise? What is the wisdom in this? I committed no other evil than saying, 'I shall make obeisance only to you.'
>
> Fifthly, when he created me and gave me both a general and a particular command, and I did not obey him, he cursed me and drove me away. Why, then, did he give me access to Adam, so that I entered paradise a second time and deceived him by my evil suggestion? Adam consequently ate of the forbidden tree, and God expelled him from paradise with me. What is the wisdom in this? Had he prevented me from entering paradise, Adam would have eluded me and would have been there for ever.
>
> Sixthly, after God had created me and given me both a general and a particular command; after he had cursed me and given me re-entrance to paradise, where a dispute took place between me and Adam, why did he give me power over his descendants in such a way that I could see them but they could not see me? Why were my

> evil suggestions able to influence them, but they had no power or influence of any kind over me? What is the wisdom in this? If God had created them and given them their nature with no one seeking to make them deviate from it, they would have lived pure, attentive and submissive. This would have been more fitting for them and more in harmony with wisdom.
>
> Seventhly, I admit all this, namely, that God created me, that he gave me both a general and a particular command, and that when I did not obey him he cursed me and expelled me from paradise; also, that when I wanted to re-enter paradise he allowed me to do so and gave me access to it; that when I did the thing I did he cast me out but gave me power over mankind. Why, then, after that, when I asked him to give me respite, did he give me respite? I said to God, 'My Lord, respite me till the day they shall be raised.' He said, 'Thou art among the ones that are respited unto the day of a known time.'[2]
>
> What is the wisdom in this? If he had destroyed me at that time, Adam and the whole of mankind would have been beyond my power, and there would have been no evil in the world. Is not the enduring of the world in right order better than the world mixed with evil?

Iblīs then added: 'So this is my argument for what I maintain on each question.'

The commentator of the Gospel says that God told the angels to say to Iblīs:

> Your first admission that I am your God and the God of creation was not truthful and sincere, for if you had indeed meant that I am the Lord of the universe you would not have asked the question why; for I am God, and there is no God but Me. I am not to be questioned as to what I do, but men are questioned as to what they do.

What I have related is found in the Torah and also in [the commentaries on] the New Testament in the way that I have described them. I have often thought and said that it is quite clear that every doubt entertained by the descendants of Adam was due to the misleading action of the accursed devil and his evil suggestions,and had developed from his doubts. As, however, his doubts are confined to seven, the major innovations and errors can also be reduced to seven. Indeed, the doubts of the heretical cannot go beyond these doubts, even though they are differently expressed and follow different paths; for these doubts are like the seeds of different kinds of errors that are found, and they can all be summed up in non-acceptance of the command after the admission of the truth, and in following personal inclination as opposed to clear instruction.

All those who disputed with Noaḥ, Hūd, Ṣāliḥ, Abraham, Lot, Sbu'aib, Moses, Jesus and Muḥammad, all followed the same pattern as the first accursed one in the manifestation of his doubt. These disputations may be summarized as a refusal to be subject to command and a refusal to accept all the lawgivers and the laws; for there is no difference between their saying, 'Is a mortal man going to show us the path?'[3] and Iblīs saying, 'Shall I make obeisance to one you have created of clay?'[4] Accordingly, the starting-point of dispute and the cause of differences is that mentioned in the word of God: 'And naught prevented men from believing when the guidance came to them, but that they said, "Has God sent forth a mortal as Messenger?"'[5] God has thus made it clear that the obstacle to faith is this idea alone.

As we have been told in the Qur'ān, when man's predecessor was asked by God, 'What prevented thee to bow thyself, when I commanded thee' He replied, 'I am better than he; Thou didst create me of fire, and him Thou didst create of clay.'[6] In the same way his successor said, 'I am better than this man who is contemptible.'[7]

Similarly, if we consider the words of their predecessors we will find them corresponding to the words of those who came after: 'So spoke those before them as these men say; their hearts are much alike.'[8] So they refused to believe what the earlier ones had rejected.

The first accursed one, then, when he imposed a judgment of reason on one who cannot be judged by reason, had either to apply the law of the Creator to the created being, or the law of the created being to the Creator. The first errs by excess, the second by default. From the first error arose the following sects: the Incarnationists, the Transmigrationists, the Anthropomorphists (Mushabbiha), and the Extremists among the Shī'a who went so far as to give a man the attributes of God. From the second error arose the schools of Qadarites, Jabrites and Mujassima who were remiss in their description of God, and bestowed upon him the attributes of created beings. The Mu'tazilites are anthropomorphists in the matter of deeds, and the Mushabbiha are incarnationists in the matter of attributes. Each of them has a one-eyed point of view, because whoever says, 'What befits us befits God, and what does not befit us does not befit God,' has made the Creator like to the created; and whoever says, 'God can be described in the same terms in which man is described', or vice versa, has strayed from the path of truth.

The root of the Qadarite doctrine is in seeking the reason for everything. This in turn is rooted in the first accursed one demanding, firstly, the reason for creation; secondly, the wisdom of command; and, thirdly, the benefit of the command to make obeisance to Adam. From this root the sect of the Khārijites developed, because there is no difference between their saying. 'There is no judgment but that of God, and we do not appoint men as judges,' and the saying of the devil, 'I shall not make obeisance except to you. Should I make obeisance to a mortal you created from clay?'[9]

Indeed, to go from the medium to either extreme is to be condemned. The Mu'tazilites went to extremes on the question of the unity of God, and fell into *ta'ṭīl* by denying God's attributes. The Mushabbiha, on the other hand, fell short and ascribed to God bodily attributes. The Rāfiḍites went into extremes in the matter of the prophethood and the imāmate, and arrived at the doctrine of incarnation. The Khawārij fell short when they refused to allow men to be appointed as judges.

If you look, you will see that all these errors spring from the errors of the first accursed one. These first errors were the origins and the later ones their manifestations. The Qur'ān refers to this in the words of God: 'Follow not the steps of Satan; he is a manifest foe to you.'[10]

The Prophet compared each of the misguided sects of his community with a misguided people of former times. Thus he said, 'The Qadarites are the Magians of this community, the Mushabbiha the Jews of the community, and the Rāfiḍites its Christians.' Speaking in general terms he said, 'You will walk along the path of former peoples in exactly the same way, so much so that if they have entered the hole of a lizard you will enter it too.'

4 An explanation of the first error that arose in the Muslim community: how it arose, in whom it arose, and in whom it was manifested

We have shown that the errors that arose in later times are precisely the same errors which occurred in the very beginning. In the same way we can show that, during the epoch of every prophet and founder of a community or a religion, the errors in his community at the end of the epoch arose from the errors of his enemies at the beginning of his epoch, that is, from infidels and unbelievers, most of whom were hypocrites. All this may be concealed from us with respect to former peoples because of the long period of time that has passed; but with respect to this community it is no secret that its errors arose from the errors of hypocrites at the time of the Prophet, who did not accept his judgment in what he commanded or forbade, and began to reason on their own accord where there was no scope for reasoning, asked questions in fields in which it was forbidden to enter or enquire, and disputed baselessly where dispute was not permitted. Consider [for example] the tradition about Dhu 'l-Khuwaiṣira al-Tamīmī when he said, 'Do justice, O Muḥammad, for you have failed to do justice.' Whereupon Muḥammad replied, 'If I do not do justice who will?' But the accursed man reiterated what he had said, and went on, 'This is a distribution in which the thought of God was not present.' This was a clear rebellion against the Prophet. If then a person who has criticized a true imām becomes a Khārijite, how much more fitting it is that one who has criticized the prophet should be called a Khārijite? Is not this criticism equivalent to holding a thing good or evil on the basis of reason, and of judging according to one's own ideas in opposition to a clear command? Is it not a contemptuous rejection of a command on the basis of some form of analogy? The Prophet at last said, 'Out of the loins of this man a people will come forth who will flee from religion as an arrow flies from the bow.'

Consider also the story of another group of hypocrites in the battle of Uḥud, who asked, 'Do we have any say in the matter?'[11] Or their words, 'If they had been with us they would not have died nor been killed.'[12] Is not this a clear expression of belief in man's power? Or consider another group of polytheists who said, 'Had God wished we would have worshipped no other beside God.'[13] Or the words of another group who said, 'Shall we give food to those to whom God would have given to eat had he wished?'[14] Is not this a clear expression of the idea of predeterminism? Consider, too, the story of another group who disputed concerning God himself, delving into the mysteries of his majesty and his actions, till God forbade them to do so, and filled their hearts with fear by the words: 'He looses the thunderbolts and smites with them whomsoever he will; yet they dispute about God, who is mighty in power.'[15]

This is what happened in the lifetime of the Prophet when he was strong, powerful and in good health. The hypocrites at the time acted deceitfully, outwardly manifesting *islām* and hiding their unbelief. Their hypocrisy, however, showed itself in their constant criticism of whatever Muḥammad did or did not do. These criticisms were like seeds from which grew a crop of errors.

As for the differences that arose among the Companions at the time of the Prophet's sickness and after his death, these are said to have been differences of personal judgment, *ikhtilāfāt ijtihādīya*, and their aim was simply to maintain the rites of the *sharī'a* and to establish religious practices.

The first dispute that took place during the Prophet's sickness, according to what the Imām Abū 'Abdullāh Muḥammad b. Ismā'īl al-Bukhārī relates on the authority of 'Abdullāh b. 'Abbās, is as follows. When the last sickness of the Prophet became acute, he said, 'Bring me an inkpot and writing material; I shall write something for you so that you will not be led astray after my departure.' 'Umar said, 'The Prophet has been overcome by pain, God's book is sufficient for us.' A noisy argument arose among those gathered; whereupon the Prophet said, 'Go away; there should be no quarrelling in my presence.' Ibn 'Abbās says, 'What a tragedy which prevented us from having some writing of the Prophet!' The second dispute during his sickness occurred in the following way. The Prophet said, 'Prepare the army of Usāma; cursed be the one who fails to join it!' Some said that they must carry out his command, especially as Usāma had already left the city. Others, however, said, 'The Prophet's sickness has become very serious; we cannot bear parting with him while he is in this condition. So we shall wait and see what happens.'

I have referred to these two disputes because critics might regard them as differences which have affected the faith. This, however, is not so. Their aim was simply to uphold religious principles at a time when hearts were unsettled, and to cool down the heat of strife which is very powerful at a time of change.

The third dispute was at the Prophet's death, when 'Umar said, 'If anyone says that Muḥammad has died I shall kill him with this sword of mine. He has been taken up to heaven as Jesus was.' Abū Bakr b. Abū Quḥāfa, however, said, 'Whoever worshipped Muḥammad, Muḥammad is dead; whoever worshipped the God of Muḥammad, the God of Muḥammad is living; he has not died and shall not die.' He then recited the words of God:

> Muḥammad is naught but a Messenger; Messengers have passed away before him. Why, if he should die or is slain, will you turn about on your heels? If any man should turn about on his heels, he will not harm God in any way; and God will recompense the thankful.[16]

People then accepted what Abū Bakr was saying, and 'Umar said, 'It is as though I had never heard this verse till Abū Bakr read it.'

The fourth dispute concerned the place of the Prophet's burial. The emigrés from Mecca wanted to take him back to Mecca, for this was where he grew up, this was where his people dwelt, and this was where he also stayed. The Anṣār of Medīna wanted to bury him in Medīna, because that was where he migrated and where he received help. Some wanted to take him to Jerusalem, because that was the burial place of the prophets, and it was from there that his ascension to heaven took place. Finally, all agreed to bury him in Medīna when the saying of the Prophet was remembered that the prophets are buried where they die.

The fifth dispute arose over the imāmate. The greatest dispute, indeed, in the community has been that over the imāmate; for no sword has ever been drawn in Islam on a religious question as it has been drawn at all times on the question of the imāmate. It was easily resolved by the help of God in the early days when a difference arose about it between the emigrés and the Anṣār. The Anṣār said, 'There should be one *amīr* chosen from amongst us and one from amongst you,' and unanimously nominated their chief Sa'd b. 'Ubāda al-Anṣārī. Abū Bakr and 'Umar, however, corrected this immediately by going together to the meeting-place of Banū Sā'ida. 'Umar says:

> On our way I was preparing a speech in my mind. When we reached the meeting-place I attempted to speak; but Abū Bakr said, 'Stop, 'Umar!' He then praised God, and spoke all that I was preparing in my mind as though he was reporting the unseen. Then before the Anṣār could enter into discussion, I stretched out my hands to him and swore allegiance to him. Everyone else did likewise and the discord ended. This episode of the swearing of allegiance to Abū Bakr occurred unexpectedly, and God saved Muslims from its evil outcome. If anyone should do the same thing again let him be put to death. Any man who swears allegiance to another without consultation with other Muslims commits an act of deception; both of them must be put to death.

The Anṣār surrendered their demands only because Abū Bakr reported the Prophet as saying that the imāms are to be from the Quraish.

That is what occurred in the meeting-place. When Abū Bakr returned to the mosque, people crowded on him and readily swore allegiance to him, with the exception of some of the Banū Hashim and of Abū Sufyān of the Umayyads. 'Alī b. Abū Ṭālib, however, was occupied in carrying out what the Prophet had ordered him to do, that is, to prepare him for burial, perform the burial itself, and remain by his grave, without entering upon any dispute or argument.

The sixth dispute was on the question of Fadak and its inheritance from the Prophet, when Fāṭima was claiming it as heiress, or even as owner. She was finally persuaded to abandon her claim by the famous tradition of the Prophet: 'We prophets do not bequeath an inheritance; what we leave behind is in charity.'

The seventh dispute was over the question of fighting those who refused to pay the zakāt. Some said, 'We shall not fight them in the same way as we fight unbelievers'; but others said, 'On the contrary, we shall fight them.' Abū Bakr at last said, 'If they do not give me the hobbling-cord they used to give the Prophet, I shall fight them.' He thereupon made preparations to do battle with them. All the Companions, too, agreed with him. 'Umar, during his caliphate, exercising his personal judgment, returned the captured property, and released the prisoners and captives.

The eighth dispute was over Abū Bakr's appointment of 'Umar as caliph at his death. Some said to him, 'You have placed over us a man of very harsh and unbending disposition.' The dispute ended when Abū Bakr said, 'If God were to ask me on the day of judgment I would say, "I have placed over them the best man amongst them."' During 'Umar's reign a number of differences arose, as, for example, on the question of the right of inheritance of a grandfather, of brothers and of distant relatives. There was also the question of compensation for the loss of fingers and teeth, and the punishment of crimes about which no clear instruction had been handed down.

Of all their affairs their conflict with the Greeks and Persians was the most important at this period. God granted victory to the Muslims who took many captives and much booty, with everyone following the directions of 'Umar. The message spread, the word of God became supreme, the Arabs submitted, and the resistance of the non-Arabs was weakened.

The ninth dispute was over the question of consultation, *shūra*, [instituted by 'Umar for the election of a caliph], different views being expressed about it. All agreed to swear allegiance to 'Uthmān and everything was in order. Islam continued to be preached in his time, many conquests were made and the treasury was full. 'Uthmān treated people well and showed himself generous. However, his relatives among the Umayyads stirred up the fires of hell, and he was consumed in the conflagration; they acted unjustly and cruelly, and he reaped the fruits of their cruelty. In his reign many disputes arose, and he was blamed for many incidents which should be laid to the account of the Umayyads.

Among these disputes was 'Uthmān's giving permission to al-Ḥakam b. Umayya to return to Medīna after the Prophet had driven him away from it. Al-Ḥakam used to be referred to as the one expelled by the

Prophet. He had previously appealed to Abū Bakr, and 'Umar even expelled him a further forty leagues from his abode in the Yemen.

'Uthmān also exiled Abū Dharr to al-Rabdha, gave his daughter in marriage to Marwān b. al-Ḥakam and allowed him to keep a fifth of the booty from Africa, which was equivalent in value to two hundred thousand dinars. He gave refuge to 'Abdullāh b. Sa'd b. Abū Sarḥ who was his nursing foster-brother, though the Prophet had declared his blood forfeit. 'Uthmān also appointed him as governor of Egypt and all its provinces. Again he appointed 'Abdullāh b. 'Āmir as governor of Baṣra where he did what he did.

The governors of 'Uthmān's provinces were as follows: Mu'āwiya b. Abū Sufyān, the governor of Syria; Sa'd b. Abū Waqqāṣ, the governor of Kūfa, who was followed by Walīd b. 'Uqba and Sa'īd b. al-'Āṣ; 'Abdullāh b. 'Āmir, the governor of Baṣra, and 'Abdullāh b. Sa'd b. Abū Sarḥ, the governor of Egypt. They all utterly abandoned him, till at last he met his fate, and he was unjustly murdered in his house. As a result of the cruelty to which he was subjected civil strife broke out which is not yet fully settled.

The tenth dispute took place during the reign of 'Alī, the Commander of the Faithful, after he had been unanimously accepted and allegiance had been sworn to him. To begin with, Ṭalḥa and Zubair went to Mecca and induced 'Ā'isha to go to Baṣra with them. They subsequently fought a battle against 'Alī, known as the Battle of the Camel. However, both later had a change of heart and repented, for 'Alī reminded them of something which they remembered. While fleeing from battle Zubair was killed by a bow-shot of Ibn Jarmūz, who is now in hell, because the Prophet said, 'Give the murderer of Ibn Ṣafīya the news that he will go to hell.' Ṭalḥa was struck dead by an arrow from Marwān b. al-Ḥakam while fleeing from battle. As for 'Ā'isha she had been induced to act as she did, but afterwards regretted it and repented.

As for the dispute between 'Alī and Mu'āwiya, the Battle of Ṣiffīn, the opposition of the Khārijites who forced 'Alī to accept arbitration, the treachery of 'Amr b. al-'Āṣ to Abū Mūsa al-Ash'arī and the continuation of the dispute till his death – all these are well known. Similarly the dispute between 'Alī and the Khārijites, the assembling of the latter at Nahrawān, their turning against him, their vilifying of him and their entering into an armed conflict against him – all this also is well known. On the whole 'Alī was on the side of the truth, and the truth on his side. 'Alī witnessed in his times not only those who rebelled against him, such as Ash'ath b. Qais, Mis'ar b. Fadakī al-Tamīmī, Zaid b. Ḥuṣain al-Ṭāī and others, but also those who went to extremes in his favour, as

'Abdullāh b. Saba' and his followers. From these two groups arose innovation and error. Thus the words of the Prophet came true: 'Two kinds of people will perish because of you: those who bear you an intense love and those who bear you an intense hatred.'

Subsequently the disputes became grouped under two headings. One was the dispute over the question of the imāmate and the other the dispute on matters of doctrine. The dispute over the imāmate was based on two different points of view. One was to assert that the imāmate was established by agreement and election; the other to hold that it was established by decree and appointment. Those who believed that the imāmate was established by agreement and election believed in the imāmate of anyone on whom the community, or a significant section of the community, had agreed. This could be anyone in general provided, as some held, that he was a Quraishite; or, as others maintained, that he was a Hāshimite, and so on. Those who held the first alternative accepted the imāmate of Mu'āwiya and his descendants, and after them the caliphate of Marwān and his descendants. The Khārijites on their part always agreed on an imām from amongst themselves, provided he lived according to their beliefs and followed the path of justice in his dealings with them. Otherwise they deserted him and deposed him, or even put him to death.

Those who maintained that the imāmate was established by appointment differed after the death of 'Alī, some holding that he appointed his son Muḥammad b. al-Ḥanafīya: these are the Kaisānīya. These, however, differed among themselves after the death of Muḥammad b. al-Ḥanafīya. Some maintained that he had not died, but that he would return and fill the earth with justice. Others, on the contrary, said that he had died, and that the imāmate had been transmitted to his son Abū Hāshim. These again differed among themselves. Some believed that the imāmate remained in Abū Hāshim's descendants from one appointment to another. Others, however, held that it had been transferred to another, but differed as to who that other was. Some said this other was Bayān b. Sam'ān al-Nahdī, others 'Alī b. 'Abdullāh b. 'Abbās. Others again said that it was 'Abdullāh b. Ḥarb al-Kindī, and others 'Abdullāh b. Mu'āwiya b. 'Abdullāh b. Ja'far b. Abū Ṭalib. They all agreed, however, that religion consists of obedience to a man. Hence they interpreted the laws of *sharī'a* in terms of a particular person, as will shortly be seen in our treatment of the sects.

Those who did not believe in the imāmate of Muḥammad b. al-Ḥanafīya believed in the appointment of Ḥasan and Ḥusain. They maintained that the imāmate cannot belong to two brothers except in the case of

Ḥasan and Ḥusain. These also differed among themselves. Some confined the imāmate to the descendants of Ḥasan, and so after Ḥasan's death believed in the imāmate of his son Ḥasan, followed by that of Ḥasan's son 'Abdullāh, of 'Abdullāh's son Muḥammad, and lastly, Muḥammad's brother Ibrāhīm – the two imāms who rose up during the reign of Manṣūr and were killed. Some believed that Imām Muḥammad would return. Some, however, transferred the appointment to the descendants of Ḥusain, after whose death they believed in the appointment of his son 'Alī b. Ḥusain Zain al-'Ābidīn. After this they differed. The Zaidīya believed in the imāmate of his son Zaid. They believed too that any Fāṭimid who rises in revolt, and is also a scholar, pious, brave and generous, is an imām who must be followed. They also permitted the return of the imāmate to the descendants of Ḥasan. Some of them came to a halt at a certain imām and believed in his return. Others permitted the imāmate to continue, and believed in the imāmate of every person who in his time had the required qualities. A description of their views will be given presently in detail.

As for the Imāmīya they believed in the imāmate, by appointment, of Muḥammad b. 'Alī al-Bāqir, followed by that of Ja'far b. Muḥammad al-Ṣādiq, also by appointment. After al-Ṣādiq, however, they differed among themselves concerning his sons as to which of them was the appointed one. There were five of these: Muḥammad, Ismā'īl, 'Abdullāh, Mūsā, and 'Alī. Some maintained the imāmate of Muḥammad. These are known as the 'Ammārīya. Others believed in the imāmate of Ismā'īl, and denied that he died during the life of his father: these are known as the Mubārakīya. Some went no further and believed in his return. Some permitted the imāmate to continue in his descendants, by one appointment after another, to our own day. These are called the Ismā'īlīya. Some believed in the imāmate of 'Abdullāh, known as the Snub-nosed, and in his return after death, for he died without leaving any issue. Some believed in the imāmate by appointment of Mūsā, whose father is reported to have said, 'The seventh is your *qā'im*; he is the namesake of the one who brought the Torah.'

These, too, differed among themselves. Some went no further than Mūsā and believed in his return, for they maintained that he did not die. Others did not commit themselves regarding his death: these are called the Mamṭūra. Others held his death for certain and permitted the imāmate to continue in his son 'Alī b. Mūsā al-Riḍā: these are known as the Qaṭ'īya. These again differed after his death with respect to each of his descendants.

The Twelvers carry on the imāmate from 'Alī al-Riḍa to his son

Muḥammad, from Muḥammad to his son 'Alī, from 'Alī to his son Ḥasan and, finally, to Ḥasan's son Muḥammad, the *qā'im*, the Awaited One, the twelfth imām. They believe that he is living, that he has not died, and that he will return to fill with justice an earth which is now filled with injustice. Others carry on the imāmate to Ḥasan al-'Askarī, after whom they either believe in the imāmate of his brother Ja'far, not going beyond him, or they express some doubt about Muḥammad. They are continually confused, either carrying on the imāmate or bringing it to an end: in the latter case believing either in return after death, or in concealment and return after concealment.

This is a summary of the differences on the question of the imāmate; details will be given when the sects are discussed.

The following are the differences in doctrinal matters. In the last days of the Companions there arose the heresy of Ma'bad al-Juhanī, Ghailān al-Dimashqī and Yūnus al-Aswārī, which maintained the power of man and refused to ascribe good and evil to divine decree. Wāṣil b. 'Atā', a pupil of Ḥasan al-Baṣrī, followed in their footsteps. His pupil was 'Amr b. 'Ubaid who further developed the question of man's power. 'Amr was an emissary of Yazīd al-Nāqiṣ, during the Umayyad period, but afterwards he became a friend of Manṣūr whose imāmate he accepted. Manṣūr once praised him by saying, 'I threw grain out to the people and all gathered it up except 'Amr.'

The Wa'īdīya amongst the Khārijites, the Murji'a amongst the Jabrīya, and the Qadarīya all embarked upon their heresies at the time of Ḥasan. Wāṣil separated himself from the last group by expressing a belief in the intermediate position. Thus he and his followers became known as Mu'tazilites. Zaid b. 'Alī became the pupil of Wāṣil, from whom he learnt his doctrine. As a consequence all the Zaidīya became Mu'tazilites. Those who rejected Zaid b. 'Alī because he held views contrary to those of his ancestors on doctrinal matters, as well as on the question of association and dissociation, became known as the Rāfiḍites: they were a group from Kūfa.

After this the Mu'tazilite leaders studied the works of the philosophers as they became available during the reign of Ma'mūn. They then introduced the methods of the philosophers into theology, which they made into a branch of science. They gave it the name of *kalām*: either because the chief question on which they spoke and disputed was that of *kalām* (God's word), by which the whole discipline was called; or in imitation of the philosophers, who called one of their branches of learning Logic, for Logic and *kalām* are synonymous.

Abu 'l-Hudhail al-'Allāf, who was their greatest teacher, agreed with the philosophers that God is knowing with knowledge, but that his knowledge is his essence; similarly, he is powerful with power, but that his power is his essence. He is the author of heresies on the questions of the divine word and will, of men's deeds, of belief in man's power, of man's appointed time and of man's sustenance, as will be made clear when we are explaining his views. A number of disputations took place between Abu 'l-Hudhail and Hishām b. al-Ḥakam on the question of anthropomorphism. Abū Ya'qūb al-Shaḥḥām and al-Ādamī, who were followers of Abu 'l-Hudhail, agreed with him in all his views.

During the reign of Mu'taṣim, Ibrāhīm b. Sayyār al-Naẓẓām went to excess in following the views of the philosophers, and separated himself from his predecessors by his Shī'ite heresies and his innovations on the question of man's power. He also separated himself from other Mu'tazilites on certain questions, as we shall mention. Among his followers were Muḥammad b. Shabīb, Abū Shimr, Mūsā b. 'Imrān, al-Faḍl al-Ḥadathī and Aḥmad b. Khābiṭ. Al-Aswārī agreed with him in all his heresies. So also did the Iskāfīya, the followers of Abū Ja'far al-Iskāfī, and the Ja'farīya, the followers of the two Ja'fars, Ja'far b. Mubashshir and Ja'far b. Ḥarb.

Next came the innovations of Bishr b. al-Mu'tamir; as for example, a belief in secondary effects in which he went to excess, being inclined to naturalist philosophy. He also held the belief that God has power to punish a child, but if he does so he is unjust. He held other such views peculiar to himself. Abū Mūsā al-Murdār, 'the Mu'tazilite monk', became his pupil, but differed from him in his denial of the miraculous nature of the Qur'ān from the point of view of language and style. It was in his time that persecution of the Orthodox theologians reached its height because of their belief in the eternity of the Qur'ān. Among his pupils were the two Ja'fars; Abū Zufar and Muḥammad b. Suwaid, the followers of al-Murdār; Abū Ja'far al-Iskāfī and 'Īsā b. al-Haitham, the followers of Ja'far b. Ḥarb, 'the Scarred One'. Among those who went to excess in the doctrine of man's power are Hishām b. 'Amr al-Fuwaṭī and his disciple al-Aṣamm. Both also attacked the imāmate of 'Alī, saying that an imāmate is not valid without the consent of the whole community. Both held too that it is impossible for God to know things before they come to pass. They deny also that the non-existent is a thing. Abu 'l-Ḥusain al-Khayyāṭ and Aḥmad b. 'Alī al-Shaṭawī were followers of 'Īsā al-Ṣūfī, and afterwards attached themselves to Abū Mujālid. Ka'bī was a disciple of Abu 'l-Ḥusain al-Khayyāṭ; his views are in every respect the same as those of his master.

Mu'ammar b. 'Abbād al-Sulamī, Thumāma b. Ashras al-Namīrī and

Abū 'Uthmān 'Amr b. Baḥr al-Jāḥiẓ, were all contemporaries and held similar views, though in some matters they had opinions of their own which we shall mention in due course. The later Mu'tazilites, as Abū 'Alī al-Jubba'ī, his son Abū Hāshim, Qāḍi 'Abd al-Jabbār and Abu 'l-Ḥusain al-Baṣrī, have given a summary of the teachings of their masters; but on some matters they follow their own opinions, which shall be considered further on.

The golden age of *kalām* began with the 'Abbāsid caliphs, Hārūn, Ma'mūn, Mu'taṣim, Wāthiq, and Mutawakkil, and closed with Ṣāḥib b. 'Abbād and a group of Dailamites. About the middle of this period there arose a group of Mu'tazila, such as Ḍirār b. 'Amr, Ḥafṣ al-Fard and Ḥusain al-Najjār, who belonged to the later school, and who differed from their masters on a number of questions.

There also appeared at the time of Naṣr b. Sayyār a man called Jahm b. Ṣafwān who propounded his unorthodox views on predetermination, *jabr*, in the city of Tirmidh. He was put to death at Marw by Sālim b. Aḥwaz al-Māzinī towards the close of the Umayyad period.

In each period there were differences of opinion between the Mu'tazilites and the Orthodox on the question of the attributes. The Orthodox were accustomed to argue not according to a scholastic method but by relying on authoritative statement. The Orthodox were called the Ṣifātīya. Some of them maintained the existence of the attributes of God in terms of entities subsisting in him, while some likened his attributes to those of creatures. All of them followed the literal meaning of the Qur'ān and *sunna*. They also argued with the Mu'tazilites over the question of the eternity of the world, again relying on the literal sense. 'Abdullāh b. Sa'īd al-Kullābī, Abu 'l-'Abbās al-Qalānisī and Ḥārith b. Asad al-Muḥāsibī were more exact in their thinking, and more skilled in scholastic argument.

A debate took place between Abu 'l-Ḥasan 'Alī b. Ismā'īl al-Ash'arī and his teacher on the question of what constitutes good and evil. Ash'arī forced his teacher to recognize certain consequences of his position, to which he could give no answer. Ash'arī, thereupon, left him and joined the Orthodox, whose position he supported by the scholastic method. In this way a school of his own arose. His method was followed by a number of scholars, as, for example, Qāḍi Abū Bakr al-Bāqillānī, Abū Isḥāq al-Isfarā'īnī, and Abū Bakr b. Fūrak. There is not much difference of opinion between these theologians.

[During this time] there appeared a man from Sijistān who manifested a certain show of piety, named Abū 'Abdullāh Muḥammad b. Karrām. He was a man of little learning, but had taken from various sects a confused mixture of ideas, which he put into his book and spread among the vulgar of Gharja, Ghūr and in the country of Khurāsān. His teaching was systematized and developed into a school. He was supported by Maḥmūd b. Subuktegīn, the Sultan, who on account of the Karrāmīya persecuted the Traditionalists and the Shī'ites. Muḥammad b. Karrām's school closely resembled that of the Khārijites; they are crude corporealists, except for Muḥammad b. al-Haiṣam who does not go as far as the others do.

5 The reason which made necessary the arrangement of this book on arithmetical principles: reference will also be made in this chapter to arithmetical procedures

Since the basis of arithmetic is precision and conciseness, and my aim in writing this book is to deal with all beliefs with brevity, I have chosen the most comprehensive method of arrangement; and in pursuing my aims and purposes I have followed arithmetical procedures in the divisions and subdivisions of my book. I intend to explain the methodology of this science and the number of its divisions, lest it should be thought that, since I am a jurist and a theologian, I would be a stranger to its ways and lack understanding of its significance and its symbolism. Therefore I have chosen the soundest and best of arithmetical procedures, and given for it the clearest and most concrete of proofs. I made it [i.e. the division of the book] correspond to the science of numbers, my chief desire being to derive benefit from it.

Grades of arithmetic begin with one and end with seven; they do not go beyond that. The first grade is the 'beginning of arithmetic', *ṣadr al-ḥisāb*. It is the first object of division. From one point of view it is an odd number without a pair, but from another point of view it is a whole, and admits division. From the point of view of its being a whole it is divisible, and as such may be divided in two parts. The form of the extension must have two extremes under which may be written general details, general measurements, definition, movement, transference, aspects of the whole viewed in general terms, statements about the subject and what is connected with it. Under this should be written prominently at the left corner the numbers constituting the whole.

The second grade is the root, *al-aṣl*, and its form is determined, *muḥaqqaq*. It is the first division made on the first whole. It is even, not odd; it must be restricted to two parts, and not extended to a third; the form of its extension must be shorter than the 'beginning', for the part is smaller than the whole. Underneath this will be written what is particular to it, as orientation, classification, and other specifications. This form has a pair which is like it in extension, but it need not be its equal in measurement.

The third grade stems from the root, and its form, too, is determined. It is the second division which the first and the second subject undergo, and which cannot be less than two parts, not more than four. Those writers who exceed this number fall into error and show their ignorance of mathematics, as we shall shortly show. The form of its extension has to be shorter than that of the 'root'. Underneath it also must be written fully and clearly whatever is appropriate to it.

The fourth grade is called *al-maṭmūs*, the effaced, and its form is ط . It may exceed four, but it is better if it is limited to a minimum. It is shorter in extension than the previous one.

The fifth grade is called *al-ṣaghīr*, the small, and its form is ص. It may go to the maximum limit of division and subdivision. It is shorter in extension than the previous one.

The sixth grade is called *al-mu'waj*, the curved, and its form is ، . This also may be subdivided till no further subdivision is possible.

The seventh grade is called *al-mu'aqqad*, the knotty, and its form is لـلـ . It extends from one side to the other, not that it is the 'beginning of arithmetic', but the 'conclusion' which looks like the 'beginning'.

These are the symbols of arithmetic and the total number of its divisions. Every division has its like corresponding to it and its pair equalling it in extension. This should never be lost sight of. Arithmetic is both a record of past events and an indication of the future.

We shall explain now the quantitative aspect of these forms: why the divisions are restricted to seven; why the 'first beginning' is an odd number having no pair in form; why the 'root' is divisible only into two and not into three; why the next division is restricted to four, and why the other divisions are unlimited.

The scholars who have discussed the science of numbers and arithmetic differ among themselves regarding 'one'. Is it part of number? Or is it the starting-point of number, not itself being included in number? This difference of opinion is due to the wide meaning of the word one; for the word one is used and understood as that of which number is composed – two, for example, has no other meaning than one plus one; likewise with regard to three and four. The word one, however, may also be used as meaning that from which numbers proceed, that is, one is the cause of number and not part of it; in other words, it does not enter into the composition of number.

Oneness may even be regarded as an aspect pertaining to all numbers; not in the sense that number is composed of it, but that every existing thing is one in its genus, in its species, and in its individuality. Thus we say 'One mankind', or, 'One individual'. Likewise in number itself: thus three in its threeness may be said to be one 'three'.

In the first sense oneness is part of numbers, in the second sense the cause of numbers, and in the third sense an aspect pertaining to numbers. But none of these three meanings of one is applicable to God. God is one in a way different from that in which other things are one. These unities and multiplicities are derived from him. It is impossible, moreover, for him to be divided in any way.

The majority of scholars speaking on numbers agree that one is not included in number and, therefore, the first root of number is two. Number is divided into even and odd. The first odd number is three, and the first even number is four; beyond four number is a combination of these. Thus five is composed of the root number and the odd number, and is called the round number. Six is composed of two odd numbers, and is called the complete number. Seven is composed of odd and even numbers, and is called the perfect number. Eight is composed of two even numbers; it is the beginning of another series of combinations about which we do not intend to speak.

The 'beginning of arithmetic' corresponds to one, inasmuch as it is the cause of number and not part of it. Therefore it is unique and has no counterpart. Since the 'root' of number is two, its determination is limited to only two divisions; and since number is divided into odd and even, the determinations on this basis are limited to four [numbers], the first odd number being three and the first even number four; these are the limit. The other numbers will be composed of these. Therefore the universal elements in numbers are one, two, three and four; these are the limit. Numbers beyond these are composed of them without a limit to their composition. The remaining sections, therefore, cannot be restricted to a definite number but go as far as calculations will go. Beyond this the application of number to the numbered, and of the prime to the composite, belongs to another science. We shall discuss this when we treat of the views of the ancient philosophers.

Conclusion

When the introductory sections have been completed as well as possible we shall begin to treat of the views of mankind from the time of Adam to our own day, hoping that no view or belief will be omitted. Under every chapter and division we shall write what is appropriate to it, so that it will be clear why a particular heading was used for each chapter. Under every sect mentioned we shall indicate what views and beliefs are common to all the sub-sects, and under every sub-sect what is peculiar to it and held only by its followers.

We shall give an account of all the various divisions of Islamic sects, which total seventy-three. On the various sub-sects outside the Community we shall restrict ourselves to those better known for their systems of thought. We shall treat first those meriting to be treated first, and place at the end those meriting to be placed there.

The art of arithmetic requires that opposite the ends of the lines all the explanatory comment be written; the art of writing on its part requires that the margin should be left free, as is customary among writers. Accordingly I have paid attention to the requirements of both these arts. I have arranged the chapters according to arithmetical principles and left the margins as is customary among writers. I seek the help of God and in him I trust. He is sufficient for me, for he is the best of Guardians.

Prelude

The beliefs of mankind: those belonging to revealed religions and communities, and those following human ideas and philosophies

Our treatment shall cover Islamic sects and others who have a truly revealed book, as the Jews and Christians; those with a book of a somewhat similar kind, as the Magians and the Manicheans; those who have penal laws and statutes but no book, as the first Sabaeans; and, finally, those who have neither book nor penal laws nor religious laws, as the early philosophers, atheists, star-worshippers, idol-worshippers and Brahmins. We shall mention the founders and followers of each. We shall quote the original sources and refer to the writings of each group, and shall follow their terminology after we have become acquainted with their methods, and made an investigation of their basic principles and conclusions.

The true division [in religion], like that between negative and positive, is, we maintain, that mankind with regard to beliefs is divided into those who follow a revealed religion and those who follow human ideas and beliefs. When a man holds a belief or expresses an opinion he is either acquiring it from someone else, or is following his own ideas. One who acquires knowledge from someone else is the one who submits and obeys. Religion means obedience, and the one who submits and obeys is the religious man; one who follows his own independent judgment is an innovator and a heretic. There is a saying of the Prophet that the one who seeks counsel will not be unhappy, but the one who follows his own counsel will not be happy.

It may happen sometimes that the one who acquires a belief from another is simply a blind follower, who by chance has a religion because he had parents or teachers who had false beliefs. These he followed without reflecting whether they were true or false, and without discerning between the sound and the unsound. Such a one receives no benefit, for he has made no gain nor acquired any knowledge, nor followed a teacher after due discernment and conviction. 'Such as have testified to the truth, and that knowingly'[1] is a necessary condition for following another. This ought to be remembered.

It may also happen that the one following his own ideas derives them from knowledge he has already acquired. If he is aware of the source from which they were derived and the method by which they were derived, he will not, strictly speaking, be following his own ideas, for he has derived his ideas from knowledge already acquired. 'Those of them whose task it is to discover would have known the matter'[2] is a principle of great importance. It is those who follow an absolutely independent course who deny the prophethood of the prophets, such as, for example, the philosophers, Sabaeans and Brahmins. They do not believe in religious laws and divine commandments, but instead make rational laws by which they may live. Those who derive their knowledge from others are the ones who believe in the prophethood of the prophets. Those who believe in religious laws do also believe in rational laws, but the reverse is not true.

Part I

Introduction

Followers of religions and members of religious communities: Muslims, people of the book and those with something similar to a book

We are treating here of the meaning of the words *dīn, milla, shir'a, minhāj, islām, ḥanīfīya, sunna* and *jamā'a*. These are modes of expression that are found in the Qur'ān; each by reason of etymology and usage has a specific meaning and signifies a certain reality. We have already explained the meaning of the word *dīn*, namely, that it is obedience and submission; as God says, 'Religion with God is Islām.'[1] Sometimes it is used in the meaning of recompense. There is a saying, '*kamā tadīnu tudānu*,' which means 'As you do so shall you be recompensed.' It may also be used in the meaning of reckoning on the day of judgment. God says, 'That is the true religion.'[2] Accordingly the *mutadayyin* is one who submits, who is obedient, and who believes in recompense and reckoning on the day of judgment. God says, 'I have chosen Islām for your religion.'[3]

Since man needs to live together with others of his species to provide for his subsistence and also to prepare himself for his eternal destiny, this corporate living has to be of a kind that will ensure mutual defence and co-operation; by mutual defence he will be enabled to keep what is his, and by mutual co-operation to obtain what he does not possess. This form of corporate living is the *milla*. The special path leading to it is called the *minhāj, shir'a* or *sunna*. The agreement on that *sunna* is called *jamā'a*; as God says, 'To every one of you we have appointed a right way and an open road.'[4]

The creation of the *milla* and the prescribing of the way is not possible except through one chosen by God, whose genuineness is manifested by certain signs. Sometimes the sign is contained in the message itself, sometimes it accompanies the message, and sometimes it comes after it.

Let it be remembered that the greatest *milla* was that of Abraham, which was called the Ḥanīfīya. It is opposed to Sabaeanism as a kind of antithesis. How this is so we shall mention later. God speaks of 'the *milla* of your father Abraham.'[5]

The *sharī'a* began with Noah; as God says, 'He has laid down for you as religion that he charged Noah with.'[6] But laws and commandments began with Adam, Shīth and Idrīs. All Sharī'as and religions, all religious ways and paths, reached their culmination through Muḥammad, in that *sharī'a* which is the most perfect, most beautiful and most excellent; as God said, 'Today I have perfected your religion for you, and I have completed My blessing upon you, and I have chosen Islam for your religion.'[7]

It is said that to Adam was given names and to Noah the meaning of these names, but to Abraham was given both names and their meanings; to Moses was given revelation and to Jesus the deeper understanding of revelation; but to Muḥammad was given both revelation and its deeper understanding, according to 'the creed of your father Abraham'.[8] The mode of the first prophetic affirmation and its perfection through the second in such a way that each affirmation confirmed past religions and religious ways; the establishment of correspondence between the divine word and the creatures, and of harmony between religion and nature – all this is proper to the prophets; no one else shares this honour with them. It is said that God established his religion on the model of his creation so that his creation would lead man to his religion and his religion to his creation.

Section I
Muslims

Introduction

Introduction I

We have already explained the meaning of *islām*, and we shall now explain the difference between *islām, īmān* and *iḥsān*. We shall show the first, the intermediate and the final stages [of faith] by means of the famous tradition about the interrogations of Gabriel, when he appeared in the garb of a bedouin and sat so close to the Prophet that their knees touched. He said to the Prophet, 'O Apostle of God, what is *islām*?' The Prophet replied, 'To bear witness that there is no God but Allāh, that I am a messenger of God, to observe prayer, pay the zakāt, fast in the month of Ramadān and perform the pilgrimage if you are able to do so.' Gabriel said, 'You have spoken the truth.' He then asked, 'What is *īmān*?' The Messenger replied, 'To believe in God, his angels, his scriptures, his messengers, the Last Day; to believe also in the *qadar* (determination of good and evil).' Gabriel said, 'You have spoken the truth.' He then asked, 'What is *iḥsān*?' The Prophet replied, 'To worship God as though you see him, but if not, to know that he sees you.' Gabriel said, 'You have spoken the truth.' He finally asked, 'When is the Hour?' The Prophet replied, 'The one who is asked about it does not know more than the one asking.' Gabriel then arose and departed, and the Prophet said, 'That was Gabriel who came to teach you about your religion.' In this way the Prophet distinguished between the meaning of *islām* and *īmān*. *Islām*, however, is sometimes used in the sense of outward submission, and in this sense there is no difference between the faithful and the hypocrite. God says, 'The bedouins say, 'We believe.' Say, 'You do not believe;' rather say, 'We submit.''[1] Thus the Qur'ān distinguishes between the two words.

Since *islām* in the sense of outward submission is something common to all, this is the beginning. If it is accompanied by sincerity, and if one believes in God, his angels, his scriptures, his messengers and the Last Day; and if he also believes and affirms that all good and evil are determined by God, that is, that what befell him could not have been avoided by him, and what did not befall him could not have befallen him: such a one is a true believer, *mu'min.*

Thus when submission and faith are brought together, and outward effort is united with inner vision so that the unseen becomes the seen, the final stage is reached. Thus *islām* is the beginning, *īmān* the intermediate stage and *iḥsān* the final stage. Used in this way the word *muslim* includes those who attain to salvation as well as those who perish in hell. Sometimes the word *islām* is used together with *iḥsān*, as when God says, 'Whoever submits his will to God in sincerity.'[2]

It is in this sense also that we may understand God's words: 'I have chosen Islam for your religion.'[3] As also in the following verses: 'Religion with God is Islam;'[4] 'When his Lord said to him 'Submit,' he said, 'I have submitted to the Lord of all being;'[5] 'See that you die not save in submission.'[6] In this sense the word *islām* is used only for those attaining to salvation.

God knows best.

Introduction II

Those who are engaged in *uṣūl* (root matters) differ among themselves with regard to the unity of God, his justice, 'promise and warning', revelation and reason. We shall now go on to speak of the meaning of *uṣūl, furū'* (branches) and other such words.

Some theologians say that *uṣūl* means the knowledge of God in his oneness and his attributes, and the knowledge of the prophets with their signs and proofs; but, in general, every question whose discussion leads to the determination of truth belongs to *uṣūl*. Now since religion consists of knowledge and obedience, knowledge being the root and obedience the branch, whoever treats of the knowledge and unity of God is an *uṣūlī* (theologian), and whoever treats of obedience and law is a *furū'ī* (jurisconsult). *Uṣūl* is the subject of scholastic theology, and *furū'* is the subject of jurisprudence. Some scholars believe that whatever is within the sphere of the intellect, and can be attained by reflection and argumentation, belongs to *uṣūl*; and whatever belongs to the sphere of probability, and is reached through analogy, *qiyās*, and personal endeavour, *ijtihād*, belongs to *furū'*.

As regards the unity of God, the Orthodox and all the Ṣifātīya say that God is one in his essence, without division. He is one in his eternal attributes; there is no other like him. He is one and alone in his deeds; he has no associates. The Mu'tazilites say that God is one in his essence without any division or attributes. He is one and alone in his deeds and has no associates. There is no eternal being other than he and no partner in his deeds. The existence of two eternal beings is impossible. It is likewise impossible for one thing to be an object of two powers. This is the unity of God.

As for justice, according to the Orthodox, God is just in his deeds in the sense that he disposes freely of what is his own and is under his dominion, doing as he pleases and judging as he wills; for justice consists in putting everything in its due place, and disposing freely of what is under one's dominion according to one's pleasure and knowledge. Injustice is the opposite of this. For God, therefore, any injustice in his judgment or in his way of acting is inconceivable. According to the Mu'tazilites, on the other hand, justice is that which reason manifests as in accord with wisdom, and which consists in acting in a manner that is right and in promoting the good.

As for 'promise and warning' the Orthodox say that promise and warning are God's eternal word. God promised a reward for what he commanded and warned against what he forbade. Whoever attains to salvation and deserves a reward does so because of God's promise; whoever perishes and deserves punishment does so because of God's warning. God is not obliged to do anything on the basis of reason. The Mu'tazilites, on the contrary, say that there is no eternal word. God in fact commanded and forbade, promised and warned, through a created speech. Whoever attains to salvation and deserves reward does so on account of his own deeds; whoever perishes and deserves punishment does so on account of his own deeds. Reason in its wisdom requires this.

As for revelation and reason, the Orthodox say that all obligations are known through revelation, though all knowledge comes through the intellect. In other words, the intellect does not discern the goodness or evil of things, nor make demands, or impose obligations; revelation, on the other hand, does not give information, that is, it does not cause knowledge, but imposes obligations. The Mu'tazilites, however, say that all knowledge as well as all obligation comes through reason; to show gratitude, for example, to one bestowing favours is obligatory before receiving revelation. Goodness and evil are intrinsic qualities of what is good and evil.

These are the basic matters which are the subject of discussion among the theologians. We shall give a detailed account of the views of each group. Every science has a subject and various matters connected with it, which, as far as possible, we shall mention with the help of God.

Introduction III
The Mu'tazilites and others, namely, the Jabrites, the Ṣifātīya and combinations of these

The sects of the Mu'tazilites and Ṣifātīya are utterly opposed to each other. The same may be said of the Qadarites and Jabrites, the Murji'a and Wa'īdīya, the Shī'ites and Khārijites. This opposition between one group and another has at all times manifested itself. Each sect has had its own body of ideas and its own books composed by its adherents. Each has had a state authority which supported it, and powers which submitted to it.

Chapter 1

The Mu‘tazilites

Introduction

The Mu‘tazilites are called the followers of divine justice and unity. They are also known as the Qadarīya and ‘Adlīya. They themselves, however, hold that the word Qadarīya is ambiguous, and say that it should be used of those who believe that the *qadar* (determination) with respect to good and evil is from God. They thereby wished to avoid the ignominy commonly attached to the name because of a tradition that ‘the Qadarīya were the Magians of this community’. In this they were unanimously opposed by the Ṣifātīya on the ground that Jabrīya and Qadarīya are contradictory terms: how, they asked, can one contradictory term be applied to another? The Ṣifātīya further appealed to the saying of the Prophet that the Qadarīya are the adversaries of God in the matter of determination. According to them, one who believes in submitting himself to God and entrusting himself to him, while at the same time attributing all events to a determined fate and unalterable decree, cannot conceivably dispute about *qadar*: making a division between good and evil, attributing good to the action of God and evil to that of man.

Common doctrines

1 God is eternal: eternity is his special characteristic

The Mu‘tazila deny altogether the eternal attributes. According to them God is ‘knowing’ by his essence, ‘powerful’ by his essence, ‘living’ by his essence: not by ‘knowledge’ or ‘power’ or ‘life’ considered as eternal attributes or entities, *ma'ānī*, subsisting in him. This is so because if the attributes shared in the eternity of God, which is his special characteristic, they would also share in his godhead.

They are all of the opinion that the speech of God is temporal and created in a place. It consists of letters and sounds, and these are recorded in books by means of their likenesses which manifest them. Again, what is found in a place is an accident which at once disappears.

They all hold that will, hearing and sight are not entities subsisting in the divine essence. They differ, however, in their explanation of the meaning of attributes and their manner of existence, as we shall explain later.

They are unanimous in denying that God can be seen by the eyes in Paradise. They also deny the possibility of any description of him in anthropomorphic terms, such as assigning him direction, place, form, body, abode, movement, transition, change, or emotion. Hence, the ambiguous verses of the Qur'ān with such descriptions must be interpreted in a metaphorical sense. This is what they mean by Unity.

2 Man has power over his good and bad deeds and is also their creator

Man, therefore, deserves reward or punishment in the next life for what he does in this one. One cannot ascribe to God evil and injustice or an act of unbelief and sin, because if he created injustice he would be unjust; likewise, if he created justice he would be just. They are agreed also that God does only what is right and good, *ṣalāḥ*, and being wise he must do what is good for man; but as regards doing what is best for man, *aṣlaḥ*, or bestowing grace, *luṭf*, upon him, the necessity of this is disputed amongst them. This they call Justice.

3. When a believer departs from this life, obedient to God's law and repentant, he merits reward, *thawāb*, and recompense, *'iwaḍ*, but the bestowal of favour, *tafaḍḍul*, is something over and above reward. When, however, a man departs from this life unrepentant of grave sins, he merits eternal damnation, though his punishment will be lighter than that of the unbeliever. This is what they call 'promise and warning', *al-wa'd wa'l-wa'īd.*

4. Even before revelation is received, man is under an obligation to acquire a fundamental knowledge of God and to show him gratitude for benefits received. Man is obliged also by reason to know good and evil; he is likewise under an obligation of doing the good and avoiding the evil. Obligations made known to men by God are signs of his graciousness, revealed to them through his prophets for their trial and probation:

'So that those who died might die after a clear sign [had been given], and those who lived might live after a clear sign [had been given].'[1]

The Mu'talzites disagree, however, on the question of the imāmate. Some of them hold that it is decided by appointment, while others say it is decided by election, as we shall explain when discussing the view of each individual sect.

We shall consider now the particular views of the various sub-sects of the Mu'tazilites.

1 The Wāṣilīya

These are the followers of Abū Ḥudhaifa Wāṣil b. 'Aṭā' al-Ghazzāl, 'the Lisper'. Wāṣil was a pupil of Ḥasan al-Baṣrī under whom he studied history and various branches of learning during the reigns of 'Abd al-Malik b. Marwān and Hishām b. 'Abd al-Malik. A number of Wāsil's followers are still to be found in Maghrib, in the district where Idrīs b. 'Abdullāh al-Ḥasanī led an uprising during the reign of Abū Ja'far al-Manṣūr.

This Mu'tazilite school is known as the Wāṣilīya. It has four basic doctrines which are as follows:

(1) *A denial of the attributes of God, such as knowledge, power, will and life*. In the beginning this doctrine was undeveloped and was explained by Wāsil b. 'Aṭā' in simple terms as follows: It is universally agreed that the existence of two eternal gods is impossible; so to assert the existence of an eternal entity, or an eternal attribute [in God], would be to say that there were two gods.

The followers of Wāṣil went more deeply into this question after studying the works of the philosophers. They concluded by reducing all the attributes of God to knowledge and power, which they maintained were his essential attributes. According to Jubbā'ī these attributes are aspects of the eternal essence; according to Abū Hāshim they are its modes. Abu 'l-Ḥusain al-Baṣrī, on the other hand, tended to reduce all the attributes to one, namely, knowledge. This was also the view of the philosophers, which we shall later discuss more fully. The Orthodox, however, opposed the Mu'tazilites on the ground that the attributes are found mentioned in the Qur'ān and the traditions.

(2) *A belief in 'qadar'*. In this way they followed Ma'bad al-Juhanī and Ghailān of Damascus. Wāṣil b. 'Aṭā' himself expounded more fully the doctrine of *qadar* than he did that of the attributes. According to him God is wise and just; evil and injustice cannot be attributed to him. God cannot will of his creatures the contrary of what he commands them;

he cannot determine what they do and then punish them for doing it. Hence man is the author of good and evil, belief and unbelief, obedience and disobedience; and it is he who will be requited in accordance with his deeds. Over all these things, therefore, God has given him power.

Man's acts comprise the following: movement, rest, deliberation, reflection and knowing. It is impossible, moreover, for a man to be ordered to do something which he cannot do, nor feel within himself the capacity to do. Whoever denies this denies the obvious. This was confirmed from the Qur'ān.

I have seen a letter said to have been written by Ḥasan al-Baṣrī to 'Abd al-Malik b. Marwān in response to his enquiry about *qadar* and *jabr* (predetermination). In his reply Ḥasan al-Baṣrī expressed a view similar to that of the Qadarites, supporting it with verses of the Qur'ān and proofs from reason. This letter, however, may have been written by Wāṣil b. 'Aṭā' himself, as Ḥasan was not one to oppose the belief of the Orthodox that the determination, *qadar*, of good and evil is from God, a way of speaking almost universal among them. Curiously enough, these words which are found in tradition are interpreted as referring to misfortune and well-being, adversity and prosperity, sickness and health, death and life, and other similar things which come from God: not, however, good and evil, right and wrong, which are the products of man's own action. A number of Mu'tazilites have also mentioned this interpretation in their writings on others of their school.

(3) *The intermediate position.* The origin of this doctrine is as follows. One day someone went to Ḥasan al-Baṣrī and said to him:

> O Imām! There are some today who say that grave sinners are unbelievers. For them grave sin is unbelief by which one is cast out of the community. This group is the Wa'īdīya section of the Khārijites. On the other hand, there are others who defer judgment on grave sinners. For them grave sin does not adversely affect a person as long as he has faith. Deeds, they hold, do not form an integral part of faith; sin, therefore, does not adversely affect one having faith, just as obedience is of no avail to one without faith. These are the Murji'a (the 'Postponers'). What in your opinion should we believe?

While Ḥasan was considering this Wāṣil interrupted and said, 'I do not regard the grave sinner as a believer in an absolute sense, nor yet an unbeliever in an absolute sense; he is, in my opinion, in an intermediate position, neither believer nor unbeliever.' After this he arose and moved away to another pillar of the mosque where he began to explain what he had said to a group of Ḥasan's followers. Ḥasan then remarked, 'Wāṣil has separated himself from us. From then on Wāṣil's followers were known as the Mu'tazila (the 'Separatists').

Wāṣil explains his position as follows. The word *īmān* designates good qualities, and one endowed with these is called a *mu'min*, a word of commendation. A sinner, on the other hand, does not have these good qualities, and so does not merit praise; he is not, therefore, called a *mu'min*. He is not, however, in the strict sense, also an unbeliever, because it cannot be denied that he professes the faith and also performs certain good deeds. Nevertheless, if he departs from this life in the state of unrepentant grave sin, he will be condemned to hell forever; for hereafter there will be only two classes of men: 'One in paradise and the other in hell.'[2] His punishment, however, will be lighter than that of the unbeliever and his grade in hell will not be as low. In this opinion Wāṣil is followed by 'Amr b. 'Ubaid, who also agrees with him on the question of *qadar* and the denial of the attributes.

(4) *Views on the opposing parties in the battles of the Camel and Ṣiffīn.* According to Wāṣil one of these parties was in the wrong, but which one cannot be specified. He holds a similar view on 'Uthmān, on those responsible for his death, and on those also who deserted him. One of these parties, he said, is certainly sinful, just as of two parties execrating one another one is certainly sinful, but which one cannot be determined. Wāṣil's views on a sinner are already known. About the status of the conflicting parties the least that can be said is that their testimony is inadmissible. Consequently, Wāṣil does not regard the testimony of 'Alī, Ṭalḥa and Zubair, even in insignificant matters, as admissible. It is possible that 'Uthmān and 'Alī are both wrong.

Such are the views of Wāṣil, head of the Mu'tazila and founder of this school of thought, on the leading figures among the Companions of the Prophet and Imāms of the family.

'Amr b. 'Ubaid agreed with Wāṣil, but he added (with regard to the question of declaring one of the two parties a sinner, without specifying either) that if two men from either party, for example, 'Alī and another one of his followers, or Ṭalḥa and Zubair, gave testimony, their testimony would not be admissible. Accordingly he regards both of them as sinners whose place is hell.

'Amr was a transmitter of Ḥadīth and was well known for his asceticism, while Wāṣil was highly esteemed among the Mu'tazilites for his learning and culture.

2 The Hudhailiya

These are the followers of Abu' l-Hudhail Ḥamdān b. al-Hudhail al-'Allāf, 'Shaikh of the Mu'tazila', who advanced the sect by his exposition and defence of its doctrines. He himself learnt Mu'tazilism from 'Uthmān b. Khālid al-Ṭawīl who in turn was a pupil of Wāṣil b. 'Aṭā'. Some say that Wāṣil was taught by Abū Hāshim 'Abdullāh b. Muḥammad b. al-Ḥanafīya, but according to others he was a pupil of al-Ḥasan b. Abu 'l-Ḥasan al-Baṣrī.

Abu 'l-Hudhail differs from the main body of the Mu'tazilites on the ten following points:

(1) *God is 'knowing' with knowledge and his knowledge is his essence; he is 'powerful' with power and his power is his essence; he is 'living' with life and his life is his essence*. This opinion was derived by Abu 'l-Hudhail from the philosophers, who held that God is one in his essence without any kind of multiplicity. As to the attributes they are not additional to his essence in the form of entities subsisting in it, but his essence itself. They may be regarded either negatively or as concomitants, as will be explained later. The difference between saying that God is knowing with his essence and not by knowledge, and that he is knowing by knowledge which is his essence, is that the first proposition denies the attributes, while the second affirms either an essence which is identical with the attributes, or an attribute which is identical with the essence. Abu 'l-Hudhail's theory that these attributes are aspects of the essence agrees with the Christian notion of the hypostases, or with the modes of Abū Hāshim.

(2) *There are acts of will which have no substrate; by these acts God is 'willing'*. Abu 'l-Hudhail was the first to introduce this notion which was adopted by his successors.

(3) With regard to God's speech, some of it is not in a place, such as his word 'Be'; but some of it is in a place, such as an order or prohibition, information or enquiry. From this it seems as though he held that the creating word is different from the word of command.

(4) Abu 'l-Hudhail's views on *qadar* are the same as those of other Mu'tazilites, except that he is a Qadarite with regard to this life, but a Jabrite with regard to the next. According to him, whatever is done by those dwelling in the everlasting abodes of heaven or hell is done necessarily: man in the next life has no power over his actions, but all are created by God. If any of these acts were men's own acquisition, they would have to be responsible for them.

(5) The movements of those who dwell eternally in heaven or hell will

cease, and will be followed by an everlasting rest and stillness. In this state of rest those in heaven will experience all their pleasures and those in hell all their suffering. This approaches the view of Jahm who maintained that heaven and hell would come to an end. Abu 'l-Hudhail was forced into this position in order to overcome a difficulty about the beginning of the universe, namely, that phenomena which have no beginning are like those which have no end as they are both infinite. To this he replied: 'I do not believe in a movement that has no end, just as I do not believe in a movement that has no beginning; all will turn into an everlasting rest.' He seemed to think that the problem with regard to movement did not exist with regard to rest.

(6) *'Capacity' is an accident, and something more than health and physical integrity*. According to Abu'l-Hudhail there is, besides, a difference between mental acts and bodily acts. It is impossible to have mental acts without corresponding power and capacity to act while performing these acts. This, however, is possible in the case of bodily acts where, he says, capacity precedes the act; thus man acts through capacity in the first moment, but the act comes into being only in the second moment. The moment of 'will do', *yaf'alu*, is other than the moment of 'having done', *fa'ala.*

Whatever is occasioned, *tawallada*, by man's deed is also his deed, except perception of colour, taste, smell and other things whose nature, *kaifīya*, is unknown. The understanding and knowledge which are aroused in another through information and instruction are, according to Abu 'l-Hudhail, created in him by God and are not the acts of a human agent.

(7) With regard to one who has not yet received revelation Abu 'l-Hudhail says that he is under obligation from reason to know God beyond any doubt; if he fails in this respect, then he merits eternal punishment. He is also duty bound to know the goodness of the good and the evil of the evil, with the consequent obligation of pursuing the good, such as truth and justice, and avoiding the evil, such as lying and injustice. Abu 'l-Hudhail also holds that there are acts of obedience which are not directed towards God nor seek to please him; such are, for example, the intention of initiating an enquiry [into the existence of God] and the first enquiry itself, for God is not yet known. The act is, nevertheless, an act of worship.

With regard to one undergoing an interrogation he says that if he does not know how to reply evasively and to dissemble, it is lawful for him to tell a lie, and the guilt of lying is not imputed to him.

(8) *Man's appointed time of death and his sustenance*. Abu 'l-Hudhail

says that even if a man had not died a violent death he would nevertheless have died at this time: a man's life-span cannot be prolonged or shortened. As to sustenance this may be understood in two ways. In the first place it may be taken as referring to all beneficial things created by God of which it can be said that they were created by him as sustenance for man. If, therefore, it were said that men have eaten and benefited from what God did not create as sustenance, this would be an error, because it would mean that in material things there was something not created by God. Secondly, it may be understood as referring to those things about which God has made a pronouncement as to their sustenance for man: those things whose use is allowed by God are sustenance, and those forbidden by him are not sustenance; that is, man is not commanded to partake of them.

(9) According to Ka'bī, Abu 'l-Hudhail also held that God's will is other than the thing willed. God's will to create a thing is his creation of it; but his creation of the thing is not the thing itself. His creation is his word, and this word is not in a substrate. He also says that God has not ceased to be hearing and seeing, that is, that he continues to hear and see. Similarly, he has not ceased to be forgiving, merciful, bountiful, a creator and provider, rewarding and punishing, a friend and foe, commanding and forbidding, in the sense that he continues to manifest all these characteristics.

(10) Ka'bī also relates that according to Abu 'l-Hudhail a proof cannot be established about something not now present except with the testimony of twenty witnesses, of whom one or more must belong to the elect. There will always be such people on earth who are God's friends, blameless men who never lie or commit grave sins. It is they who are the proof and not the collective report, because it is possible for a great number of men to lie if they are not God's friends, or if there is not amongst them a single blameless man.

Abu 'l-Hudhail was followed by Abū Ya'qūb al-Shaḥḥām and al-Ādamī who adopted his teachings. He died at the age of a hundred years in AH 235, at the beginning of the caliphate of al-Mutawakkil.

3 The Naẓẓāmīya

These are the followers of Ibrāhīm b. Sayyār b. Hāni' al-Naẓẓām who had studied many of the writings of the philosophers, and effected a fusion of philosophy with Mu'tazilite *kalām*. Al-Naẓẓām differed from other Mu'tazilites in the following points:

(1) He goes beyond the general Mu'tazilite position that *qadar* (the determining power) with respect to good and evil, belongs to men by saying that we cannot attribute to God power with respect to evil and sin; these, moreover, are not within his power. In this he opposes his fellow Mu'tazilites who maintained that God, indeed, has power over them, but he is not their author because they are evil. Naẓẓām considers that as 'evil' is an essential quality of the evil, and, therefore, the doing of it cannot be ascribed to God, the mere possibility of God's doing evil is also evil and is, therefore, not attributable to God; for we cannot attribute the power to do evil to the One who is just. Naẓẓām makes matters worse by saying that God has power to do what he knows to be for the good of his creatures, but no power to do in this world what is not for their good.

Such are Naẓẓām's views about what concerns God's power in this world. As for the next world, he holds that we cannot ascribe to God power to increase in any way the punishment of hell, or in any way to decrease it. Similarly, God cannot decrease the joys of heaven nor cast anyone out of it. None of this is within his power.

The objection was put to Naẓẓām that if this were so God would be obliged by his nature to do what he does, whereas one who truly has power is able to choose between doing and not doing. He replied: 'What you object to about the power to act applies also to the act itself; for, according to you, it is impossible for God to perform this act, even though it is within his power; so there is no difference.'

Naẓẓām adopted this view from the ancient philosophers who had maintained that one who is generous cannot withhold anything, and not do it. Accordingly, only what God has created and brought into existence is within his power. If God knew of anything better or more perfect that was within his power to create as regards the order, arrangement and usefulness of things, he would have created it.

(2) On the question of will, Naẓẓām's view is that will cannot in reality be attributed to God; therefore, when in theology a will is ascribed to him because of his deeds, what is meant is that he creates them and brings them into being in accordance with his knowledge. When he is said to will the deeds of men what is meant is that he commands them to be done or forbids them. It was from Naẓẓām that Ka'bī took this view about divine will.

(3) All man's deeds are movements only; even a state of rest is a movement in tendency, *i'timād*. Knowledge and will are movements of the mind. By movement is not meant local motion, but rather any form of change, as the philosophers say; as, for example, a change of quality, quantity, position, place, time and the like.

(4) Naẓẓām agrees with the philosophers that in reality man is a soul and spirit, while the body is the instrument of the soul and its mould. Naẓẓām, however, did not fully understand the thought of the philosophers and inclined towards the view of the naturalists among them; namely, that the spirit is a fine substance which permeates the body and penetrates all its parts, just as water is diffused through all the parts of the rose, or oil through sesame, or fat through milk. He adds that it is the spirit which has power and capacity, life and will; its capacity, moreover, lies in itself and exists before the act.

(5) Ka'bī relates of Naẓẓām the opinion that every act which is beyond the limit of human power is God's deed, simply by reason of the intrinsic nature of the thing. For example, God gave a stone its nature and bestowed upon it its peculiar character; so that when a stone is thrown it moves with an impetus imparted to it, and when the impetus is exhausted the stone will naturally return to its proper place. Naẓẓām had confused views on the nature of substances and their laws, differing both from the theologians and philosophers.

(6) Naẓẓām agreed with the philosophers in their denial of indivisible particles and proposed the theory of 'leaps'. The difficulty was once put to him that an ant crossing from one end of a rock to the other would thus have traversed an unlimited space, but how could that which is finite traverse the infinite? He replied that it could be done partly by walking and partly by leaps. He took the example of a rope tied round a piece of wood which is across the centre of a well. The rope is fifty yards long and fastened to it is a bucket. Another rope also fifty yards long has a hook attached to it. By means of this hook the first rope is drawn up and in this way the bucket reaches the top of the well. The bucket has, therefore, covered one hundred yards in the same time as the rope pulling it, which is fifty yards long. This is only possible, he said, because the passage is made partly by leaps. Naẓẓām did not realise that a leap is also traversing the distance and is equal to the distance itself. The difficulty, therefore, remains unanswered. The difference between walking and leaping amounts to no more than a difference between fast and slow time.

(7) Substances are composed of an aggregation of accidents. Naẓẓām also agrees with Hishām b. al-Ḥakam that colours, tastes and smells are bodies. At times he declares that bodies are accidents, at other times that accidents are nothing but bodies.

(8) God created all existing things as they are now in the one act of creation: minerals, plants, animals and men. His creation of Adam did not precede that of his posterity except that some of them were put in

a latent condition in others. The order of their precedence is simply the result of their coming forth from this hidden state, not that of their creation and coming into being at that time. Naẓẓām adopted this view from those philosophers who believe in this manner of latency and appearance. He is always inclined to follow the naturalists rather than the metaphysicians.

(9) The miraculous nature of the Qur'ān, according to Naẓẓām, consists in giving information about past and future events, in averting temptations to challenge the Qur'ān, in [God's] forcibly preventing the Arabs from engaging in such attempts and rendering them incapable. Had they been left to themselves, they would have been able to produce a chapter like one in the Qur'ān with its beauty, eloquence and style.

(10) Naẓẓām holds that the agreement of the community, *ijmā'*, is not authoritative in religious law. Similarly, analogy, *qiyās*, in matters of *sharī'a* is not authoritative. Only the words of the sinless imām are authoritative.

(11) Naẓẓām is inclined to adopt the Rāfiḍite views and to be disparaging of the leading Companions. He says in the first place that there is no imāmate without designation and appointment that are explicit and public. The prophet designated 'Alī on a number of occasions, and did this so explicitly that there could be no longer any doubt about it in the community. 'Umar, however, concealed it, and it was he who was responsible for the election of Abū Bakr on the day of Saqīfa. Naẓẓām also accuses 'Umar of doubt on the day of Ḥudaibiya when he questioned the Prophet, saying: 'Are we not in the right? And are they not in the wrong?' The Prophet replied: 'Yes, that is so.' 'Umar thereupon asked: 'Why then do we show weakness in our religion?' According to Naẓẓām this was doubt and uncertainty in the matter of religion on the part of 'Umar, who was disturbed in mind about what Muḥammad had decided and ordered. Furthermore, Naẓẓām lied in saying that 'Umar struck Fāṭima in the stomach on the day Abū Bakr was installed as Caliph, causing her a miscarriage; and that he cried out: 'Burn her house and all its inmates!' when there were in the house only 'Alī, Fāṭima, Ḥasan and Ḥusain.

Naẓẓām says, too, that 'Umar exiled Naṣr b. al-Ḥajjāj from Medīna to Baṣra. He also introduced the *tarāwīḥ* [that is, the special prayer in Ramaḍān], forbade the *mut'a* (temporary marriage) during pilgrimage, and dealt harshly with governors. All these were unprecedented acts.

Naẓẓām also disparaged 'Uthmān, the Commander of the Faithful, and gave an account of his misdeeds, such as: bringing Ḥakam b. Umayya back to Medīna though he had been banished by the Prophet; exiling

Abū Dharr, a friend of the Prophet, to Rabdha; appointing al-Walīd b. 'Uqba as governor of Kūfa, though he was one of the most depraved of men; appointing Mu'āwiya to the governorship of Syria, and 'Abdullāh b. 'Āmir to that of Baṣra; giving his daughter in marriage to Marwān b. al-Ḥakam. All these men did harm to his caliphate. Naẓẓām also accuses 'Uthmān of striking 'Abdullāh b. Mas'ūd in connection with the preparation of the authoritative version of the Qur'ān, and because of 'Abdullāh's criticism of him. All of these things are the misdeeds of 'Uthmān according to Naẓẓām.

Naẓẓām further discredits himself by censuring both 'Alī and 'Abdullāh b. Mas'ūd for saying, 'This is my own personal opinion.' He also maintained that Ibn Mas'ūd was lying when he reported the Prophet as saying, 'Happy is the man who is happy in the womb of his mother.' Ibn Mas'ūd lied, too, in his account of the splitting of the moon and in his identification of the jinn with the gypsies. Naẓẓām himself, indeed, denied the jinn altogether. Other absurd accusations are made by him against the Companions of the Prophet.

(12) With regard to a rational being before revelation comes to him Naẓẓām held that, if he is a man of intelligence and capable of reflection, he must by his own reflection and reasoning acquire the knowledge of God. He also believed in the power of reason to discover the goodness or evil of all of man's actions. Again, he said that for choice to be possible there must be two contrary suggestions in a man, one urging and the other restraining.

(13) Naẓẓām expressed views also about 'promise and warning'. He maintained, for example, that if a person steals or misappropriates a hundred and ninety-nine dirhem, he does not become a *fāsiq* till the amount reaches at least two hundred dirhem, the minimum amount at which alms becomes compulsory; only then is he a *fāsiq*. The same principle applied to the minimum amount of other possessions subject to zakāt. In regard to the hereafter he held that God's favour to children will be the same as his favour to animals.

Aswārī agrees with Naẓẓām in all these points, but adds that God cannot be said to have power to do what he knows that he will not do, nor power to do what he has made known he will not do. Man, however, has power to do these things because man's power extends to two contrary courses of action, even though it is obvious that only one of these contraries will be realized, and not the other. Abū Lahab continued to be addressed by God even though he had made it known that: 'Burnt soon will he be in a fire of blazing flame.'[3]

Abū Ja'far al-Iskāfī and his associates agree with Naẓẓām on this, and add that God has no power to do injustice to adults endowed with reason, but he can be said to have power to do injustice to children and the insane. Both Ja'far b. Mubashshir and Ja'far b. Ḥarb follow Naẓẓām without adding anything, except that Ja'far b. Mubashshir says that among the *fāsiqs* of the Muslim community there are some who are worse than atheists and Magians. He maintained that the agreement of the Companions on the penalty to be imposed on wine-drinkers was an error, because where a prescribed penalty is concerned only a [Qur'ānic] text or determination based on tradition is authoritative. He also considered that if a person steals a single grain of wheat he becomes a *fāsiq* and loses the faith.

Muḥammad b. Shabīb, Abū Shimr and Mūsā b. 'Imrān were followers of Naẓẓām, but differed from him on the question of 'warning' and 'the intermediate position'. According to them one guilty of a grave sin does not lose the faith merely by committing a grave sin. Ibn Mubashshir used also to say about 'warning' that the meriting of punishment and an everlasting abode in hell could be known by reason before being known by revelation.

Among the followers of Naẓẓām were al-Faḍl al-Ḥadathī and Aḥmad b. Khābiṭ. Ibn al-Rāwandī says that they believed that the world has two creators, one of these being eternal, namely, God, and the other created, namely, the Messiah. This they said because of God's words in the Qur'ān: 'When you formed from clay the likeness of a bird.'[4] Ka'bī denied this, particularly of al-Ḥadathī, because of the high esteem in which he held him.

4 The Khābiṭīya and the Hadathīya

The Khābiṭīya were the followers of Aḥmad b. Khābiṭ, and the Ḥadathīya of al-Faḍl al-Ḥadathī. Both in turn were followers of Naẓẓām and studied the works of the philosophers. They added to the teachings of Naẓẓām three new heresies.

(1) They assign to the Messiah one of the divine prerogatives, agreeing with the Christians in their belief that he is the one who will call mankind to a reckoning in the next life. He is the one meant by God's words: 'Your Lord comes with angels in their ranks.'[5] He is also the one who will come in shadowing clouds, and who is referred to by the words of God: 'Until your Lord comes.'[6] Again, he is the one of whom the Prophet spoke when he said, 'God created Adam in the image of the Most

Merciful.' Also when he said, 'The Most Powerful will put his foot in the fire.' Aḥmad b. Khābiṭ maintained that the Messiah put on a body of flesh, that is, [Shahrastānī comments], the eternal Word became incarnate, as the Christians say.

(2) *The belief in transmigration of souls*. They hold that God created men healthy, sound in body and intelligent, in an adult state, and in a world other than this one in which they now live. He created in them the full knowledge of himself and showered on them his blessings. It is impossible for the first of God's creatures to be anything but intelligent and thinking beings, able to draw a lesson from experience, whom, from the beginning, God placed under an obligation to show gratitude to him. Some of them obeyed him in all that he had commanded and some disobeyed in all; others, again, obeyed in some things and not in others. Those who obeyed in all things God allowed to remain in heaven where he had placed them from the beginning. Those who were disobedient in all things God cast out of heaven and put in a place of punishment, namely, hell. Those who were partly obedient and partly disobedient God sent to this world and clothed them in these gross bodies. He also subjected them to adversity, suffering, hardship and comfort, pain and pleasure. In this life, too, he gave them different forms, some having the form of men and some of animals according to the measure of their sins. Those who had sinned less and obeyed more were given a body more beautifully formed and their sufferings were less. Those whose sins were more were given a body less beautiful in form and suffered more. Henceforward these will not cease to be an animal over and over again, one form succeeding another, as long as their acts of obedience and disobedience remain. Such is the essence of the doctrine of the transmigration of souls.

A contemporary, Aḥmad b. Ayyūb, a leader of the Mu'tazila, and also a pupil of Naẓẓām, said the same as Aḥmad b. Khābiṭ on the transmigration of souls and the creation of all things at the one time. He added, however, that when the level of an animal is reached obligation disappears; the same is true also when the level of a prophet or angel is attained – the obligation likewise disappears. These states are thus states of reward or punishment.

The Khābiṭīya and the Ḥadathīya also believe that there are five different worlds of which two are abodes of reward. In one of these worlds there are food, drink, consorts, gardens and rivers. In the other, which is higher than this one, there is no eating nor drinking nor consorting, but only spiritual pleasure, repose and ease, having nothing of a bodily nature. The third is the world of punishment alone and that

is the fire of hell, where there are no grades, but all are equal. The fourth is the world of the beginning in which creatures were created before coming down to the earth: this was the first paradise. The fifth is the world of trial, the one in which men are placed under certain obligations after having acted wrongly in the previous one. The constant cycle of rebirths will not end in this world till both the scales of good and evil are full. When the scale of goodness is full, all deeds become deeds of obedience and the obedient soul becomes pure goodness. It is then taken to paradise without a moment's further delay in this world, for to defer payment would be unjust on the part of the All-sufficient. As the tradition says, 'Give a man his wages before his sweat dries.' On the other hand, when the scale of evil is full all deeds become deeds of disobedience, and the disobedient soul becomes pure evil. It is then cast into hell without a moment's delay. This is the meaning of God's words: 'When their term is reached, not an hour can they cause delay, nor (an hour) can they advance it.'[7]
(3) Their interpretation of all that has been said in tradition about the vision of God (such as the saying of the Prophet: 'You will see your Lord on the day of judgment as you see the moon by night when it is full, and you will suffer no harm in seeing him'), is in terms of the vision of the First Intellect, the first being that was created by God. This is the Active Intellect, from which forms emanate to existing things. It is this which is meant by the Prophet when he said:

> The first thing God created is the Intellect. Having created it, he said to it, 'Come forward', and it came forward; then he said, 'Step back', and it stepped back. God now said, 'By my power and glory, I have not created anything better than you. By you I give honour and by you I give disgrace; by you I bestow and by you I withhold.'

Accordingly it is this Intellect which will appear on the day of judgment when the veils will be removed between it and the forms which have emanated from it. Thus they will see it like the full moon at night. He who created the Intellect, however, will not be seen at all, for no comparison is possible except between created things.

Ibn Khābiṭ says that every species of animal forms a separate community, according to God's words: 'There is not an animal that lives on the earth, nor a bird that flies on its wings but forms part of communities like you.'[8] To every community, moreover, there is a messenger of its own kind; as God says, 'There never was a community without a warner having lived among them.'[9]

The views of Ibn Khābiṭ and Faḍl al-Ḥadathī on transmigration are different from those of others, as though they had mixed up the ideas of the metempsychosists, the philosophers and the Mu'tazila.

5 The Bishrīya

These are the followers of Bishr b. al-Mu'tamir, one of the greatest scholars of the Mu'tazilites. It was he who introduced the doctrine of secondary effects, *tawallud*, in which he went to extremes. He differed from other Mu'tazilites on six points:

(1) He maintained that colour, taste, smell and other sense perceptions as hearing and sight may result as secondary effects of a man's action if their causes are the result of his action. This view he took over from the Naturalists, except that they do not differentiate between primary and secondary effects. Possibly they do not look upon power as the theologians do, since, in their view, the potentiality, *quwwa*, of action and the potentiality, *quwwa*, of receiving an effect are different from the notion of power, *qudra*, held by the theologians.

(2) According to Bishr capacity, *istiṭā'a*, consists of sound constitution, health of limb and freedom from infirmities. He goes on to say, 'I do not maintain that man acts with this capacity in the first moment nor in the second moment; but I say that man acts, and the act does not take place except in the second moment.'

(3) God has power to punish a child, but if he actually did so he would be unjust to the child; however, it would not be right to speak in this way of God. Rather, if God did punish the child, we should say that the child was a rational adult and a sinner on account of a sin he had committed; he would, therefore, be deserving a punishment. This, however, is a contradictory statement.

(4) Ka'bī says of Bishr that he held that God's will is one of God's acts. It has two aspects, that of an attribute of essence and that of an attribute of action. With regard to the will as an attribute of his essence, it means that God does not cease willing all his own deeds and all the acts of obedience of his servants. This is because he is wise, and one who is wise cannot know what is good and beneficial and not will it. As to the will as an attribute of action, if it is related to his own act at the time of bringing it into being, it means his creation of the act. This attribute precedes creation because that which causes a thing cannot be simultaneous with it. If, on the other hand, God's will is related to man's deed, then this is a command.

(5) God has grace, *lutf*, which, if bestowed, all men on earth would

believe and deserve reward, as they would if they believed without grace though in this case more so. It is not, however, obligatory on God to give his grace to men. Similarly, there is no obligation on God to do what is best, *al-aṣlaḥ*, because there is no limit to the good within his power. Nothing, in fact, can be said to be the best because there can be always something better. God must, however, give man power and capacity [to believe], and remove from him obstacles to belief through a summons and a prophetic message.

A thinking being knows God before revelation by reflection and reasoning. Moreover, since he is free in his choice of action there is no need of two contrary suggestions, because contrary suggestions do not come from God but from the devil. The first thinking being was not preceded by a devil casting doubt in his mind; even if he had been, the same question would arise with regard to the devil.

(6) Whoever repents of a grave sin and commits it again deserves punishment for the first sin also, because his repentance was accepted on condition that he did not sin again.

6 The Mu'ammarīya

These are the followers of Mu'ammar b. 'Abbād al-Sulamī, one of the most hair-splitting of the Qadarites in the subtlety he displayed in his denial of the attributes, and in denying that the determination of good and evil comes from God. He declared that anyone who did not hold these doctrines was an unbeliever and astray.

Mu'ammar differed from other Mu'tazilites on a number of points. Among these are the following:

(1) God did not create anything except bodies. Accidents are produced by bodies. These occur either naturally, as when fire causes burning, or the sun causes heat, or the moon causes colour; or they are the results of option, as when animals move or come to rest, come together or disperse. It is strange that the coming into existence of the body and its annihilation are, according to him, accidents. How, then, can he say that these two accidents are produced by bodies? On the supposition that God did not bring the accidents into being, then surely neither did he bring the bodies into being nor annihilate them, for coming into being is an accident. It would, therefore, follow that God did not act at all.

Mu'ammar has to face the further problem of whether God's speech is an accident or a body. If he says that it is an accident, it is God who has created it, because, according to him, the speaker is the one who produces the speech. Or, he must admit that God's speech is not an accident. If, therefore, he says that it is a body, then he has contradicted his assertion that it was created in a place, because a body cannot subsist in a body. If he does not believe in the affirmation of eternal attributes, nor in the creation of accidents, it will follow on his view that God has no speech at all. But if God has no speech, then he neither commands nor forbids. If, however, there is neither command nor prohibition, neither is there any religious law. Thus his views lead to a position which is utterly disgraceful.

(2) Mu'ammar says that accidents of every kind are infinite in number. He also holds that every accident which inheres in a subject does so by reason of an 'entity' which necessitates its inherence there. This would clearly lead to an infinite regress. Because of this view Mu'ammar and his followers were called 'Believers in Entities'. Mu'ammar further maintained that movement is opposed to rest: not, indeed, in its essence, but by an entity which necessarily brings about this opposition. In the same way the likenesses and unlikenesses of similar things, and opposition of contraries, are all due to an entity.

(3) Mu'ammar said, according to Ka'bī, that God's will for a thing is both other than God and other than God's creation of it; again, it is neither a command nor a communication nor an injunction. Mu'ammar, therefore, is speaking of something ambiguous and unintelligible. He further says that man has no acts other than acts of his will, either direct or indirect. Those acts, therefore, which are subject to God's command, such as standing up or sitting, movement or rest – whether these relate to good or evil – are to be ascribed to his will neither directly nor indirectly. This is very strange, though it is in keeping with his views on the nature of man.

According to Mu'ammar man is an entity or a substance other than a body. He is knowing, powerful, free and wise. He is neither moving nor at rest, neither changing nor enduring, neither seen nor touched nor felt nor known by any sense; nor does he occupy one place rather than another; nor is he confined within the limits of space and time, but he is ruler of the body, and his relationship with it is one of direction and management. Mu'ammar adopted this idea from the philosophers who maintained the existence of the human soul as a certain kind of entity, namely, a substance subsisting by itself without a permanent place of abode. They also maintained the existence of other rational beings of the same kind, such as the separated intellects. Because of his sympathy with the teaching of the philosophers Mu'ammar distinguished between the acts of the soul, which he called man, and those of the matrix which is his body. He went on to say that the act of the soul is will only, and that the soul is man; therefore, the act of man is will. All besides that, such as movement, rest and tensions, are acts of the body.

(4) It is related of Mu'ammar that he objected to saying that God is *qadīm* (eternal), because the word *qadīm* is taken from *qaduma, yaqdumu*, hence *qadīm* (active participle). It is, therefore, a verb, as for example, 'He took from it both what had become old, *qaduma*, and what was new, *ḥadutha*.' He also said that *qadīm* implies priority in time, whereas God's existence does not belong to the sphere of time.

Mu'ammar is also reported to have said that creation is different from the thing created, and bringing into being is other than what is brought into being. According to Ja'far b. Ḥarb he also asserted that it is impossible for God to know himself, because this would mean that the knower and the known are not identical. Similarly, it is impossible for God to know anything other than himself; just as it may further be said that it is impossible for him to have power over existing things inasmuch as they are existing. Possibly this is wrongly reported, because no intelligent man could say such an absurd thing.

Mu'ammar, however, was inclined to follow the philosophers, according to whom God's knowledge is not a passive knowledge, that is, consequent upon the object known, but an active one. Inasmuch, therefore, as God is an agent he is a knower; it is his knowledge that causes the act. God's knowledge is necessarily connected with existing things at the moment of their coming into existence, but it is impossible that it should be connected with what is non-existent as long as it remains non-existent. The philosophers also maintain that God is knowledge and intellect, and that in him intellect, subject of intellection and object of intellection are one and the same thing. Ibn 'Abbād, therefore, means that we should not say that God knows himself, because this would imply a distinction between the knower and the known; nor that God knows things other than himself, because this would mean that his knowledge was caused by other than himself. Either, then, the report is incorrect, or it should be interpreted in the above way. We, however, are not followers of Ibn 'Abbād, so we need not attempt to give an explanation.

7 The Murdārīya

The Murdārīya were the followers of 'Īsā b. Ṣubaiḥ known as Abū Mūsā al-Murdār. 'Īsā b. Ṣubaiḥ himself was a pupil of Bishr b. Al-Mu'tamir, from whom he received his theological instruction. He lived an ascetic life and was known as 'the Mu'tazilite monk'. He differed from other Mu'tazilites on several points.

(1) On the question of power he said that God can lie and do injustice; and if he did lie or commit an injustice then he would be a lying and unjust God. [The author adds] God is far above this.

(2) With regard to secondary effects he held the same view as his master, but added that one act may proceed from two agents as a secondary effect.

(3) With respect to the Qur'ān he held that men have power to produce something similar to it in diction, style and excellence of composition. He also went to extremes in his belief in the creation of the Qur'ān, and declared an unbeliever anyone who said it was eternal, accusing him of maintaining that there were two eternal beings. He also regarded as an unbeliever anyone who was associated with the ruling prince. Such a one, according to him, should neither inherit nor bestow an inheritance. Again, he held that one who maintained that a man's actions were created by God was an unbeliever; so also is one who said that God would be seen by the eyes. He went into such extremes in declaring people unbelievers that he called them unbelievers even when they said there is only one God. Ibrāhīm b. al-Sindī once asked him about all men on earth. He replied that all were unbelievers. Ibrāhīm thereupon asked, 'Will then paradise, which is as spacious as heaven and earth together, contain only you and three of your followers?' He was confounded and made no reply.

Among the pupils of Abū Mūsā al-Murdār were also the two Ja'fars, Abū Zufar and Muḥammad b. Suwaid. Ja'far b. Ḥarb al-Ashajj was supported by Abū Ja'far Muḥammad b. 'Abdullāh al-Iskāfī and 'Īsā b. al-Haitham. Of the two Ja'fars Ka'bī relates that they held that God created the Qur'ān in the Preserved Tablet, and that it cannot be removed, since it is impossible for one thing to be in two places at the same time. What we read is a copy of what is already written in the Preserved Tablet, and this [reading] is our act and our creation. 'Of the different views of the Qur'ān,' Ka'bī says, 'this is the one I prefer.'

On the ability of reason to know good and evil, the two Ja'fars held that it is evident from reason that before revelation man has an obligation to know God, as well as all his commandments and attributes; it is also man's duty to know that, if through his remissness he fails to know God and show him gratitude, he will suffer eternal punishment. Thus they held that reason manifests the necessity of eternal punishment.

8 The Thumāmīya

The Thumāmīya were the followers of Thumāma b. Ashras al-Numairī, who, though himself living an altogether irreligious and dissolute life, believed that a fasiq will suffer eternally in hell if he dies unrepentant; such a one, he said, while living, is in an intermediate position.

Thumāma differed from his fellow Mu'tazilites on certain points. He said, for example, that secondary effects have no agent. The reason is that it is impossible to ascribe them to a primary agent because it would mean that an act could be ascribed to a dead person; as when, for instance, a man having set a cause in operation died, and the secondary effect afterwards followed. Again, these secondary effects cannot be ascribed to God, because this could lead to ascribing an evil act to God, which is impossible. Finally, in confusion, he said that secondary effects have no agent. He also said that unbelievers, polytheists, Magians, Jews, Christians, Manichees and atheists will all be turned to dust on the day of judgment. This is true also of animals, birds and the children of believers.

Again, according to Thumāma, a capacity is sound constitution, health of limbs and freedom from infirmity. Moreover, it exists before the act. Knowledge is a secondary effect of reflection, and, as such, like other secondary effects, it is an act without an agent. Thumāma also believed, as other Mu'tazilites do, in the power of reason to know good and evil, and in the obligation to acquire such knowledge before revelation. He added, however, that among unbelievers there are some who do not know their creator, and, therefore, they are free from blame. He further said that all this knowledge is necessary for man, and if a man did not know God necessarily, he would not be commanded to know him. Such a one would have been created as a lesson and object of ridicule, and would be comparable to all the animal world. He also held that man's only act is will, and everything else is an event without a cause.

Ibn al-Rāwandī relates that Thumāma said, 'The world is God's creation by reason of his nature.' Perhaps he meant by this what the philosophers mean by saying that God created by necessity of nature and not according to his will. According to this belief he would be bound to maintain, as the philosophers do, that the world is eternal, because what is necessarily caused necessarily co-exists with its cause.

Thumāma lived at the time of Ma'mūn with whom he stood in good standing.

9 The Hishāmīya

The Hishāmīya are the followers of Hishām b. 'Amr al-Fuwaṭī. Hishām goes to greater extremes on the question of *qadar* than do other Mu'tazilites. He refrained from ascribing actions to God even though this is done in the Qur'ān. Thus, for example, he says that God does not join together the hearts of the believers, but they are joined together by their own choice; though the Qur'ān says, 'You did not join their hearts together, but it was God who joined them'.[10] Similarly, he says God does not endear the faith to the believers nor make it attractive to their hearts; yet God says, 'He has endeared the faith to you and made it attractive to your hearts.'[11] He obstinately refused to ascribe to God acts of setting a stamp or placing a seal [on the hearts of men], putting a barrier and the like, though all these expressions appear in the Qur'ān. Thus, for example: 'God has sealed their hearts and their ears';[12] 'God has set a seal upon them because of their unbelief';[13] 'We have placed a barrier in front of them and behind them.'[14] I wonder what he means. Does he deny the words of the Qur'ān and the fact of their revelation by God? If so, he has fallen into open unbelief. Or does he deny that the literal meaning of the words are to be ascribed to God, and say that these, therefore, must be interpreted? If that is so, then his view is essentially the same as that of other Mu'tazilites.

Another of his innovations concerns the proof of God's existence. According to him accidents do not prove that God is a creator and, moreover, they cannot furnish such a proof. Bodies, however, do prove that God is a creator. This too is very strange.

Another unusual view concerns the imāmate. An imām, he said, may not be appointed in time of civil war and strife, but may be appointed only when there is concord and peace. Similarly Abū Bakr al-Aṣamm, one of his followers, used to say, 'The imāmate is valid only when there is universal consent of the community.' By this he wished to discredit the imāmate of 'Alī, because the homage paid to him was rendered during the period of civil war without the agreement of all the Companions, since everywhere there were some opposed to him.

Hishām also held the unusual view that heaven and hell are not yet created, because there is no advantage in their existence if they are both empty, and if no one is enjoying them or suffering in them. This became the accepted view of the Mu'tazilites.

Hishām believed, too, in the 'final acts', *al-muwāfāt*, and maintained that faith at death is all that matters. He said that whoever is obedient to God all his life, but in God's knowledge he will [at last] do something, even if it be a grave sin, [but not *kufr*], which will bring to nought his deeds, such a one does not deserve the promise of a reward. The converse is also true.

Hishām was followed by 'Abbād, a Mu'tazilite, who was unwilling to use the expression 'God created an unbeliever', because the word unbeliever denotes two things: 'unbelief' and 'man', whereas God does not create unbelief. He also said that the gift of prophecy is a recompense for [good] deeds, and will continue to be bestowed as long as the world lasts. 'Abbād also maintained, according to Ash'arī, that we cannot say that God still speaks or that he no longer speaks. Al-Iskāfī agrees with him in this, and both say that God cannot be called a 'speaker'.

Hishām al-Fuwaṭī also held that before things come into existence they are non-existent, and in that state they are not things. When, however, after having existed, they cease to exist, they may be called things. Accordingly we cannot say that God always had knowledge of things before they existed, since before they existed they cannot be called things.

Hishām permitted the ambushing and the killing of his opponents, and the plundering and stealing of their goods, on the ground that they were unbelievers, and that, therefore, their blood and property were forfeit.

10 The Jāḥiẓīya

The Jaḥiẓīya are the followers of 'Amr b. Baḥr Abū 'Uthmān al-Jāḥiẓ who was one of the most distinguished of the Mu'tazilites, and one of their chief writers. He had studied many of the works of the philosophers, and incorporated many of their views in his writings. These are noted for their literary excellence and exquisite charm and wit, which won for them wide publicity. Jāḥiẓ was a contemporary of [the caliphs] al-Mu'taṣim and al-Mutawakkil.

Jāḥiẓ differed from other Mu'tazilites on a number of points. All knowledge, according to him, is natural and necessary, and none of it comes from man's own activity. Man's only part is his will. All his actions proceed from him by necessity of nature, a view which was also held by Thumāma. On the other hand it is also said of him that he rejected altogether the concept of will, and denied that it belonged to the genus of accidents. He said that if the person performing an act is not unaware of it and knows what he is doing, then he is indeed willing; but when the will relates to the deed of another, that is simply a desire for it.

Jāḥiẓ also held with the naturalist philosophers that bodies have natures, with activities proper to them by reason of their nature. He said, too, that it is impossible for a substance to become nothing; accidents, indeed, change, but substances are not annihilated. He further maintained that those who go to hell would not be punished eternally, but would be transformed into the nature of fire. He held, too, that the fire of hell attracts its inhabitants to itself without anyone being made to enter it.

Jāḥiẓ's denial of attributes agrees with that of the philosophers, whilst he follows the general Mu'tazilite view in maintaining that man has power over good and evil. Ka'bī tells us of him that he maintained that God can be said to be willing in the sense that he cannot be unaware or ignorant of what he is doing, and that he cannot be compelled or coerced.

Again, in the opinion of Jāḥiẓ, all intelligent men know that God is their creator; they know also that they are in need of a prophet. Because of this knowledge they are liable to judgment. Men are of two kinds: those who know the unity of God and those who are ignorant of it. Those in ignorance are excused, but those with knowledge are liable to judgment.

Jāḥiẓ goes on to say that if anyone accepts the religion of Islam and believes that God is not a body nor form; that he cannot be seen by the eyes; that he is just, not committing wrongs nor willing sins; and, if having this belief and certainty, he professes it fully, he is truly a Muslim. If, however, knowing all this, he denies and rejects it, and maintains instead anthropomorphism and predeterminism, he is certainly a polytheist and infidel. If anyone has not thought about these things, and merely believes that God is his Lord and Muḥammad is the messenger of God, such a one is a believer; no blame attaches to him, nor is more than this to be required of him.

According to Ibn al-Rāwandī, Jāḥiẓ said that the Qur'ān has a body, which may sometimes take the form of a man and sometimes that of an animal. This view is like that reported of Abū Bakr al-Aṣamm who held that the Qur'ān was a created body.

Jāḥiẓ denied accidents altogether. He also denied the attributes of God. In general the views of Jāḥiẓ are just the same as those of the philosophers, except that he and his followers are more inclined to the naturalists than to the metaphysicians.

11 The Khayyāṭīya and the Ka'bīya

These are the followers of Abu 'l-Ḥusain Ibn Abū 'Umar al-Khayyāṭ, the teacher of Abu 'l-Qāsim b. Muḥammad al-Ka'bī.[15] Both belonged to the Mu'tazilite school of Baghdād and held the same views, except that Khayyāṭ goes to extremes in maintaining that the non-existent is a thing.

According to Khayyāṭ a thing is that which can be known and about which information can be given; that substance is a substance even in its non-existence; similarly, that an accident is an accident even in its non-existence. The same can be said about all kinds of genera and species. He even went so far as to say that blackness is blackness even in its non-existence. The only exceptions are the attribute of existence, and those attributes which are concomitants of existence, or of coming into existence. For the non-existent he uses the word *al-thubūt* (the affirmed). He denies the attributes of God as other Mu'tazilites do, and also holds the common Mu'tazilite views on *qadar*, revelation and the use of reason.

Ka'bī differs from his teacher on the following points: God's will is not an attribute subsisting in his essence; nor does he will by his essence; nor is his will an occurrence either in a substrate or not in a substrate. When we say of God that he is willing we mean that he is knowing and powerful, not coerced in his action nor averse to it. When it is said that he wills his acts this means that he creates them in accordance with his knowledge; and when it is said that he wills the acts of men it means that he commands them and approves of them. God's hearing and seeing are interpreted in a similar way. His hearing, therefore, means that he knows all that is audible, and his sight that he knows all that is visible. Ka'bī has the same view as other Mu'tazilites on God's vision of himself, that is, he denies it in the literal sense and gives it another meaning. The others, however, maintain that God sees himself as well as all things visible, and, therefore, his seeing of them is something more than his knowing of them. This, however, is denied by Ka'bī who said that when we say that God sees himself and sees visible things we only mean that he knows both.

12 The Jubbā'īya and The Bahshamīya

These are the followers of Abū 'Alī Muḥammad b. 'Abd al-Wahhāb al-Jubbā'ī and his son Abū Hāshim 'Abd al-Salām, both of whom belonged to the Mu'tazilites of Baṣra. They differed from other Mu'tazilites as well as from each other on a number of things. The points on which they differed from other Mu'tazilites are as follows:

They maintained that there occur acts of will which are not in a substrate and by which God can be said to be willing. There is also a glorification not in a substrate when God wills to glorify himself. Similarly, there will be annihilation not in a substrate when God wills to annihilate the universe. What is most characteristic of these attributes, [namely, not in a substrate], is also applicable to God, as he likewise is not in a substrate. To maintain, [Shahrastānī says], the existence of accidents, or what may be regarded as accidents, which are not in a substrate, is like maintaining the existence of substances, or what may be regarded as substances, which are not in a place. This resembles the view of philosophers, inasmuch as they maintain the existence of an intellect, which is a substance, not in a substrate nor in a place; likewise with regard to the Universal Soul and the separated intelligences.

They hold that God is a speaker with a word which he creates in a substrate. The word, according to them, consists essentially of articulated sounds and ordered arrangement of letters. The speaker is the one who produces the word and not the one in whom the word subsists. Jubbā'ī differs, however, from other Mu'tazilites, especially in saying that God creates his own 'word' in the place of recitation whenever a man recites the Qur'ān. When it was objected to him that thus God's 'word' is not what is recited or heard, he admitted this impossible thing, and maintained something which is both unintelligible and unheard of, namely, that there are two 'words' in one place.[16]

Both denied that God will be seen by the eyes in heaven. They also held that a man's act is his creation and production; moreover, good and evil, obedience and disobedience, are to be attributed to him entirely and to him alone.

Capacity exists before the act and is a power over and above a sound constitution and health of limb; nevertheless, a physical constitution is a prerequisite for entities requiring life for their existence.

Jubbā'ī and Abū Hāshim also agree that knowledge [of God], gratitude to the Benevolent, and knowledge of good and evil are obligatory on man through reason. They further maintain that there is a law, *sharī'a*, based on reason; they reduce the prophetic *sharī'a* to determinations of laws and to the prescription of assigned times for acts of worship: these are such that cannot be arrived at by reason and speculation. Thus, for example, reason and wisdom require that the Wise One reward the obedient and punish the disobedient, but the duration [of reward or punishment] in time or eternity is known by revelation. *Īman* (faith), according to them, is a word of praise; it means qualities of virtue which when found in a person entitle him to be called a *mu'min* (believer). Whoever commits a grave sin is at once to be called a *fāsiq* (sinner), neither believer nor unbeliever; if he does not repent but dies in that sin he will abide in hell for ever.

Both agree that God does not keep back his grace, *lutf*, from men, nor anything which is good, *ṣalāḥ*, and which is best, *al-aṣlaḥ*, for them, which if granted, would, he knows, lead to obedience and repentance. The reason for this is that God is omnipotent and omniscient, generous and wise; who suffers no loss by giving; whose treasures are not diminished by being bestowed, and whose possessions are not increased by being withheld. The best, *al-aṣlaḥ*, however, is not the most pleasant, but it is that which is most rewarding in the next life and most fitting in the present one, even though it may be painful and far from pleasant; such as, for example, cupping, blood-letting and taking medicines. It would be untrue to say, on the other hand, that God has power to do what is better for man than what he actually does.

Obligations are all acts of grace; as, likewise, are God's sending of prophets, his laying down of laws and regulations, and his pointing to the right way.

Jubbā'ī and Abū Hāshim disagree on the following points:

With regard to the attributes of God Jubbā'ī holds that God is knowing by his essence, is powerful, living and so on by his essence. The meaning of the expression 'by his essence' is that God does not need in his knowing either an attribute which is knowledge, or a 'mode' by which he is knowing. According to Abū Hāshim, on the other hand, God is knowing by his essence in the sense that he has a mode, which is an attribute, recognizable over and above his being an existing essence. The attribute, however, can only be known along with the essence and not apart from it. Thus he maintained that there are modes which are attributes neither existing nor non-existing, neither known nor unknown; that is, in themselves they are not known as attributes, but are known only with the essence. Reason recognizes a necessary distinction between knowing a thing in itself and knowing it with an attribute. So one who knows the essence of God does not *ipso facto* know that he is knowing. Similarly, one who knows substance does not *ipso facto* know that it is in a place and is a substrate of accidents.

There is no doubt that man recognizes that existing things are similar in some respects and dissimilar in others, and knows that that in which they are alike is other than that in which they differ. These are reasonable propositions which no intelligent person would deny. Now these [points of similarity and dissimilarity] are not reducible to the essence, nor to accidents as distinct from the essence, for this would lead to accidents inhering in accidents; therefore, they must be modes. Thus the 'knowing' of the knowing One is a mode [of the essence] which is an attribute over and above his being an essence; that is, what is meant by knowing is other than what is meant by the essence. The same can be said about his being powerful, living and the like. Abū Hāshim, moreover, maintains another mode for God which necessitates these modes.

Abū Hāshim's father and others who denied these modes opposed this view, reducing similarity and dissimilarity to words and generic names. They asked, 'Are not these modes similar in being modes and dissimilar in their individual characteristics? We can say the same thing about the attributes. This would lead to maintaining that modes have modes, which would mean a *processus in infinitum*.' Therefore, they argued that these modes are reducible either to mere words, originally invented to apply to many things, and not signifying an entity or an attribute existing in the essence embracing these things and common to them, which would be impossible; or to aspects and mental considerations, derived from instances of similarity and dissimilarity. These aspects, however, such as affinities and relationships, proximity, distance and the like, are, as is commonly agreed, not regarded as attributes. This view is followed by Abu 'l-Ḥusain al-Baṣrī and Abu 'l-Ḥasan al-Ash'arī.

Al-Jubbā'ī and his followers go on further to say that the non-existent is a thing. Those who maintain that it is a thing, as we have already seen that some Mu'tazilites do, do not deny to that thing any attributes except that of existence. Accordingly they do not ascribe to God's power any effect in the bringing into being of the attributes except that of giving them existence. Existence, however, according to those who deny modes is nothing more than a word; but, according to those who hold the existence of modes, it is a mode which cannot be described either as existent or non-existent. These views, as you see, are contradictory and absurd. Of those who deny modes there are, nevertheless, some who regard the non-existent as a thing, but do not apply to it the attributes of genera.

According to Jubbā'ī the special characteristic of God is eternity. Anyone sharing in the particular also necessarily shares in the more common. [Shahrastānī says], I wonder how it is possible for him to speak meaningfully of sharing and not sharing, of common and particular, while he denies the modes. This, indeed, on the view of Abū Hāshim, would be consistent. When, however, we look into the nature of eternity it means only having no beginning; and it would be impossible to regard a negation as the special characteristic of God.

Jubbā'ī and Abū Hāshim disagree as to God's attributes of hearing and seeing. According to Jubbā'ī to say that God is hearing and seeing means that he is living and has no imperfection. He is opposed in this by his son and other Mu'tazilites. His son holds the view that God's hearing is a mode; so also is his seeing. That he is 'seeing' is a mode other than that he is 'knowing', for these are two different statements, with different meanings, different relations and different effects. Other Mu'tazilites, however, say that God's hearing and seeing means that he apprehends what is visible and audible.

Father and son also differ on some aspects of the question of grace. There may be someone, for example, of whom God knows that if he believed with grace his reward would be less because his effort would be less, but if he believed without grace his reward would be greater because his effort would be greater. Of such a one Jubbā'ī says that it would not be fitting for God to impose an obligation upon him without grace, nor to treat him like one about whom he knows that he would not be fully obedient except with grace. He adds that if God were to impose an obligation on him without grace, he would inevitably be making his situation worse rather than removing his weakness. Abū Hāshim disagrees with Jubbā'ī on some aspects of this question. According to him it would be fitting for God to impose an obligation on such a man to follow the more difficult path, and believe without grace.

Jubbā'ī and Abū Hāshim differed also on the question of inflicting suffering for the sake of compensation, *'iwaḍ*. Jubbā'ī says that God may inflict suffering undeservedly with a view to compensation. In this way he explains the suffering of children. His son says that inflicting suffering is fitting, provided that it is followed by compensation and at the same time a lesson is drawn.

Jubbā'ī's views on compensation may be explained in two ways. One is that God may bestow a favour, *tafaḍḍul*, what he bestows as compensation, except that he knows that it would be of no benefit to bestow compensation unless it is first preceded by suffering. The other is that it would be good to do this for compensation is due, whereas what God bestows as favour is not due. Reward, *thawāb*, however, according to them, is different from favour in two ways. Firstly, it honours and exalts the one rewarded, along with heavenly bliss. Secondly, it is something more than favour. It would not be right, therefore, to regard compensation as being the same as reward, because compensation does not differ from favour in either quantity or quality.

Jubbā'ī's son says that it is fitting for God to bestow gratuitously as a favour what he bestows as compensation, although compensation comes to an end and is not lasting. According to Jubbā'ī it is possible for God to do justice to a person oppressed by another by giving him compensation from his own bounty, but only if the oppressor does not have any compensation due to him for anything which he may have suffered. Abū Hāshim, however, says that justice is not rendered by bestowing favour, because bestowing favour is not obligatory upon God. Jubbā'ī and his son both hold that God has no obligation towards men in this world, if he does not lay commands upon them through reason and revelation. If, on the other hand, he does command them to do what is known by reason as obligatory and to avoid what is evil (while at the same time having created in them an inclination towards evil and an aversion from good, and built evil dispositions into them), then it is obligatory upon him, whilst imposing obligations upon them, to perfect their reason, to show signs, to bestow power and capacity, and to provide the necessary means so as to remove the obstacles to performing what he has commanded. It is also obligatory upon God to grant them whatever is most conducive to doing what he has commanded them, and deterring them from doing the evil which he has forbidden. On many aspects of this question they are most confused.

Conclusion

The views of all the Mu'tazila of Baghdād on the prophethood and imāmate differ from those of the Mu'tazilites of Baṣra. Some of their leaders incline to the Rāfiḍites and others to the Khārijites.

Jubbā'ī and Abū Hāshim both agree with the Orthodox on the question of the imāmate, holding that it is by election. They also agree that the Companions differ in their degree of excellence in conformity with their order in the imāmate. However, they deny altogether that saints work miracles, whether they be Companions or others. They go to extremes in asserting the sinlessness of the prophets, not only in regard to greater sins but also lesser ones. Jubbā'ī does not even allow that they are tempted to sin, though his opinion here is open to interpretation. Later Mu'tazilites, as Qāḍī 'Abd al-Jabbār and others, followed the school of Abū Hāshim.

Abu 'l-Huṣain al-Baṣrī, however, opposed Abū Hāshim in this matter. He explained the arguments of the leading Mu'tazilites, and consequently rejected the views of Abū Hāshim as fabrications and falsehood. He differed from the later Mu'tazilites, on a number of points, such as denying modes, and denying that the non-existent is a thing or that colours are accidents. He also asserted that existing things differ from each other by their essences. This is a consequence of his denial of modes. He also reduced all of God's attributes to his knowing, his being powerful and his apprehending. He is inclined, too, to the view of Hishām b. al-Ḥakam that things are not known before they exist. He is philosophical in his views, but he spread his ideas among the Mu'tazila in the form of theology. In this manner they became known amongst them, for only a little was known to them of these ways of thought.

Chapter 2

The Jabrīya

Introduction

Jabr is a doctrine which denies that a deed is in reality to be attributed to man, and ascribes it to God. There are two main groups of Jabrites:

(i) the pure Jabrīya who do not allow any deed at all to man, not even the power to act;
(ii) the moderate Jabrīya who admit that man has power, but maintain that it is a power which is in no way effective.

If, however, one maintained that this created power in man has some effect on the act and calls it an 'acquisition', *kasb*, such a one cannot be called a Jabrite; though, according to the Mu'tazilites, those who do not hold that this created power has any independent influence in originating or causing acts are Jabrīya. In this case, however, these Mu'tazila would have to give the name Jabrite to other Mu'tazila who maintain that a generated act has no agent, because, according to them, the created power has no influence on such an act.

Writers on heresies regard the Najjārīya and the Ḍirārīya as Jabrīya, just as they look upon the Kullābīya as Ṣifatīya. As for the Ash'arites, they are sometimes considered as Hashwīya and sometimes as Jabrīya. We have heard the Jabrīya themselves recognize the Najjārīya and Ḍirārīya as fellow Jabrīya. As, however, they have said nothing about the others we have included them among the Ṣifātīya.

1 The Jahmīya

The Jahmīya are the followers of Jahm b. Ṣafwān, and adherents of pure determinism, a heresy which first arose in Tirmidh, and on account of which Jahm was put to death by Sālim b. Aḥwaz al-Māzinī in Marw in the last days of the Umayyad Caliphate.

Jahm agreed with the Mu'tazila in denying the eternal attributes, but he also added other doctrines. These are as follows:

(1) It is not lawful to apply to God an attribute which is also applicable to creatures, because this would imply likeness between God and creatures. He, therefore, denies that God is living and knowing, but maintains that he is powerful, an agent and a creator, because to no creature can be attributed power, action and creation.

(2) God has cognitions which are not eternal and these cognitions are not in a substrate. According to Jahm it is not right to say that God could know a thing before he created it, for the question would arise whether his knowledge remained as it was before or not. If it remained as it was this would imply lack of knowledge in God, because knowledge that a thing will come into being is other than knowledge that it has come into being. If it did not remain as it was, then it would have changed, and that which changes is created, not eternal. In this question Jahm is in agreement with Hishām b. al-Ḥakam, whose views have already been explained. He goes on to say that, since it is proved that there is a cognition which comes into being, one of two things is possible. The first possibility is that this cognition comes into existence in God's essence. This, however, would lead to a change of his essence, and thus God would be a substrate for changes. The second possibility is that this cognition comes into being in a substrate, and it would, accordingly, be an attribute of this substrate, not of God. Thus it becomes evident that God's knowledge has no substrate. Jahm maintains, therefore, that there are non-eternal cognitions in God corresponding in number to the objects known.

(3) With regard to created power Jahm says that a man does not have power over anything, nor can he be said to have capacity [to act]. Man is absolutely determined in his deeds. He has neither power, nor will, nor choice. God creates deeds in man just as he produces actions in all inanimate objects, and it is only in a metaphorical sense that, as with inanimate objects, deeds can be ascribed to man: as when we say, for example, that a tree bears fruit, that water runs, that a stone moves, that the sun rises and sets, that the sky becomes overcast and sends forth rain, that the earth moves and brings forth vegetation, and so on. Rewards and punishments, moreover, are determined just as all deeds are. Again, once the principle of determination has been established it follows that what is commanded is also determined.

(4) All motion in heaven and hell will come to an end. Paradise and hell will both pass away after those who have gone to paradise have enjoyed its bliss, and those who have gone to hell have suffered its torments. The reason for this is that we cannot imagine movements which will never end, just as we cannot imagine movements which have no beginning. The words of the Qur'ān: 'They shall dwell in it for ever',[1] are to be interpreted as an hyperbole for the sake of emphasis, and not meant to be understood in the literal sense of eternity; as, for example, when we say, 'May God make that man's kingdom eternal.' Jahm defended his doctrine that eternity will come to an end with the words of the Qur'ān: 'They will be in it eternally as long as there are heaven and earth, except as thy Lord pleases.'[2] This verse, he pointed out, contains both a condition and an exception, whereas the eternal and everlasting do not admit of either condition or exception.

(5) If a man has knowledge [of God] but outwardly denies him, this denial does not make him an unbeliever because it does not take away his knowledge. Hence he remains a believer. Jahm further says that faith is not made up of parts, that is, it cannot be divided into belief, words and deeds. Again, those who have faith do not surpass one another in degrees of faith; therefore, the faith of the prophets and that of the people are on the same level – knowledge does not differ in degrees.

The early masters bitterly attacked Jahm, accusing him of absolute denial of the divine attributes.

Jahm also agreed with the Mu'tazila in denying the beatific vision, in maintaining that the Qur'ān is created, and in holding that knowledge is obligatory upon reason before revelation.

2 The Najjārīya

The Najjārīya are the followers of Ḥusain b. Muḥammad al-Najjār, whose views were adopted by most of the Mu'tazila in the district of al-Rayy. They fall into various groups, as Barghūthīya, Za'farānīya and Mustadrika, but they do not differ on the fundamental points to which we have referred. They are in agreement with the Mu'tazila in denying the attributes, namely: knowledge, power, will, life, hearing and seeing; however, they agree with the Ṣifātīya in holding that God creates deeds.

Najjār maintained that God wills himself inasmuch as he knows himself. He was, therefore, faced with the consequence that God wills all things, and this he admitted. God wills, he says, good and evil, benefit and harm. To say that God is willing means that he is not forced or coerced. Najjār also says that God is the creator of all man's deeds, good and bad, right and wrong: man on his part acquires these deeds. He further maintains that the created power has a certain effect on these deeds; this he calls acquisition, *kasb*, as Ash'arī does. He agrees, too, with Ash'arī that capacity exists with the act.

On the question of the beatific vision, Najjār denies that God can be seen with the eyes, for this to him is impossible. However, he says that God may change into an eye the power of knowledge that is in the heart, and men will know God through that eye; this will be called seeing.

Najjār also holds that the word of God is created, but differs from the Mu'tazila on a number of points. According to him, for example, God's word when it is recited is an accident, and when it is written a body.

On the question of God's word the Za'farānīya, strangely enough, believe, on the one hand, that it is other than himself, and that whatever is other than himself is created; but, on the other hand, they hold that whoever says that the Qur'ān is created is an unbeliever. Perhaps they mean by that that there is a difference [between the Qur'ān and the word of God], otherwise their statements would be obviously contradictory.

The Mustadrika, however, say:

> We believe that God's word is other than himself, and that it is created. The Prophet, however, has said that God's word is not created, and all our predecessors are in agreement with this statement. We are, therefore, willing to accept that, but interpret their opinion that it is not created as follows: it is uncreated in this pattern of words and sounds, but created in other than these words; one is a copy of the other.

Ka'bī relates of Najjār that he says that God is everywhere both in essence and existence, not merely through knowledge and power. This leads him to many absurdities. With regard to a thinking being before revelation he holds the same position as the Mu'tazila, that is, that he must gain knowledge through reflection and reasoning. *Īmān*, according to him, is belief. Again, whoever commits a grave sin, and dies in it without repentance, will be punished for it; however, he will come out of the fire of hell, because it would not be just to make him equal to an unbeliever by an eternity of punishment.

Muḥammad b. 'Īsā, known as Barghūth, Bishr b. Ghiyāth al-Muraīsī and Ḥusain al-Najjār closely resemble one another in their ideas. They all maintain that God is 'willing', and has not ceased willing everything that he knows will take place, good or bad, belief or unbelief, obedience or disobedience. Most of the Mu'tazila, however, deny this.

3 Ḍirārīya

The Ḍirārīya are the followers of Ḍirār b. 'Amr and Ḥafṣ al-Fard. Both of them agree in denying the positive nature of the attributes, and maintain that God is knowing and powerful in the sense that he is not ignorant nor impotent. Both hold that God has a quiddity which is known to himself alone. They say that this view was taken from Abū Hanīfa and some of his followers. What is meant by it is that God knows himself directly, not by proof or testimony; we, on the other hand, know him through proof and testimony. They maintain that man has a sixth sense by which he will be able to see God on the day of reward in paradise.

Both also say that man's deeds are in reality created by God and man in reality acquires them. Thus it is possible for an act to be produced by two agents. It is possible, too, for God to change accidents into bodies. Capacity and incapacity also are parts of the body, and therefore a body, which certainly continues to exist for two moments, *zamānain.*

Both hold that, since the time of the Prophet, authority lies in consensus alone; therefore, whatever religious laws are handed down from the Prophet by traditions reported by only one authority are not to be accepted. It has been reported of Ḍirār that he refused to recognize the version [of the Qur'ān] by Ibn Mas'ūd and also that by Ubayy b. Ka'b, and categorically denied that God has revealed it. He also held that before revelation is received nothing is obligatory upon a thinking being through reason alone; obligation arises only when a prophet comes, and commands or forbids him. Again, reason cannot show that anything is obligatory upon God.

Ḍirār also maintains that the imāmate may be held by other than a Quraishite. He even says that if there are two candidates, a Quraishite and a Nabataean, we should prefer the Nabataean, because as he has a small following and is less powerful, it would be easier for us to depose him if he acts contrary to the *sharī'a*. The Mu'tazilites, on the other hand, though they grant that the imāmate may be held by other than a Quraishite, do not hold that preference may be given to a Nabataean over a Quraishite.

Chapter 3

The Ṣifātīya

Introduction

Most of the pious leaders of the early community maintained eternal attributes of God, such as knowledge, power, life, will, hearing, seeing, speech, majesty, glory, generosity, beneficence, honour, grandeur. Moreover they did not differentiate between essential and operative attributes, but spoke of both in the same way. They also believed in such Qur'ānic descriptives as 'two hands' and 'a face'. They did not interpret them, but simply said, 'These attributes have been mentioned in the Qur'ān, and, therefore, we shall call them revealed attributes.' As the Mu'tazilites deny the attributes and the early leaders, *salaf*, maintain them, the latter are called *Ṣifātīya* (Attributists), but the Mu'tazilites *Mu'aṭṭila* (Strippers). Some of the early leaders so exaggerate the existence of attributes that they make them analogous to the attributes of created things. Others restrict themselves to operative attributes.

Concerning the revealed attributes, there were two schools of thought among the early leaders. One school interpreted them in a way that could be suggested by the words themselves. The other group abstained from interpretation. They said:

> We know from reason that there is nothing like God; therefore, God does not resemble any created thing, nor does any created thing resemble him. This we are sure of. We do not know, however, the meaning of the words applied to him in such statements as: 'The Beneficent sat on the throne',[1] 'I created with my hand',[2] 'God came',[3] and the like. We need not know the explanation of these verses, nor how to interpret them; but we are obliged to believe that God has no partner and that there is nothing like him: that we have shown beyond doubt.

Some later thinkers went beyond what the early leaders had said, maintaining that the attributes must be understood literally and explained just as they had been revealed, without any attempt to interpret them or hesitation in accepting them literally. These fell into pure anthropomorphism, which was contrary to what the early leaders believed.

A strict form of anthropomorphism had existed amongst the Jews; not, indeed, amongst all of them, but in a section of them amongst the Qarrā'ites, who found in the Torah many words which would suggest such a conception. The Shī'a of our faith also fell into one of two extremes: one was to make some of the imāms like God, the other to make God like a man. When the Mu'tazilites and scholastic theologians arose, some of the Shī'ites abandoned their extreme views and adopted Mu'tazilism; some of the early leaders, on the other hand, adopted a literal interpretation and became anthropomorphists.

Among those early leaders who did not follow the principle of interpretation or adopt anthropomorphism was Mālik b. Anas. According to him we know that God sits on the throne, but how is unknown. To believe that he sits on a throne is necessary; to ask how is a heresy. Aḥmad b. Ḥanbal, Sufyān al-Thaurī and Dāwūd b. 'Alī al-Asfahānī and their followers held the same view. By the time of 'Abdullāh b. Sa'īd al-Kullābī, Abu 'l-'Abbās al-Qalānisī and al-Ḥārith b. Asad al-Muḥāsibī, all of whom were among the early leaders, scholasticism had been adopted by them, and the beliefs of the early leaders were supported by scholastic reasoning and theological arguments. Some taught and others wrote. Finally an argument took place between Abu 'l-Ḥasan al-Ash'arī and his teacher on a question concerning the 'good' and the 'best'. As a result of this argument Ash'arī went over to the early leaders and supported their views with scholastic methods. Ash'arī's views and methods were adopted by the Orthodox, and the name Ṣifātīya was now given to the followers of Ash'arī.

As the Mushabbiha (anthropomorphists) and the Karrāmīya also affirmed attributes we have included them among the Ṣifātīya as two different groups.

1 The Ash'arites

The Ash'arites are followers of Abu'l-Ḥasan 'Alī b. Ismā'īl al-Ash'arī, a descendant of Abū Mūsā al-Ash'arī. I have heard of the strange coincidence that Abū Mūsā al-Ash'arī held the same views as Abu 'l-Ḥasan al-Ash'arī. In a discussion that once took place between Abū Mūsā al-Ash'arī and 'Amr b. al-'Āṣ, 'Amr asked Abū Mūsā, 'To whom shall I go for an explanation of God's actions?' Abū Mūsā replied, 'You may come to me.' Thereupon 'Amr asked, 'Does God predetermine what I do and then punish me for it?' Abū Mūsā said 'Yes.' 'Why?' 'Amr asked. Abū Mūsā replied, 'Because he does not do you an injustice.' 'Amr was silent and made no answer.

Ash'arī maintains that if a man reflects on his creation, that is, on how he came into being and passed through various stages, step by step, till he reached the fully developed form; and if he knows for certain that by himself he could not have planned his own creation and his development from step to step, nor his own evolution from an undeveloped to a fully developed form, he would be forced to acknowledge that he has a creator who is all powerful, knowing and willing. For it is impossible to imagine that these well-ordered acts could proceed from nature alone, since the signs of a deliberate choice, order and perfection are manifest in them.

God, therefore, has attributes which are known from his acts: these attributes cannot be denied. Just as his acts show that he is knowing, powerful and willing, so also do they show that he has knowledge, power and will. There is no difference in the validity of what is inferred, whether it be manifest or hidden. Moreover, 'the one knowing', as used of God, has in reality no meaning other than that he has knowledge; 'the one powerful' no meaning other than that he has power; 'the one willing' no meaning other than that he has will. Thus through knowledge come order and perfection, through power things occur and come into being, through will comes the determination of time, measure and form. When these attributes are ascribed to the essence, they cannot be conceived unless we say that the essence is 'living' with 'life', as we have already shown.

Ash'arī put to silence those who denied the attributes with an argument they could not answer. You agree with us, he said, that God is knowing and powerful. This can be understood in only two ways: either the two notions expressed by these two attributes are one, or they are more than one. If they are only one, then God must know by his power and be powerful through his knowledge. It would follow, therefore, that whoever knows only God's essence would know, nevertheless, that he is knowing and powerful. This, however, is not true. Therefore we know that these aspects are different from one another.

Now this difference is due either to the words alone, or to a mode, or to an attribute. It cannot, however, be due to the words alone, because reason demands that there must be two different concepts corresponding to two different words. Even if we supposed that the words did not exist, reason would not doubt what it has conceived. Again, the difference is not due to the mode; because to hold that there is an attribute which cannot be described as either existing or non-existing involves maintaining something intermediate between existence and non-existence, between affirmation and denial, which is impossible. It is clear, therefore, that the difference between the two aspects is due to an attribute which subsists in the essence. This last is what Ash'arī believed.

Qāḍī Abū Bakr al-Bāqillānī, one of Ash'arī's followers, rejects his master's views regarding modes. He himself affirmed the modes. He held, nevertheless, that attributes are entities subsisting in the essence and not modes; for according to him, the modes which were maintained by Abū Hāshim are the same as what we call attributes, especially as he affirmed a mode which necessitates the existence of these attributes.

Aub 'l-Ḥasan said that God is knowing with knowledge, powerful with power, living with life, willing with will, speaking with speech, hearing with hearing and seeing with sight, though he has a different opinion with regard to God's 'enduring'. These attributes, Ash'arī says, are eternal and subsist in the essence of God. It cannot be said that they are he or other than he; nor can it be said that they are not he, nor that they are not other than he.

It has been shown that God speaks with an eternal speech, and wills with an eternal will, by the proof already given that God is a sovereign, and a sovereign is one who commands and forbids; therefore, God is commanding and forbidding. Now he commands either with an eternal command or with a created command. If it is with a created command then this command is either created in God's essence, or in a substrate, or not in a substrate. It cannot, however, be created in his essence, because this would mean that God would be a substrate for created things, and that is impossible. Nor can it be created in a substrate, because in that case it is the substrate which would be the subject of attribution. Nor, again, can it be created in no substrate, because that would be absurd. Therefore it is clear that God's command is eternal, that it subsists in him and is his attribute. The same kind of argument can be given for willing, hearing and seeing.

God's knowledge is one and is connected with all that is known: the impossible, the possible, the necessary, the existent and the non-existent. His power is also one, connected with all things possible and proper for existence. His will is one, connected with all things capable of individualization. His word is one: it is command, prohibition, statement, interrogation, 'promise and warning'. All these, however, are merely aspects of his word, and do not imply numerical division of the word itself or its expressions. The sentences and words which are revealed through the tongues of angels to the prophets are signs of the eternal word: the sign itself is created and originated, but what is signified by it is eternal. The difference between reading and what is read, between reciting and what is recited, is like the difference between the words spoken and the one spoken of. The words spoken are created, and the one spoken of is eternal.

Ash'arī with this subtle distinction opposed a group of Ḥashwīya who maintained that even the letters of the words are eternal. According to Ash'arī speech is an entity which subsists in the mind and is other than its verbal expression, the verbal expression being a human attempt to manifest it. The speaker, therefore, according to Ash'arī (unlike the Mu'tazilites, for whom the speaker is the one who produces the speech), is the one in whom speech subsists; hence the verbal expression is called speech either in a metaphorical sense, or because the word is common to both the entity existing in the mind and its expression.

God's will is one and eternal, and is connected with all things that are willed, not only God's own deeds but also the acts of his creatures. God's will is connected with the deeds of men inasmuch as they are created by him, but not inasmuch as they are acquired by them. It is in this sense that Ash'arī held that God wills all things good and bad, beneficial and harmful. In accordance with his will and knowledge, he willed of his creatures what he knew, and this he ordered the pen to write in the Sacred Tablet. This is his command, decree and determination, which cannot be changed or altered. Whatever is contrary to God's knowledge and his decree cannot happen.

According to Ash'arī it is possible for God to command what is beyond the power of man to perform, not only on account of the reason we have already mentioned, but also because for Ash'arī capacity is an accident, and an accident does not endure for two moments. At the time of command the one commanded does not have power to execute the command, because the one commanded is one who will have the power to do what he has been commanded. However, to command one who has no power at all to do what is commanded is impossible, even if it were found clearly written in the Book.

Man has power over his acts because he experiences in himself an obvious distinction between movements such as trembling and shuddering, and those which are voluntary. This difference is due to the fact that voluntary movements are brought into being through power, and as a result of the choice of the one possessing that power. On the basis of this Ash'arī says that the acquired act is the one possible through the power present, and the one that occurs 'under' the created power. According to Ash'arī's principle, however, the created power has no effect on the bringing into being [of an act], because from the point of view of coming into being there is no difference between substance and accident. If this created power had an influence on coming into being it could influence the coming into being of everything created, so that it would be able to bring into being colours, tastes, smells and even to produce substances and bodies. This would lead to the possibility of heaven falling on earth through the created power. God, indeed, has established a custom of creating the resultant act, either immediately subsequent to the created power, or under its mantle, or with it; when man has willed it and wholly directed himself to it, this is called 'acquisition'. Accordingly the act will be the creation of God; that is, it is originated and brought into being by him. It will also be man's acquisition, having taken place 'under' his power.

Qāḍī Abū Bakr al-Bāqillānī has taken the matter a little further. According to him it has been proved that the created power is not capable of bestowing existence. However an act in its attributes and aspects is not limited to coming into being alone, but it has other aspects also, such as, for example, in the case of a substance, its being a substance, occupying a place and receiving an accident. Similarly, an accident has the aspects of being an accident, being coloured, being black and so on. For those who affirm modes these aspects in their view are modes. Bāqillānī holds that the aspect of an act's coming into being with or 'under' the created power is a special relationship [between the two], and this is called acquisition. It is this acquisition which is an effect of the created power.

Bāqillānī further says that if it is possible, as the Mu'tazilites say, for antecedent power or capability to have an effect on the state of an act, namely, its coming into being and receiving existence, or on any other aspect of the act, why should it not be possible for the created power to have an effect on a state which is an attribute of what comes into being, or on some aspect of the act, for example, giving the movement a specific form? In other words what is understood by movement as such, or by an accident as such, is other than what is understood by standing up or sitting down; these are two different modes. Thus every act of standing up is a movement but not every movement is a standing up. We know that a clear distinction is made between saying, for example, that a man brought [something] into being, and saying that he prayed or fasted or sat or stood. Just as we may not attribute to God any aspect of an act which is attributable to man, so also we may not attribute to man what is attributable to God. In this way the Qāḍī affirms an effect produced by the created power. The effect of this power is the particular mode – one of the aspects of an act – which has come into being through the connection of the created power with the act. It is due to this aspect alone that reward or punishment is meted out, because existence as such does not merit them. This is particularly so for the Mu'tazilites, for whom it is the aspect of good and evil which deserved recompense, good and evil being two essential attributes apart from existence. Thus an existing thing from the point of view of its existence is neither good nor evil.

Bāqillānī goes on to say:

> If it is possible for you to maintain the existence of two attributes which are two modes, then it is also possible for me to maintain one mode to which the created power is connected. If someone says that this is a mode which is unknown, we have already answered this objection in explaining, as far as possible, its manner of existence, in defining what it is, and giving an illustration of it.

Imām al-Ḥaramain Abu 'l-Ma'ālī al-Juwainī has gone somewhat further in this point. According to him to deny the created power and capacity is contrary to reason and experience; on the other hand, to maintain a power which has no effect at all is equivalent to denying the power altogether. Similarly, to maintain the effect of power on a mode, not on an act, is equivalent to the denial of effect; particularly as modes, on the Mu'tazilite principle, cannot be predicated as existing or non-existing. A man's act must, therefore, be ascribed in a true sense to his own power, though not in the sense of bringing it into being and creating it. The reason for this is that creation expresses the idea of self-sufficiency in bringing a thing into being out of nothing; whereas man, although feeling in himself power and capacity, also feels in himself a lack of this self-sufficiency. Thus the act in its existence is dependent upon the power [in man], and this power in its existence is dependent upon another cause, the relationship of that power to this cause being the same as the relationship of the act to that power. Similarly, this cause will be dependent upon yet another cause till it reaches the cause of all causes. This final cause, therefore, is the creator both of the causes and the things caused, and is absolutely independent; for every other cause, however independent it may be in some respects, is dependent in other respects. God is the only one who is absolutely independent, lacking in nothing whatever. This opinion was adopted by Juwainī from the metaphysicians, and introduced by him into scholastic theology.

According to the principles of Juwainī this account of the relationship of the cause to the thing caused is not confined to the act and power of man, but applies to all created things that come into existence. On that basis, [Shahrastānī says], we would have to believe in the law of nature, and assert that bodies and their natures have an effect in bringing into existence other bodies and their natures. This, however, is not the doctrine of the Islamic schools. How indeed would it be possible? Even according to the philosophers a body does not have any effect in bringing into existence another body. They hold that it is not possible for a body to proceed from a body, nor from any power in a body, because a body is composed of matter and form; if a body produced an effect it would do so with both of its components, that is, with both matter and form. Matter, however, of itself does not exist, and, therefore, if it produced an effect it would do so with its non-existence; but, as the latter is impossible, so, too, must be the former. Consequently, the contrary is true, namely, neither the body, nor any power in the body, can produce an effect in another body.

The more profound of the philosophers have gone beyond a consideration of bodies and power in bodies to a consideration of whatever is contingent of itself. According to them that which is contingent of itself cannot bring anything into being, because if it did so it would be in conjunction with contingency. As contingency of itself is non-existential, the contingent left to itself is, therefore, nothing. Accordingly, if contingency produced an effect conjointly with nothing it would mean that nothing had an effect on existence; that, however, is impossible. Therefore there is in reality no cause that gives existence except the Being necessary of itself. All other causes prepare for the reception of existence, but are not themselves the causes of existence itself. An explanation of this will be given later on. If these ideas are the origins of Juwainī's views it is difficult to see how the act can really be ascribed to causes.

We return now to the view of the founder of the school. According to Abu 'l-Ḥasan 'Alī b. Ismā'īl al-Ash'arī, if God is actually the Creator, and none other is associated with him in the work of creation, then that which most characterizes God is his power to create. This, indeed, is the meaning of his name Allāh. Abū Ishāq al-Isfarā'īnī, on the other hand, holds that God's most proper characteristic is his 'being', *kawn*, which necessarily distinguishes him from all other beings. Some of the Ash'arites say that we know for certain that there is nothing that exists which does not differ in some way from all other things, for otherwise it would mean that all existing things are alike and have the same characteristics. Now God is an existent. He must, therefore, be distinguished from other existents by a characteristic that is particular to him, though the mind cannot attain knowledge of it. Moreover, it has not been made known through revelation. We, therefore, they say, go no further.

Is it possible, then, for the mind to have some notion of what this characteristic may be? On this question, too, there is a difference of opinion. The latter view [that God has a particular characteristic] is like that of Ḍirār, except that Ḍirār uses the word 'quiddity', *māhīya*. This term, however, is objectionable.

Ash'arī holds the view that every existent can be seen, because it is existence which enables a thing to be seen. God exists, therefore he can be seen. We also know from revelation that the believers will see him in the hereafter; as God says, 'On that day there shall be joyous faces looking at their Lord.'[4] Similar verses and traditions may be found. Ash'arī says, however, that the vision of God does not entail direction, place, form, or face to face encounter either by impingement of rays or by impression, all of which are impossible.

Two views are reported of Ash'arī about the nature of the beatific vision. One is that this vision is a special kind of knowledge in the sense that it is related to existence rather than to non-existence; the other that it is a perception beyond knowledge, which does not require an effect on the thing perceived, nor an effect derived from it.

Ash'arī also maintains that hearing and seeing are two eternal attributes of God. They are perceptions beyond knowledge, connected with their proper objects provided they exist. He holds also that hands and face are attributes that are reported of God; for, as he explains, revelation speaks of them, and, therefore, they must be accepted as they are revealed. He follows the early community in not attempting to interpret them, though according to one opinion reported of him he allows interpretation.

Ash'arī's views also in regard to 'promise and warning', names and judgments, *al-asmā' wa 'l-aḥkām*, revelation and reason, are opposed to the Mu'tazilites in every respect.

Ash'arī holds that *īmān* is inner belief; as for its verbal expression and external practice, these are 'branches' of belief. Whoever, therefore, believes in his heart (acknowledging the unity of God, recognizing the prophets and sincerely believing all that they have made known from God), such a one's *īmān* is valid; if immediately afterwards he dies with this *īmān* he will be regarded as a believer and be saved. Nothing will make him cease to be a believer except the denial of one of these truths. Whoever commits a grave sin, and dies without repentance, his judgment will rest with God. Either God in his mercy will forgive him, or the Prophet will intercede on his behalf; as the Prophet himself has said, 'I shall intercede for all those of my community who have committed grave sins.' God, however, may punish him as his sin deserves, and afterwards in his mercy place him in paradise. It is impossible that he should remain eternally in hell with the unbelievers, because revelation has made known to us that whoever has in his heart a particle of faith will be taken out of hell. Ash'arī, however, says:

> I do not maintain that if such a one repents it becomes obligatory upon God, by the dictate of reason, to accept his repentance, because it is God who imposes obligation. Nothing, therefore, is obligatory upon him. Nevertheless, revelation says that the repentance of those who repent will be accepted, and the prayers of those in need will be heard. God is the sole master in the affairs of his creatures. He does what he pleases and judges as he wills. If he were to put them all in hell, it still would not be unjust, because injustice lies in disposing of something not one's own or using a thing improperly. God being the absolute master of all things injustice cannot be conceived of him, nor can it be attributed to him.

Ash'arī goes on to say that whatever is of obligation is so because of revelation. Reason does not impose any obligation, nor does it declare anything good or bad. Knowledge of God is, indeed, acquired by reason, but it is through revelation that it becomes of obligation to know him; as God says, 'We shall not punish unless we first send a prophet.'[5] Similarly, that man should show gratitude to the Bountiful, and that God should reward the obedient and punish the disobedient, are obligations made known by revelation, not by reason.

From reason nothing can be judged obligatory upon God: neither the good, the best, nor even the bestowal of grace. This is because reason may consider one thing necessary from one point of view, but from the other point of view may consider its opposite necessary. The imposing of a command is not obligatory upon God, because no benefit accrues to him from it, and no harm is thereby averted from him. He has the power to requite men by rewards or punishment, and the power to bestow favours upon them gratuitously out of generosity and graciousness. Reward, favour, grace are all gratuitously bestowed by him. All punishment and chastisement is just: 'God is not asked about what he does, though they are asked.'[6]

God may send prophets: it is not impossible for him to do so, but neither is it obligatory. However, after the prophets have come it is obligatory upon God to support them with miracles and to protect them from dangers, because one listening to a prophet must have a way of recognizing the genuineness of the prophet's claim. It is also necessary that obstacles [to preaching the message] be removed so that there should be no contradiction in God's command [to the prophet]. A miracle is an act of an extraordinary kind, offering a challenge which cannot be met. As supporting evidence it fulfils the role of verbal confirmation. A miracle is of two kinds: one which is altogether contrary to the ordinary course of nature, and one which is beyond it. The miracles of the saints truly occur; they are a kind of confirmation of the prophets and a further verification of their miracles.

Belief and obedience come through God's help, but disbelief and disobedience through his abandonment. According to Ash'arī help lies in God's creating the power to obey, but abandonment in God's creating the power to disobey. According to some of his followers, however, help consists in facilitating the means of doing good, while the opposite is abandonment.

Information given to us in revelation about unseen things, such as the pen, the tablet, the throne, the chair, paradise and hell, are all to be understood literally, and believed as they have been revealed, because there is no inconceivability in affirming them. Similarly, the information given us about things which will happen in the hereafter, as interrogation in the grave, reward and punishment therein; or also the balance, the reckoning, the path, the division of men into two groups, one in paradise and the other in hell: all these things are true; they are to be accepted and understood literally, because their existence is not inconceivable.

The Qur'ān, according to Ash'arī, is miraculous in its diction, harmony and eloquence. This is seen from the fact that the Arabs, being given a choice between the sword and producing something comparable to the Qur'ān, chose what was more painful, because they were unable to offer anything like it. Some of Ash'arī's followers, on the other hand, hold that the miraculous nature of the Qur'ān lies in taking away motives [for emulation] – thus preventing attempts to produce anything comparable – and in its information about things unseen.

Succession to the imāmate is by consensus and election, not by decree or appointment. Had there been a decree it would not have remained unknown, seeing that there were abundant motives for reporting such a decree. The companions agreed in the hall of Banū Sā'ida on the choice of Abū Bakr. They also agreed on 'Umar after Abū Bakr had appointed him. They agreed, too, on 'Uthmān after consultation, and, lastly, they agreed on 'Alī. The degrees of excellence of these imāms are according to their order in the imāmate.

With regard to 'Ā'isha, Ṭalḥa, and Zubair, Ash'arī says:

> We hold only that they repented of their error, and that Ṭalḥa and Zubair are among the ten who were given the good news of paradise. Of Mu'āwiya and 'Amr b. al-'Āṣ we simply say that they had rebelled against the rightful imām and that 'Alī then fought them as rebels. As for the People of Nahrāwān, they are heretics who had forsaken the faith as the Prophet had foretold. 'Alī was right at all times, and the truth was always with him.

2 The Mushabbiha (Anthropomorphists)

It should be recalled that the Traditionalists of the early community, when they saw the deep penetration of the Mu'tazilites into theology, and their opposition to the *sunna* which had been witnessed during the reign of the pious caliphs; and when they saw also that the Mu'tazila were supported by some of the Umayyad princes in their belief in free-will, and by a number of 'Abbāsid caliphs in their denial of the divine attributes and assertion that the Qur'ān was created: when they saw all this, they wondered how to define the views of the Orthodox in regard to the ambiguous verses of the Qur'ān and some of the sayings of the Prophet. As for Aḥmad b. Ḥanbal, Dāwūd b. 'Alī al-Asfahānī and some of the leaders among the Orthodox, they followed the early Traditionalists, such as Mālik b. Anas and Muqātil b. Sulaimān, and took a safe path, saying:

> We believe in whatever is reported in the Book and the *sunna*, and we do not try to interpret it, knowing for certain that God does not resemble any created things, and that all the images we form of him are created by him and formed by him.

They avoided anthropomorphism, *tashbīh*, to such an extent that they said that if a man moved his hand while reading the word of God, 'I created with my hands';[7] or, if he pointed with his two fingers while reporting the saying of the Prophet: 'The heart of the believer is between the two fingers of the Merciful One', the hand must be cut off and the two fingers torn out. They said:

> We refrain from offering an exegesis and interpretation of such verses for two reasons. The first is the prohibition expressed in the Qur'ān in the following words: 'But those in whose hearts is perversity follow the path thereof that is allegorical, seeking discord,

> and searching for its hidden meanings, but no one knows its hidden meanings except God. And those who are firmly grounded in knowledge say, 'We believe in it [the Book]; the whole of it is from our Lord', and none will grasp the message except men of understanding.'[8] Therefore we avoid perversity. The second reason is that an interpretation, as we all agree, is an opinion, and it is not lawful to give an opinion about the attributes of God; for we may sometimes interpret the verse in a way not intended by God, and thus we would fall into perversity. Rather we say, as do those who are firmly grounded in knowledge, 'The whole is from our Lord.' We believe in what is literally said, and we believe also in its hidden meaning, but we leave the knowledge of it to God; we are not commanded to know it, because it is not one of the requirements of *īmān*, nor one of its basic elements.

Some are even more circumspect. They would not, for example, translate into Persian words such as 'the hand', 'the face', 'taking the seat', and the like. If, in order to refer to them they needed an expression, they would use the revealed expression, word by word. This to them is the safe method, free from all anthropomorphism.

A group of extreme Shī'ites, on the other hand, and a group of Traditionalists, the Ḥashwīya, profess anthropomorphism; as, for example, the Hishāmīya among the Shī'ites, Muḍar, Kuhmus, Aḥmad al-Hujaimī and others of the Ḥashwīya. According to them God has a form and possesses limbs and parts which are either spiritual or physical. It is possible for him to move from place to place, to descend and ascend, to be stationary and to be firmly seated. The views of the Shī'ite anthropomorphists will be given in the chapter on the extreme Shī'ites. Those of the Ḥashwīya Anthropomorphists are as follows.

Ash'arī has reported on the authority of Muḥammad b. 'Īsā that Muḍar, Kuhmus and Aḥmad al Hujaimī allow the possibility of men touching God and shaking his hand; also that sincere Muslims may embrace him in this world as well as in the next, provided they attain in their spiritual endeavours to a sufficient degree of purity of heart and genuine union with God. Ka'bī reports of some of them that they say that God can be seen even in this life, and that God and men may visit one another.

Dāwūd al-Jawāribī is reported to have said: 'Do not question me about the pudendum or the beard, but you may ask me about anything else.' He also said:

> God is body, flesh and blood. He has members and limbs, such as

> hands and feet, head and tongue, two eyes and two ears; nevertheless, he is a body unlike other bodies, with flesh unlike other flesh, and blood unlike other blood. This is true also of his other attributes: he does not resemble any creature, nor does any creature resemble him.

He is also said to have held that God is hollow from the top to his breast, while the rest of him is solid; also that he has long, black and curly hair.

Words in the Qur'ān like *istiwā'* (being seated), *wajh* (face), *yadain* (two hands), *janb* (side), *majī'* (coming), *ityān* (coming), *fawqīya* (being above) and the like, are understood by the Anthropomorphists literally, that is, as they are understood when used of bodies. The same applies to words found in traditions, such as the word *ṣūra* (form) in the saying of the Prophet: 'Adam was created in the form of the Most Merciful'; or his other sayings: 'Till the Most Powerful puts his foot in the fire'; 'The heart of the believer is between the fingers of the Most Merciful'; 'God moulded the clay of Adam with his hand for forty days'; 'God put his hand or his palm on my shoulder'; 'Till I felt the coldness of his fingers on my shoulders.' These and the like they understand in the same sense as would be understood of bodies.

The Anthropomorphists have invented lies and added them to the traditions, attributing them to the Prophet; these were taken mostly from the Jews to whom anthropomorphism is natural. They go as far as to say that God's eyes were sore and the angels went to console him; that he wept over the deluge of Noah till his eyes became red; that the throne creaks under him like a new saddle on a camel; that he overlaps the throne by four inches. The Anthropomorphists also report that the Prophet said, 'God met me, shook hands with me, wrestled with me and put his hand between my shoulders, until I felt the coldness of his fingers.'

In addition to anthropomorphism they hold that the syllables, sounds and written characters of the Qur'ān are all pre-existing and eternal. According to them an utterance which is composed neither of letters nor words is unintelligible. In support of their position they appeal to traditions. For example, they quote a saying of the Prophet that God will call out on the day of judgment in a voice which will be heard by men of all ages. They also quote a saying that Moses used to hear God's words like the sound of a dragging chain. They maintain that the early Muslims believed that the Qur'ān is God's uncreated word, and that whoever says it is created does not believe in God.

> Moreover, they say, the only Qur'ān we know is the one before us, the one which we see and hear, recite and write. Those who differ

from us on this question, as for example, the Mu'tazila, agree with us that this which we hold in our hands is God's word, but they disagree with us that it is eternal. This, however, is against the consensus of the community. The Ash'arites, on the other hand, agree with us that the Qur'ān is eternal, but will not grant that this which is in our hands is God's word. This also is contrary to the consensus of the community, which is that this is, indeed, God's word. Further, to maintain the existence of God's word as an attribute subsisting in his essence, which we neither see nor write nor read nor hear, is also contrary in every way to the consensus of the community.

We believe, therefore, they say, that what is between the two enclosing covers is the word of God revealed by the mouth of Gabriel. It is this which is found in the written texts; it is this which is written in the Preserved Tablet; it is this which the believers will hear from God in paradise without veil or intermediary. That is the meaning of God's saying: 'Peace shall be the word spoken by a Merciful Lord',[9] or his word to Moses: 'O Moses, truly I am God, the Lord of all the universe.'[10] Likewise his communication to men without an intermediary is shown in his words: 'God spoke to Moses direct',[11] or, 'I chose you above other men for my message and word.'[12] The Prophet, too, is reported to have said that God wrote the Torah with his hands, created the garden of Eden with his hands, and created Adam with his hands. The Qur'ān itself says, 'We inscribed for him upon the tablets all manner of precepts and instructions concerning all things.'[13]

The Anthropomorphists also say, 'We do not add anything of our selves, nor do we pursue questions which the early community had not raised. They said, 'What is between the two covers is God's word. This is also what we say.' They supported their argument with the words of God: 'If any of the polytheists seek your protection, protect him till he hears God's word.'[14] They then add that it is certain that what he heard is only what we read. They also cite other words of God, as: 'This is indeed a Qur'ān most honourable, in a Book well-guarded, which none shall touch but those who are clean – a revelation from the Lord of the worlds';[15] '(It is) in Books held in honour, exalted, kept pure and holy, (written) by the hand of scribes, honourable and devout';[16] 'We have indeed revealed it in the Night of Power';[17] 'Ramadān is the month in which the Qur'ān was sent down',[18] and similar verses.

Some of the Anthropomorphists are disposed towards the doctrine of incarnation. They say that it is possible for God to appear in human form, as Gabriel did in the form of a bedouin, or, as when he appeared to Mary, in the form of a handsome man. This is what the Prophet meant when he said, 'I saw my God in the most beautiful form.' Again, in the Torah Moses is reported to have said, 'I spoke with God face to face, and he said such and such to me.' The extreme Shī'ites also believe in incarnation, either partial or complete, as we shall explain when giving a detailed treatment of their views.

3 The Karrāmites

The Karrāmites are the followers of Abū 'Abdullāh Muḥammad b. Karrām. We have included Abū 'Abdullāh among the Ṣifātīya because he was one of those who believed in attributes, though he finally became an upholder of corporealism and anthropomorphism. We have already mentioned in what way he belonged to the Sunnites and in what way he did not.

There are twelve different groups of Karrāmites. The six principal ones are the following: the 'Ābidīya, the Tūnīya, the Zarīnīya, the Isḥāqīya, the Wāḥidīya and the one which is closest [to the Orthodox], namely, the Haiṣamīya. Each of these sects has its own viewpoint. However, as their theories are not the work of recognized scholars, but rather foolish and ignorant men who cannot even speak clearly, we have not treated them separately. We have mentioned only the views of the founder of the school, and merely indicated the different opinions which have developed from them.

Abū 'Abdullāh declares that God is firmly seated on the throne and that he is in person on the upper side of it. He uses the word 'corporeal of God, and says in his book, *'Adhāb al-qabr*, that God is one in his essence and one in substance, and that he is in contact with the upper side of the throne. In his view it is possible for God to move, change his position and descend. Some of the Karrāmites say that God occupies part of the throne, but others say that he occupies the whole of it.

The later followers of Karrām held the opinion that God is directly above the throne. Beyond that they differed among themselves. The 'Ābidīya maintained that between God and the throne there is a measure of distance such that, if this space could be imagined as filled with substances, these would touch God. Muḥammad b. al-Haisam, on the other hand, said that between God and the throne there is unlimited space, and that God is eternally separate from the universe. He denied that God has a location and is directly above the throne, and asserted that God is above the throne but is removed from it.

Most of the Karrāmites used the word body of God. Those who believe in God's nearness to the throne maintain that his being a body means that he exists by himself. This according to them is the definition of body. From this they developed the view that any two things which exist by themselves must either be in contact with each other or separate from each other. Hence some of them maintain that God is in contact with the throne, and others that he is separate from it. Sometimes they give the following explanation: every two existing things must be so related to each other that either both occupy the same place as an accident and its substance, or one is beside the other. God, however, is not an accident because he is self-subsistent; hence he must be on one of the sides of the universe. However, the highest and most noble side is the upper side; therefore we say that God in his person is on the upper side. If he is seen, he will be seen from that side.

The Karrāmites differ also in regard to the extremities of God. Some of the corporealists believe that God has extremities on all six sides; others maintain that God has extremities on the lower side only; others deny extremities altogether, but say that God is Great. These latter differ as to the meaning of greatness. Some say that his greatness means that despite his oneness God is on all parts of the throne: the throne is under him, and he is above all of it in the same way as he is above part of it. Some say that his greatness means that despite his oneness he touches on one side more than one thing, that is, he touches all the parts of the throne, for he is Most High and Great.

They all believe that it is possible for a number of accidents to inhere in God's essence. One of their doctrines is that whatever occurs in his essence does so by his power; whatever occurs outside his essence does so through his origination. By origination they mean both bringing into existence and annihilating, which occur in his essence through his power expressed by his words and acts of will. By the thing originated they mean substances and accidents, which are distinct from God's essence. They distinguish between creating and what is created; between bringing into existence, that which is brought into existence, and that which brings into existence; similarly, between annihilating and that which is annihilated. A created thing, therefore, comes into existence through creation, and creation itself takes place in God's essence through his power. Likewise that which is annihilated passes into nothingness through annihilation, which also takes place in God's essence through his power.

They hold that there are many occurrences in God's essence; such as, for example, the giving of information about past or future events, the revealing of books to the prophets, stories, 'promise and warning', commands. In this category also are acts of hearing and seeing in regard to things audible and visible; or bringing into being and annihilation, which are God's word and will; for example, his saying 'Be' to the thing that he wills to be. His willing the existence of a thing and his word to that thing 'Be' are two forms. Muḥammad b. al-Haiṣam understands bringing into being and annihilaton in terms of will and choice, which are connected in the Qur'ān with the divine utterance; as God said, 'To anything which We have willed, We but say to it 'Be', and it is';[19] or, again, 'Verily, when he wills a thing, his command to it is 'Be', and it is.'[20]

According to most of the Karrāmites creation means God's word and will, though they differ in details. Some maintain that for every thing that exists there is an act of bringing into being, and for every thing that is annihilated there is an act of annihilation. Others hold that one act of bringing into being is sufficient for two things of the same genus, but if they are of different genera there would be required a corresponding number of acts bringing into being. They were accordingly faced with the consequence that, if every thing or every genus needed an act of bringing into existence, then each act would need a corresponding power; there would, therefore, have to be numerous powers corresponding to numerous acts. Some then said that the number of powers would correspond to the number of genera of things originated. Most of them, however, were of the view that the number of powers corresponded to the number of genera of occurrences in God's essence, namely *kāf, nūn*, will, hearing and seeing, that is, five genera. Some of them explained God's hearing and seeing by his power to listen and to look. Some maintained for God an eternal hearing and seeing; as for listening and looking, however, these they said were relations to perceived things.

The Karrāmites also maintain that there is in God an eternal will which is connected with the universal aspect of all things caused and with all the occurrences in his essence. They affirm also that there are originated acts of will for the details of things brought into being. They all agree that the occurrences [in God] do not bestow a descriptive quality on God, nor are they his attributes. These occurrences, such as his utterances, his acts of will, of hearing and of seeing, take place in his essence, but he is not on that account speaking, willing, hearing or seeing. Nor does he by creating these occurrences become an originator or a creator. He is a speaker only by his [attribute of] being 'one-who-wills'. This means he has a power over all these things.

One of the principal beliefs of the Karrāmites is that the accidents (occurrences) which God causes in himself must continue to exist, that is, it is not possible for them to cease to exist. The reason for this is, that if it were possible for these accidents to cease to exist, God would be a subject of a series of accidents, and so in this respect would be like a substance. Moreover, if we suppose that the accidents cease to exist this would occur either through power, or through annihilation created by God in his essence. It is not possible, however, for their non-existence to be brought about through power, because this would lead to the affirmation of the non-existent in his essence, whereas existent and the non-existent are as such mutually exclusive. If, indeed, it were possible for a non-existent thing to come about in his essence through his power without the instrumentality of annihilation, then it would be possible for all non-existent things to come about through his power. Moreover, this [non-existent] would have to be removed for the sake of whatever is brought into existence, so that what is being brought into existence may come into being in his essence. This according to them is impossible. On the other hand, if these accidents were annihilated through annihilation, it would be possible to suppose that annihilation could be annihilated. This would, however, entail an infinite regress. Through this kind of reasoning they reached the position that it is impossible for anything coming into being in God's essence to cease to exist.

Another of their principles is that the thing caused comes into existence in the moment immediately following the act of causation, but the act of causation has no effect upon the continued existence of the thing caused. They also hold that whatever takes place in God's essence is either creative or non-creative, the creative being that which is followed by an effect. The non-creative is either informative, obligatory or prohibitive. These latter are acts inasmuch as they indicate power but have no effect. This is a full account of their views of [God as] substrate of accidents.

Ibn al-Haiṣam has tried to modify the view of 'Abū 'Abdullāh on every issue. He has changed it from the crude and ridiculous to something intelligible. For example, on the question of anthropomorphism, he says that by the word 'body' he means that God is self-subsistent. Again, he interprets 'being above' as meaning that God is Most High, between whom and the throne there is an unlimited gulf: this is the empty space of which philosophers have spoken. He denies also that sitting on the throne means being close to it, or touching it, or being established on it in person. However, on the question of the substrate of accidents, as this did not admit of any modification, he accepted it, as we have already mentioned, though it is utterly absurd.

According to the Karrāmīya there are many more accidents than the things caused, which means that in God there are innumerable accidents, more even than the things caused, which is impossible and absurd. On the question of attributes they all agree that God is knowing with knowledge, powerful with power, living with life, willing with will: all these are eternal attributes subsisting in God's essence. Sometimes they add the attributes of hearing and seeing, as al-Ash'arī had done. Sometimes they regard his hands and face also as eternal attributes subsisting in God. They say that God has a hand not like other hands, and a face not like other faces. They maintain, too, that it is possible to see him looking upwards, though not from any other direction.

Ibn al-Haiṣam maintains that the use by the Mushabbiha of such words of God as shape and form, belly and roundness, over-extended dimension, hand-shaking, embracing and the like, bear no resemblance to the things which the Karrāmīya have said: as that God created Adam with his hand, that he is settled on his throne, and that he will come on the day of resurrection to pass judgment on his creatures. He says:

> This is because we Karrāmites do not interpret any of this in a wrong sense, that is, we do not understand [God's] hands in terms of his limbs, or his being settled on the throne in the sense of his being co-terminous with the throne which seats the most Merciful; nor, again, do we understand his coming in terms of his moving about in surrounding space. We simply say what the Qur'ān has said and no more, without attempting to say how, or interpreting anything in an anthropomorphic sense. Whatever is not in the Qur'ān and tradition we do not apply to God, as do all the Mushabbiha and the Mujassima.

Ibn al-Haiṣam says also that God knows from eternity what will be and the manner in which it will be, and he wishes the fulfilment of his knowledge in the things known to him; thus his knowledge does not become ignorance. At the time he creates he wills whatever he creates with a contingent will (*irāda ḥāditha*); and to every thing that comes into being by his command, he says 'Be', and it becomes. This is the difference between bringing into being and that which is brought into being, between creating and the thing created. Further he says:

> We maintain that good and evil are both decreed by God; that God has willed things, good and evil alike. We also maintain that a man's act is his through a created power; this is called acquisition. This created power confers upon the act an aspect over and above that of being created by God. It is that aspect which gives rise to obligation and which is the source of reward and punishment.

Conclusion

All the Karrāmīya are agreed that prior to revelation reason makes known good and evil, and that the knowledge of God is obligatory, just as the Mu'tazilites do. They do not, however, hold that reason demands that God must do what is good for men or best for them, and bestow his grace on them, as do the Mu'tazilites. They say, too, that *īmān* is an acceptance by the lips alone and does not include consent in the heart or any other deeds. They distinguish between calling a person a believer inasmuch as he is subject to law and command in this life, and inasmuch as he will be subject to the laws of the next life and the recompense therein. A hypocrite, therefore, according to them, is truly a believer in this world, but he will be deserving of eternal punishment in the next. With regard to the imāmate they maintain, as do the Sunnites, that it depends upon the consensus of the community, and not on designation or appointment. They permit, however, an oath of allegiance to be taken to two imāms in two different regions. Their purpose in this was to validate the imāmate of Mu'āwiya in Syria because of the agreement there of a group of Companions; and to validate also the imāmate of 'Alī, the Commander of the Faithful, in Medīna and the two 'Irāqs, because of the agreement there, too, of a group of Companions. They think that Mu'āwiya was right in his arbitrary action in matters of the *sharī'a*, as, for example, in fighting over his demand for the murderers of 'Uthmān, and in his assumption of absolute control over the treasury funds. The fundamental point in this regard was their indictment of 'Alī for tolerating what had happened to 'Uthmān, and keeping silence. This is the vein which bled.

Chapter 4

The Khārijites

Introduction

The Khārijites, the Murji'a and the Wa'īdīya

Whoever rebelled against the legitimate *imām* accepted by the people is called a Khārijite, whether this rebellion took place at the time of the Companions against the rightfully guided *imāms*, or against their worthy successors, or against the *imāms* of any time. The Murji'a is a separate group who held distinctive views about faith and works, though they agreed with the Khārijites on some points concerning the *imāmate*. The Wa'īdīya, on the other hand, form part of the Khārijites, holding that if a Muslim commits a grave sin he is an unbeliever and will be condemned to hell forever. We have, therefore, dealt with their views in our treatment of the Khārijites.

The Battle of Ṣiffīn

We should remember that the first rebels against 'Alī, the Commander of the Faithful, were a body of his followers in the battle of Ṣiffīn. Those who most rebelled against him and strayed furthest from religion were Ash'ath b. Qais al-Kindī, Mis'ar b. Fadakī al-Tamīmī and Zaid b. Ḥuṣain al-Ṭā'ī, who went so far as to say, 'They [the enemy] are summoning us to the book of God, but you summon us to the sword.' 'Alī, however, said:

> I have a better knowledge of what is written in the Book. Go and fight the rest of the enemy forces; go and fight those who say that

God and his messenger have lied, whereas you believe that God and his messenger have told the truth.

They, however, replied, 'You must recall Ashtar from the battle against the Muslims, otherwise we shall treat you as we treated 'Uthmān.' 'Alī was therefore forced to recall Ashtar, even though the enemy had been defeated and were retreating with only a small and almost exhausted force remaining to them. Ashtar on his part obeyed the command.

The story about the arbitration is this. First of all the Khārijites compelled 'Alī to accept arbitration. Then when 'Alī wanted to appoint 'Abdullāh b. 'Abbās as his arbitrator, the Khārijites objected, saying, 'He is a relative of yours.' They forced him to send instead Abū Mūsā al-Ash'arī to judge according to the Book of God. The arbitration went against 'Alī, and when 'Alī did not accept it they rebelled against him. 'Why did you appoint men as judges?' they asked. 'Judgment belongs to God alone.' These were the rebels who afterwards assembled at Nahrawān.

Kharijite sects

The most important groups among the Khārijites are the Muḥakkima, the Azāriqa, the Najdāt, the Baihasīya, the 'Ajārida, the Tha'āliba, the Ibāḍīya and the Ṣufrīya. The others are subdivisions of these. Common to them all is dissociation from 'Uthmān and 'Alī, which they consider of greater moment than any other act of obedience. Marriages, moreover, are only allowed on this condition. They hold, too, that those who commit grave sins are unbelievers, and that rebellion against an imām who opposes *sunna* is a duty and an obligation.

1 The Early Muḥakkima

These are the ones who rebelled against 'Alī, the Commander of the Faithful, at the time of the arbitration, and assembled at Ḥarūrā' near Kūfa. Their leaders were 'Abdullāh b. al-Kawwā', 'Attāb b. al-A'war, 'Abdullāh b. Wahb al-Rāsibī, 'Urwa b. Jarīr, Yazīd b. 'Aṣim al-Muḥāribī and Ḥurqūṣ b. Zuhair al-Bajalī known as Dhu 'l-Thudayya. On the day of Nahrawān they numbered twelve thousand men, who gave themselves up to prayer and fasting. It was of these the Prophet had said, 'Prayer and fasting of any one of you compared with theirs will seem of little worth, but their faith will not reach their hearts.' These are the rebels, too, to whom the Prophet referred, saying, 'From the stock of this man there will emerge a people who will fly from religion as an arrow flies from a bow.' The first of them was Dhū 'l-Khuwaisira and the last Dhū 'l-Thudayya.

At the beginning these early Muḥakkima based their revolt on two fundamental points. The first was the innovation concerning the imāmate inasmuch as they allowed it to others than the Quraish. Whoever they chose was regarded by them as an imām, provided he ruled the people according to their ideas of justice and equity. If anyone rebelled against this imām it became a duty to oppose him. If, however, the imām became corrupt and deviated from the path of justice, it became a duty to depose him or put him to death. The early Muḥakkima were, too, strong adherents of the principle of analogy. They also considered it permissible that there be no imām at all anywhere. If need arose for one he could be either a slave or freeman, Nabataean or Quraishite.

Their second innovation lay in maintaining that 'Alī was at fault in permitting arbitration, since thereby he made men judges of the matter, whereas God is the only judge. In two ways they calumniated 'Alī. The first was in the matter of arbitration, namely, that 'Alī appointed men as arbiters. This, however, is not the truth, because it was they in fact who forced him to accept arbitration. Moreover, the appointment of men as judges was permissible, because only people themselves can be judges in such a matter, and they are men. It was on this account that 'Alī said, 'What is said is right but not what is intended.' They not only held that 'Alī was wrong, but went further and declared him an unbeliever. They also cursed him for fighting against all those who broke their allegiance to him, or who had acted wrongly, or who actually rebelled against him. 'Alī, they said, fought against those who broke their allegiance to him and confiscated their property, but did not take their wives and children captive. He fought also against those who had acted wrongly, but neither confiscated their property nor made them captive. Afterwards he agreed to arbitration. As to the rebels he not only fought them, but also confiscated their property, and took their children captive.

They found fault with 'Uthmān, too, for various things they held against him. They further discredited those who took part in the battles of the Camel and Ṣiffīn. 'Alī fought a fierce battle with them at Nahrawān from which less than ten of them escaped, whereas on the Muslim side [that is, 'Alī's] less than ten were killed. Two of the rebels escaped to 'Umān, two of them to Kirmān, two to Sijistān, two to the Peninsula and one to Tell Mauzan in the Yemen. It was because of them that Khārijite ideas made their appearance in these places and are still found there to this day.

The first Khārijite to whom allegiance was given as an imām was 'Abdullāh b. Wahb al-Rāsibī. This took place in the house of Zaid b. Ḥuṣain. Among those who swore allegiance to him were: 'Abdullāh b. al-Kawwā', 'Urwa b. Jarīr, Yazīd b. 'Āṣim al-Muḥāribī and others with them. Al-Rāsibī, not wishing to accept office, at first declined the imāmate. He received the delegates but proposed someone else, being unwilling to take the charge upon himself. They, however, were content with no one but him. Al-Rāsibī was regarded as a man of wisdom and courage. He dissociated himself from the two judges, as well as from all those who agreed with their verdict and upheld the arbitration. According to these Khārijites 'Alī, the Commander of the Faithful, had become an unbeliever because, as they alleged, he had abandoned the judgment of God and appointed men as judges. It is said that the first one to say this was a man of the family of Sa'd b. Zaid b. Manāt b. Tamīm whose name was al-Ḥajjāj b. 'Ubaidullāh, known as Burk. It was he who struck Mu'āwiya on the buttocks when he heard mention of the two judges. 'Do you set up judges,' he said, 'in the realm of God's religion? Judgment belongs to God alone; let us therefore judge as God judged in the Qur'ān.' Someone who heard what he said remarked, 'He has thrown a spear and by God he has pierced it through.' For this reason they were called the Muḥakkima. When 'Alī, the Commander of the Faithful, heard these words, he said, 'These are words of justice, but what he intended by them is injustice. They say there is no need for a government, yet there must be a government of someone, either good or bad.'

It is said that the first Khārijite sword to be unsheathed was that of 'Urwa b. Udhaina when he approached Asḥ'ath b. Qais, and said to him, 'What a disgraceful thing, O Ash'ath! What do you mean by appointing men as judges? Is a provision made by one of you more binding than a provision made by God?' Then as Ash'ath was turning away 'Urwa drew his sword and struck his mule on the rump. The mule sprang away and the Yamanites scattered. When Ahnaf saw this he went with his companions to Ash'ath and asked his pardon, which he granted.

Subsequently 'Urwa b. Udhaina escaped from the battle of Nahrawān, and lived till the days of Mu'āwiya. He once went to Ziyād b. Abīhi with his *mawlā*. When Ziyād asked him about Abū Bakr and 'Umar, he spoke well of them. When, however, he questioned him about 'Uthmān, he said, 'I was his constant supporter for six years of his caliphate, but afterwards I dissociated myself from him because of his innovations.' He then declared 'Uthmān to be an unbeliever. When Ziyād asked him about 'Alī, Commander of the Faithful, he replied, 'I supported him too till he appointed the two judges, but after that I dissociated myself from him.' He also declared 'Alī to be an unbeliever. Ziyād then asked him about Mu'āwiya; thereupon he poured abuses on the latter's head. Finally he asked him about himself. He replied, 'Your origin is uncertain and your end is a summons; in the meantime you are disobedient to your Lord.' At this Ziyād ordered his head to be struck off. He then called his *mawlā* and said to him, 'Give me an account of his life and tell the truth.' The *mawlā* asked, 'Shall I be lengthy or brief?' Ziyād replied, 'Be brief.' The *mawlā* then said, 'I did not bring his food to him during the day, nor did I ever make his bed for him at night.' This shows his way of life and his dedication, but the other shows his wickedness and his beliefs.

2 The Azāriqa

These were the followers of Abū Rāshid Nāfi' b. al-Azraq. They accompanied him from Baṣra to Ahwāz which they conquered with all its towns, as well as the districts of Fāris and Kirmān beyond it. This happened at the time of 'Abdullāh b. al-Zubair whose governors in these districts they killed.

Among the leaders of the Khārijites with Nāfi' were the following: 'Aṭīya b. al-Aswad al-Ḥanafī, 'Abdullāh b. Mākhūn, his two brothers 'Uthmān and al-Zubair, 'Amr b. 'Umair al-'Anbarī, Qaṭarī b. al-Fujā'a al-Māzinī, 'Ubaida b. al-Hilāl al-Yashkarī and his brother Muḥriz b. Hilāl, Ṣakhr b. Ḥabīb al-Tamīmī, Ṣaliḥ b. Mikhrāq al-'Abdī, 'Abd Rabbihī the elder and 'Abd Rabbihī the younger. They were at the head of about thirty thousand horsemen who held the same views and had joined their ranks.

'Abdullāh b. al-Ḥārith b. Naufal al-Naufalī sent against them the Commander of his army, Muslim b. 'Ubais b. Karīz b. Ḥabīb, but the Khārijites killed him and put his forces to flight. He then dispatched 'Uthmān b. 'Abdullāh b. Mu'ammar al-Tamīmī, but they defeated him also. He next sent Ḥāritha b. Badr al-'Itābī with a large army; he also was defeated, and the people of Basra now feared for their lives and city at the hands of the Khārijites. Al-Muhallab b. Abū Ṣufra was then sent against them. He carried on the war against the Azāriqa for nineteen years, till at last the fighting came to an end in the days of al-Ḥajjāj. Nāfi', however, died before the main battles of al-Muhallab against the Azāriqa, and in succession to him they had sworn allegiance to Qaṭarī b. al-Fujā'a al-Māzinī, whom they called the Commander of the Faithful.

The following are the eight innovations of the Azāriqa. In the first place [Nāfi‘] declared that Alī was an unbeliever. He said that God revealed of him: ‘And of mankind there is one whose conversation on the life of this world pleases you (Muḥammad), and he calls God to witness as to that which is in his heart; yet he is the most rigid of opponents.’[1] He held that ‘Abd al-Raḥmān b. Muljim, (God's curse be upon him!) was right in what he did, and said that God revealed of him: ‘And there is the kind of man who gives his life to earn the pleasure of God.’[2] ‘Imrān b. Ḥiṭṭān the Muftī, the most pious of the Khārijites and also their greatest poet, composed the following verses about the blow struck ‘Alī by Ibn Muljim:

> O blow from a repentant one, who sought by it only the pleasure of the Lord of the throne. When I think of him I look upon him as the one of all mankind who is most perfect in the sight of God.

To this innovation the Azāriqa remained faithful. They further said that ‘Uthmān, Ṭalḥa, Zubair, ‘Ā’isha, ‘Abbās and all other Muslims with them were unbelievers and would all be in hell forever.

Secondly, Nāfi‘ regarded as unbelievers those who stayed behind and did not go into battle, and he was the first to declare openly his dissociation from them, even though they agreed with his opinions. All those who did not join him [in his camp] he also looked upon as unbelievers. Thirdly, he permitted the killing of the children and womenfolk of his opponents. Fourthly, he abolished the punishment of stoning to death for adultery because this was not mentioned in the Qur'ān. He also abolished the punishment for defamation imposed on those who slandered innocent women. Fifthly, he maintained that the children of polytheists would be in hell with their parents. Sixthly, dissimulation, *taqīya*, is not lawful in word or in deed. Seventhly, God may send a prophet of whom he knows that he will fall into unbelief after becoming a prophet, or that he was an unbeliever before being a prophet. Since grave and venial sins are the same in his eyes and constitute unbelief, and since there are some in the community who consider it possible for prophets to commit grave and venial sins, it would follow that these are acts of unbelief [for the prophets also]. Eighthly, all the Azāriqa agree that whoever commits a grave sin is an unbeliever and outside the fold of Islam; such a one will be eternally in hell with other unbelievers. This view they support by the example of the unbelief of Iblīs who, they say, committed only a grave sin when he was ordered to prostrate himself before Adam but refused, even although he had acknowledged the oneness of God.

3 The Najdāt al-'Ādhirīya

These are the followers of Najda b. 'Āmir al-Ḥanafī, called by some 'Āṣim. It is told of him that he left Yamāma with his army intending to join the Azāriqa. He encountered Abū Fudaik and 'Aṭīya b. al-Aswad al-Ḥanafī with a group opposed to Nāfi' b. al-Azraq. They informed him of the dissension Nāfi' had caused both by his declaration that those who stayed behind were unbelievers, and also by his other innovations and heresies. Thereupon they swore allegiance to Najda and called him Commander of the Faithful.

The Najdāt afterwards differed among themselves with regard to Najda. Some said that he had become an unbeliever because of certain deeds which they considered blameworthy. One of them was that he had sent an army against the people of al-Qaṭīf under the command of his son, who put to death their men and captured their women. On the women the army put a price: 'If their value falls within our share there is no problem, but if not we shall give back whatever is in excess.' However, they cohabited with them before the division took place, and also appropriated the booty before it was divided. When they returned to Najda and told him about it, he said, 'It was wrong to do what you did.' They replied, 'We did not know that it was not right.' So he excused them on account of their ignorance. His followers, however, were divided on this point. Some of them agreed with him and regarded ignorance as grounds for acquittal in judgment based on *ijtihād* (personal endeavour). They said:

> Religion consists of two things. The first comprises knowledge of God and his prophets, the inviolability of the blood of Muslims (by this they meant those who agreed with them), and, in general, acceptance of all that has been revealed by God. This is obligatory upon all men and ignorance of it cannot be excused. The second comprises everything else; and in this people are excused until they know for certain what is lawful and what is unlawful.

They said also that whoever allows punishment of a *mujtahid* for making an error in matters of law, before the law is certainly established, is an unbeliever.

According to Najda the life and property of the people of the covenant and of *dhimmīs* are forfeited during the state of dissimulation. Moreover, he ordered his followers to dissociate themselves from those who forbade this. He also said that there was hope that God would forgive those of his followers who deserved the punishment prescribed by law; if he did punish them it would be elsewhere than in hell, and subsequently they would be admitted to heaven. From these, therefore, it would not be lawful to dissociate. He said, too, that whoever casts a glance [at a woman], or tells a lie, small or great, and persists in it, is a polytheist; but whoever commits adultery, drinks wine or steals, and does not persist in it, is not a polytheist. Najda was, nevertheless, extremely strict in applying the legal penalty for drinking wine.

When Najda wrote to 'Abd al-Malik b. Marwān expressing his satisfaction with him, his followers disapproved of what he had done and called upon him to repent. This he openly did, and they accordingly gave up their resentment and hostility. One section of them, however, was ashamed of this demand made on him, saying, 'We have made a mistake; we had no right to ask an imām to repent, nor had he any right to repent on our demanding that he do so.' They then repented, confessed to their error, and said to him, 'You must now repent of your repentance, otherwise we shall forsake you.' Accordingly he repented of his repentance.

Abū Fudaik and 'Aṭīya left Najda, and afterwards Abū Fudaik attacked and killed him. Abū Fudaik then dissociated himself from 'Aṭīya, who in turn dissociated himself from Abū Fudaik. 'Abd al-Malik b. Marwān then sent 'Umar b. 'Ubaidullāh b. Mu'ammar al-Tamīmī with an army against Abū Fudaik, who was killed in a battle lasting several days. 'Aṭīya's followers are called al-'Aṭwīya, among whom was 'Abd al-Karīm b. 'Ajrad, the leader of the 'Ajārida.

The followers of Najda are also called al-'Ādhirīya because in the matter of the laws of the *sharī'a* they accept ignorance as ground for excuse. Ka'bī says of the Najdāt that they permitted dissimulation in everything said and done, even in the matter of homicide. He adds that the Najdāt unanimously asserted that men have no need whatever for an imām: all that is required of them is to show mutual justice and fairness. If they should find that this cannot be achieved without the authority of an imām, and, accordingly, appoint one, this would be lawful.

The Najdāt split into two groups, the 'Aṭwīya and the Fudaikīya, who after Najda's murder repudiated one another. The Khārijites of the region, except those who continued to follow Najda, supported Abū Fudaik, while those of Sijistān, Khurāsān, Kirmān and Qūhistān, followed 'Aṭīya. It is said that Najda b. 'Āmir and Nāfi' b. al-Azraq had joined other Khārijites at Mecca against Ibn al-Zubair, but afterwards they had dispersed. A dispute arose between Nāfi' and Najda which resulted in Nāfi' going to Baṣra and Najda to al-Yamāma. The reason for the dispute was that Nāfi' said that dissimulation was not permissible, and that failure to participate in fighting was an act of unbelief. In confirmation of this view he quoted the words of God: 'There is a party of them fearing the people as they would fear God';[3] also the words: 'Men who struggle in the path of God, not fearing the reproach of any reproacher.'[4]

Najda opposed him, and said that dissimulation is permissible, citing in support the words of God: 'Unless you have a fear of them';[5] and again: 'Then said a certain man, a believer of Pharoah's folk, that kept hidden his belief.'[6] He added that non-participation in a holy war is also lawful though participation is better, if possible. He then quoted the words of God: 'God has preferred those who struggle over the ones who sit at home for the bounty of a mighty wage.'[7]

Nāfi', however, said that these verses of the Qur'ān were relevant only to the Companions of the Prophet who had no choice; but when it is possible for others to fight and they are unwilling to do so, this is unbelief; as God has said, 'Those who lied to God and his Messenger tarried.'[8]

4 The Baihasiya

These are the followers of Abū Baihas al-Haiṣam b. Jābir who belonged to Banū Sa'd b. Ḍubai'a. Al-Ḥajjāj had tried to capture him during the reign of al-Walīd but he escaped to Medīna. 'Uthmān b. Ḥayyān al-Muzanī searched for him there and having found him put him in prison. There he passed nights conversing with him, till, finally, al-Walīd's letter arrived with instructions that his hands and feet be cut off and he be put to death. These instructions were carried out.

Abū Baihas regarded Ibrāhīm and Maimūn as unbelievers because they held views different from his own about the selling of a female slave. Similarly he held the Wāqifīya to be unbelievers. He also maintained that no one is a Muslim unless he acknowledges God and his apostles, and accepts what has been revealed to the Prophet; he must also profess friendship for the friends of God and dissociation from the enemies of God. Moreover those things which God has forbidden, and against which he has added a warning, are included in what is prescribed and laid down by the Law: of these a full and clear knowledge is required, together with the obligation of avoiding them. There are other laws, however, of whose existence a Muslim should know, but he does not need a full knowledge of them until he becomes confronted with the situation in which they are applicable. One must not act in ignorance but act only with due knowledge.

Abū Baihas dissociated himself from the Wāqifīya because they said, 'We suspend judgment about a person who has done what is unlawful in ignorance of whether it was lawful or not.' According to Abū Baihas he should have known whether it was lawful or not. Faith, he held, is a knowledge both of all that is right and all that is wrong. It is, moreover, knowledge in the heart and does not consist of words and deeds. Abū Baihas, however, is also reported to have said that faith is confession and knowledge, and not simply one without the other. Most of the Baihasīya, on the other hand, hold the view that knowledge, confession and deeds all constitute faith. Some of them maintain that nothing is forbidden apart from what is revealed in the words of God: 'I do not find, in what is revealed to me, aught forbidden to him who eats thereof . . .'[9] All else is lawful.

A section of the Baihasīya are called the 'Awuīya, who in turn are divided into two sub-groups. One of these said, 'We shall dissociate ourselves from those who leave the camp to which they had migrated and return to their former state of inactivity.' The other group, however, said, 'We, on the other hand, shall befriend such people because they have returned to a state which was lawful to them.' Both the sub-groups held that if the imām becomes an unbeliever all his subjects become unbelievers, not only those actually present with him but those elsewhere also.

Another group of the Baihasīya are called the Expositors, because they believe that a Muslim bearing witness to the faith will be interrogated as to its detailed exposition and explanation. A further group, called the Questioners, say that a person becomes a Muslim by bearing witness to the two testimonies, by dissociating himself [from the enemies of God] and associating [with the friends of God], and by believing in a general way what has been revealed by God. If he does not know what God has made of obligation upon him he should enquire. There is no harm in not knowing the obligation until the situation demands a knowledge of it; then he should ask. However, if he does what is unlawful, not knowing that it is unlawful, he becomes an unbeliever. With regard to children they hold the same belief as the Tha'āliba, that is, that the children of believers are believers, but the children of unbelievers are unbelievers. They agree also with the Qadarīya in the matter of *qadar*, saying that God has given full freedom to men, and that, therefore, God does not will the deeds of men. As a result of all this most of the Baihasīya dissociated themselves from them.

Some of the Baihasīya said, 'If a man does what is unlawful, no judgment should be passed about his unbelief till the matter has been brought before the ruling imām, who will inflict upon him the prescribed punishment. For such things as have no prescribed punishment he will be forgiven.' Some of them also said that if intoxication results from a lawful drink, the intoxicated man will not be held responsible for what he said or did in that state. The 'Awnīya, on the other hand, said that intoxication is unbelief, but they did not regard it as such until another grave sin had been added to it; as for example, omitting prayer or slandering a virtuous person.

Among the Khārijites, too, are the followers of Ṣāliḥ b. Musarriḥ, but nothing original is reported of him by which he may be distinguished from the others. Ṣāliḥ rebelled against Bishr b. Marwān. Bishr dispatched against him al-Ḥārith b. 'Umaira (or al-Ash'ath b. 'Umaira al-Hamadānī), whom al-Ḥajjāj had sent against him. Ṣāliḥ was subsequently wounded in the castle of Jalūlā'. He then appointed as his successor Shabīb b. Yazīd b. Nu'aim al-Shaibānī, surnamed Abū 'l-Ṣaḥārā. Shabīb conquered Kūfa and killed twenty-four commanders in the forces of al-Ḥajjāj, all of whom were at the head of army units. Afterwards, however, he was forced to retreat to al-Ahwāz and was drowned in the al-Ahwāz river. While he was drowning he uttered the words: 'This is the ordaining of the Almighty, the All-Knowing.'[10]

Al-Yamān says that the Shabībīya are called the Murji'a of the Khārijites because they remained uncommitted in the affair of Ṣāliḥ. Shabīb is reported to have dissociated himself from Ṣāliḥ and to have left him. He then began to claim the imāmate for himself. Shabīb held the same views as the Baihasīya, which have already been mentioned. His prowess and valour, and his stand against his enemies were such as are found among no other Khārijite; his exploits are recorded in the works of history.

5 The 'Ajārida

These are the followers of 'Abd al-Karīm b. 'Ajrad who agreed with the Najdāt in their heresies. 'Abd al-Karīm is said to have been one of the followers of Abū Baihas though he later differed from him. He was alone in holding that it was an obligation to dissociate from a child till he was called to Islam, a call that must be made at the age of puberty. He also held that the children of polytheists would be in hell with their parents. Again, according to 'Abd al-Karīm, property is not a booty till its owner is killed.

The 'Ajārida associate with those who stay at home if their religious confession is known to them. They consider migration to be meritorious but not of obligation. In their opinion, also, grave sins make one an unbeliever. It is said of them that they deny that the *sūra Yūsuf* (Joseph) belongs to the Qur'ān. They maintain that it is only a story; moreover, a love story cannot form part of the Qur'ān.

The 'Ajārida split into various sects, each with its own beliefs. Since, however, they all form part of the 'Ajārida, we have given below a detailed outline of them.

(a) The Ṣaltīya

These are the followers of 'Uthmān b. Abu 'l-Ṣalt and al-Ṣalt b. Abu 'l-Ṣalt. They differ from the 'Ajārida in that they say, 'When a man becomes a Muslim we shall associate with him, but not with his children till they reach adulthood and accept Islam.' Some of them are reported to have said that they have neither friendship for, nor enmity against, the children of either polytheists or Muslims till they reach adulthood, when they will receive a call to Islam and either accept or reject it.

(b) The Maimūnīya

These are the followers of Maimūn b. Khālid who belonged to the 'Ajārida. He differed from the others, however, in maintaining that the power to do good and evil belongs to man, that a man's act is created and brought into being by himself, that capacity exists before the act. He also said that God wills good and not evil, and does not will man's disobedience. Ḥusain al-Karābīsī has mentioned in his book, where he treats of the views of the Khārijites, that the Maimūnīya allow marriage with the daughters of daughters, and with the daughters of the children of brothers and sisters. They say, however, that God has forbidden marriage with daughters and with the daughters of brothers and sisters, though not with the daughters of their children.

According to al-Ka'bī and al-Ash'arī the Maimūnīya deny that the *sūra* Yūsuf forms part of the Qur'ān. They also say that it is a duty to take up arms against the Sultan and punish him according to the law, together with all those who accept his government. It is not permissible, however, to fight against those who do not accept him unless they have helped him against the Khārijites, attacked their beliefs, or given the Sultan information about them. They also hold that the children of polytheists will be in paradise.

(c) The Ḥamzīya

These are the followers of Ḥamza b. Adrak. They agreed with the Maimūnīya on the question of power and their other heresies. They differed from them, however, in regard to the children of their adversaries and of polytheists, all of whom, according to them, will be in hell. Ḥamza was one of the followers of al-Ḥusain b. al-Raqqād from Auq who led a revolt in Sijistān.

Khalaf al-Khārijī opposed Ḥamza in the matter of *qadar* and the requirements for the choice of a leader. This led to their dissociation from one another. Ḥamza allows the possibility of two imāms at one time as long as there is no unanimous agreement [with regard to one of them], and the enemy has not yet been conquered.

(d) The Khalafīya

These are the followers of Khalaf al-Khārijī, Khārijites from Kirmān and Mukrān. They differ from the Ḥamzīya on the question of *qadar*, ascribing the determination of good and evil to God. In this respect they follow the Sunnites. They also say that the Ḥamzīya contradict themselves in holding that if God punishes men for deeds he destined them to do, or for deeds they did not perform, he would be unjust, while saying at the same time that the children of polytheists will be in hell, even though these children have done no deeds nor omitted any. Of all contradictory beliefs this is one of the most astonishing.

(e) The Aṭrāfīya

This is a group which holds the same views as Ḥamza on the question of power. However, they absolve the Aṭrāfīya from guilt if they do not adhere to that part of the *sharī'a* of which they are ignorant, as long as they do what is manifested by reason as obligatory; for they maintain, as do the Qadarīya, that there are obligations based on reason. Their leader is Ghālib b. Shādhak of Sijistān. They are opposed by 'Abdullāh b. al-Sadīwarī who dissociated himself from them. Among them is a group called the Muḥammadīya, the followers of Muḥammad b. Rizq, himself at first the follower of al-Ḥusain b. al-Raqqād, but later dissociating himself from him.

(f) The Shu'aibīya

These are the followers of Shu'aib b. Muḥammad, who with Maimūn belonged to the 'Ajārida. When, however, Maimūn expressed his views about power he dissociated himself from him. According to Shu'aib, God creates the deeds of man, and man acquires them through God's power and will. At the same time man is responsible for his deeds both good and bad, and is requited for them either by rewards or punishment. Nothing exists except by the will of God. Shu'aib accepted the innovations of the Khārijites on the imāmate and warning, and followed the innovations of the 'Ajārida in their judgments relating to children, to those who stayed away, to association and dissociation.

(g) The Ḥāzimīya

These are the followers of Ḥāzim b. 'Alī. They adopted Shu'aib's opinion that God is the creator of man's deeds and that man has no power over them except as God wills. They held also the doctrine of the final state, *al-muwāfāt*, namely, that God takes as friends those whom he knows will have faith at the end of their lives; on the other hand, he dissociates himself from those whom he knows will be without faith at the end. God does not cease to love his friends and hate his enemies. It is said of the Ḥāzimīya that they did not commit themselves in the case of 'Alī, nor clearly declare their dissociation from him, though they did so in the case of the others.

6 Tha'āliba

The Tha'āliba are the followers of Tha'laba b. 'Āmir, who was closely associated with 'Abd al-Karīm b. 'Ajrad until they differed on the question of children. Tha'laba said, 'We shall associate with children, both the younger and the older, till we observe whether or not they deny truth and approve of injustice.' Thereupon the 'Ajārida dissociated themselves from him. Tha'laba is also reported to have said that he passed no judgment with regard to children, that is, whether they were friends or enemies, till they reached adulthood and were called to the faith. If they then accepted the call, all was well; if, however, they refused, they became unbelievers. He believed also in taking the *zakāt* from slaves if they became rich, and giving them a share of it if they became poor.

(a) The Akhnasīya

These are the followers of Akhnas b. Qais who belonged to the Tha'āliba. He differed from the Tha'āliba, however, in saying:

> I shall reserve judgment with regard to all those who worship in the direction of Mecca and reside in the regions of dissimulation, except those whose faith is known, and these I shall befriend; or those whose unbelief is known, and from these I shall dissociate myself.

The Akhnasīya forbid attacking, killing and stealing in secret. Except for those known personally to be opposed to their views [they believe that] no one who worships in the direction of Mecca may be attacked till he has been called to the faith. If he resists the call, he may be attacked. It is said that they allow Muslim women to be given in marriage to the polytheists amongst them, that is, to those who have committed grave sins. In other matters they adhere to the doctrines of the Khārijites.

(b) The Ma'badīya

These are the followers of Ma'bad b. 'Abd al-Raḥmān who was a member of the Tha'āliba. Ma'bad opposed the error of al-Akhnas in allowing the marriage of Muslim women to 'polytheists'. He also opposed Tha'laba in his decision to take the *zakāt* from slaves; though he said, 'I shall not on that account dissociate myself from him, nor shall I give up my own opinion, which is the contrary of his.' The Ma'badīya also permit the different shares of alms-tax to be reduced to one when a person [the giver] is in a state of dissimulation.

(c) The Rushaidīya

These are the followers of Rushaid al-Ṭūsī; they are also called the 'Ushrīya. Their origin is as follows. The Tha'āliba used to impose a tax of one twentieth on the land watered by rivers and canals. Ziyād b. 'Abd al-Raḥmān informed them that the tax was one tenth; but at the same time it was not lawful to dissociate from those who had earlier said that it was one twentieth. Rushaid then said, 'If it is not lawful to dissociate from them we shall do as they did.' Over this question the Rushaidīya became divided into two sub-sects.

(d) The Shaibānīya

These are the followers of Shaibān b. Salama who rose in revolt at the time of Abū Muslim. The Shaibānīya gave assistance to Abū Muslim and 'Alī b. al-Kirmānī against Naṣr b. Sayyār. Shaibān belonged to the Tha'āliba, but when he helped Abū Muslim and 'Alī b. al-Kirmānī, the Khārijites dissociated themselves from him. When Shaibān was killed, some people said that he had repented. The Tha'āliba, however, said:

> His repentance is unacceptable because he killed those who had the same beliefs as we have and took their property. Unless the property had been ceded to him the repentance of one who kills a Muslim and takes his property is acceptable only if he imposes retribution on himself and returns the property.

Shaibān believed in predetermination, agreeing in this with Jahm b. Ṣafwān. He also denied created power.

It is said of Ziyād b. 'Abd al-Raḥmān al-Shaibānī Abū Khālid that he held that God had no knowledge till he created it for himself; moreover, things only become known to him when they come into being and have existence. He is also said to have dissociated himself from Shaibān, whom he declared an unbeliever on account of his assistance to Abū Muslim and 'Alī b. al-Kirmānī, which resulted in the death of many of the Shaibānīya in Jurjān, Nasā and Armenia. Those who associated themselves with Shaibān and accepted his repentance were 'Aṭīya al-Jurjābī and his followers.

(e) The Mukramīya

These are the followers of Mukram b. 'Abdullah al-'Ijlī. Mukram also belonged to the Tha'āliba, but he differed from the others in his opinion that anyone who omits prayer is an unbeliever, not because he omits prayer but because of his ignorance of God. He applied this principle to every grave sin man commits, and said that a man becomes an unbeliever on account of his ignorance of God. It is inconceivable, he maintained, that anyone who knows that God is one, that God is aware of the hidden and manifest, and that he requites man's obedience and disobedience, would fall into disobedience or dare to oppose him, as long as he does not become unmindful of this knowledge and does not cease to care about his obligation. It was about this that the Prophet said, 'An adulterer in committing adultery does not commit adultery while he is still a believer; and a thief in stealing does not do so while still a believer.' In this matter the Mukramīya oppose the Tha'āliba.

The Mukramīya believe in faith at the time of death, and hold that God is a friend of his servants or their enemy according to what they will be at the time of death, and not according to their deeds now; for, till a man reaches the end of his life, his deeds cannot be depended on to endure. 'If he remains steadfast in his beliefs,' they say, 'this is faith, and we shall befriend him. If he does not remain steadfast we shall be his enemy.' The same is true of God: his friendship or enmity are based on his knowledge of what a man will be at the time of his death. This doctrine is common to all the Mukramīya.

(f) The Ma'lūmīya and Majhūlīya

Originally these formed part of the Ḥāzimīya. The Ma'lūmīya, however, say that if anyone does not know God, with all his names and attributes, he is ignorant of him; it is only when he attains to all this knowledge that he becomes a believer. They also say that capacity is with the act and that the act is created by man. Because of this the Ḥāzimīya dissociated themselves from them. The Majhūlīya, on the other hand, say that whoever knows some of God's names and attributes, though ignorant of others, does know God. They also maintain that man's deeds are created by God.

(g) The Bid'īya

These are the followers of Yaḥyā b. Aṣdam. They were the first to say:

> We should hold for certain that whoever believes as we do shall go to paradise. We should not add, 'If God wills', for that would mean there was some doubt in our belief. Those who say, therefore, we are believers, if God wills', are doubters. We shall certainly go to paradise – of this there is no doubt.

7 The Ibāḍīya

These are the followers of 'Abdullāh b. Ibāḍ who arose in revolt at the time of Marwān b. Muḥammad. Marwān sent against him 'Abdullah b. Muḥammad b. 'Aṭīya and they fought in Tabāla. It is said that 'Abdullāh b. Yaḥyā al-Ibāḍī was closely associated with 'Abdullāh b. Ibāḍ in all that he did and said.

'Abdullāh b. Ibāḍ said:

> Those who worship in the direction of the Ka'ba but oppose us are unbelievers, not polytheists. However, marriage with them is lawful

and so also is mutual inheritance. It is lawful also to take as booty such things as their weapons and horses, but nothing else. It is unlawful, however, to kill them or take them captive by a surprise attack. This is permitted only after war has been declared and proof [of their unbelief] has been established.

The Ibāḍīya say that the territory where their Muslim opponents are is the the abode of the unity of God, and that the army camp of the Sultan is the territory of rebellion. They allow the testimony of non-Ibāḍites against Ibāḍites. They regard those who commit grave sins as monotheists, *muwaḥḥidūn*, but not believers, *mu'minūn*.

Ka'bī relates of the Ibāḍīya that they hold capacity to be an accident existing before the act; with that capacity the act takes place. The deeds of men are created by God, that is, brought into being and produced by him; but they are truly acquired by men, and not merely in a metaphorical sense. They do not call their imām the Commander of the Faithful, nor do they call themselves emigrants. They say the world will perish altogether when men who are subject to God's commandment perish. Ka'bī says that they all hold the opinion that whoever commits a grave sin becomes an unbeliever, but only in the sense of one who does not acknowledge God's favour, not in the sense of being cut off from the community. They are non-committal with regard to the children of polytheists. They consider it possible that suffering may be inflicted on them as a punishment, but also possible that by God's grace they may enter paradise.

Ka'bī also says that they believe in an act of obedience, *ṭā'a*, not directed towards God, as Abu 'l-Hudhail did. They differ, however, on the question of hypocrisy, that is, as to whether it should be called polytheism or not. They say that the hypocrites in the days of the Prophet were monotheists, but having committed grave sins they became unbelievers on account of those grave sins, not on account of polytheism. They also maintain that whatever God commands is common to all and not restricted to a few; by it God commands both believer and unbeliever. There is no distinction made in the Qur'ān in this respect. Again God does not create anything except as a sign of his oneness; by this a man must be guided by him. Some of them hold that it is possible for God to raise up a messenger without giving a sign by which he may be known, and that men may be put under an obligation to do all that is revealed to the messenger without an obligation on his part, or on God's part, to show miracles until God himself creates a sign and shows a miracle.

The Ibāḍīya also differ among themselves, as do the Tha'āliba and the 'Ajārida. [The following are the main divisions.]

(a) The Ḥafṣīya

These are the followers of Ḥafṣ b. Abu 'l-Miqdām, who differed from the other Ibāḍīya in holding that there is a state intermediary between polytheism and faith, namely, knowledge of God in his oneness. Whoever acknowledges God but does not believe in other things, as a prophet, or book, or the resurrection, heaven or hell; or whoever commits a grave sin, as fornication, theft or drinking of wine – such a one is an unbeliever, but he is free from polytheism.

(b) The Ḥārithīya

These are the followers of al-Harith al-Ibāḍī who differed from the Ibadites in following the Mu'tazilite view of *qadar*. He also held that capacity exists before the act, and that there are acts of obedience not directed towards God.

(c) The Yazīdīya

These are the followers of Yazīd b. Unaisa who believed in associating with the early Muḥakkima who arose before the Azāriqa, but in dissociating from those who came after them, with the exception of the Ibāḍīya whom he befriended. Yazīd also maintained that God would raise up a messenger from among the Persians, and would reveal to him a book written in heaven, and that this book would be revealed as a whole. He would abandon the *sharī'a* of Muḥammad and follow the religion of Sabaeans mentioned in the Qur'ān, who are not, however, the Sabaeans living in Ḥarrān and Wāsiṭ.

Yazīd befriended those of the People of the Book who accepted the prophethood of Muḥammad, even though they did not embrace his religion. Those among his associates and others who deserved the prescribed penalty he regarded as unbelievers and polytheists. According to him also every sin whether venial or grave is polytheism.

8 The Ṣufrīya Ziyādīa

These are the followers of Ziyād b. al-Aṣfar. They differ on several points from the Azāriqa, the Najdāt and the Ibāḍites. For example, they do not regard as unbelievers those who abstain from fighting, provided they agree with them in their religious beliefs. Again, they do not abandon the punishment of stoning to death; nor do they hold that the children of polytheists should be put to death; nor do they declare them unbelievers, and neither do they condemn them to hell forever.

They say that dissimulation is permissible in words though not in deeds. They maintain, too, that those deeds for which the prescribed punishment is due do not render a man liable to be described by a name other than that for which it is due; thus fornication, theft, slander make a man a fornicator, theif or slanderer, but not an unbeliever or polytheist. On the other hand in the case of those grave sins, such as omitting prayer or fleeing from battles, for which no punishment is prescribed on account of their gravity, the one guilty does become an unbeliever.

It is reported of Ḍaḥḥāk, who was a member of this group, that he allowed the marriage of Muslim women to unbelievers amongst them when they were in the territory of dissimulation, not, however, in the territory where they could openly declare their belief. Ziyād b. al-Aṣfar considered all the categories of alms as one in times of dissimulation. It is reported of him also that he said, 'In our own eyes we are believers, but we do not know. Perhaps in the eyes of God we have lost faith.' He held that polytheism was of two kinds: the first was obedience to Satan, the other worship of idols. Unbelief also is of two kinds: one consists in not acknowledging God's favours, the other in denying his Lordship. Dissociation, too, is of two kinds: one is dissociation from those who have merited the prescribed punishment – this is *sunna* [of the Prophet]; the other is dissociation from those who deny God – this is obligatory.

Conclusion

Let us conclude our treatment of Khārijite views by giving a list of the principal Khārijites. Among the early ones were 'Ikrima, Abū Hārūn al-'Abdī, Abu '-Sha'thā' and Ismā'īl b. Sumai'. Among the later ones were al-Yamān b. Rabāb, Tha'labī followed by Baihasī; 'Abdullāh b. Yazīd, Muḥammad b. Ḥarb and Yaḥyā b. Kāmil, the Ibāḍites. Among their poets were 'Imrān b. Ḥiṭṭān and Ḥabīb b. Murra, the companion of Ḍaḥḥāk b. Qais. Others were Jahm b. Ṣafwān, Abū Marwān Ghailān b. Muslim, Muḥammad b. 'Īsā Barghūth, Abu 'l-Ḥusain Kulthūm b. Ḥabīb al-Muhallabī, Abū Bakr Muḥammad b. 'Abdullāh b. Shabīb al-Baṣrī, 'Alī b. Ḥarmala, Ṣāliḥ Qubba b. Ṣubaiḥ b. 'Amr, Muwais b. 'Imrān al-Baṣrī, Abū 'Abdullāh b. Maslama, Abū 'Abd al-Rahmān b. Maslama, al-Faḍl b. 'Īsā al-Raqqāshī, Abū Zakarīyā Yaḥyā b. Aṣfaḥ, Abu 'l-Ḥusain Muḥammad b. Muslim al-Ṣāliḥī, Abū Muḥammad 'Abdullāh b. Muḥammad b. al-Ḥasan al-Khālidī, Muḥammad b. Ṣadaqa, Abu 'l-Ḥusain 'Alī

b. Zaid al-Ibāḍī, Abū ‘Abdullāh Muḥammad b. Karrām and Kulthūm b. Ḥabīb al-Murādī al-Baṣrī.

There were those, too, who remained neutral. They gave support neither to ‘Alī in his battles, nor to his opponents. They said, ‘We shall not participate in the conflict between the Companions.’ These were ‘Abdullāh b. ‘Umar, Sa‘d b. Abū Waqqās, Muḥammad b. Maslama al-Anṣārī and Usāma b. Zaid b. Ḥāritha al-Kalbī, *mawlā* of the Prophet.

Qais b. Abū Ḥāzim said:

I was with ‘Alī in all his hardships and battles until the day of Ṣiffīn. On that day he said, ‘March out against the rest of the enemy's forces; march against those who say that God and his Messenger have lied, whereas you say that God and his Messenger have told the truth.’ I knew what he thought of the people; accordingly I left him.

Chapter 5

The Murji'ites

Introduction

The word *irjā'* has two meanings. The first is postponement, as in the words of God: 'They said 'Put him off, him and his brother.''[1] that is, give him respite or delay him. The other meaning is to give hope. To use the term *al-Murji'a* in the first sense for this group is correct because they look upon deeds as secondary to intention and resolve. The term can obviously be used of them in the second sense also, because they hold that disobedience with faith is not harmful just as obedience with disbelief is not beneficial.

It is also said that *al-irjā'* means deferring the case of one who commits a grave sin to the day of judgment; in this world, therefore, no judgment is made as to whether he belongs to the people of Paradise or the people of Hell. If the word is understood in this way the Murji'a and the Wa'īdīya are two opposing sects. Some say that *al-irjā'* means bringing 'Alī down from the first to the fourth place. Understood in this sense the Murji'a and the Shī'a became two opposed sects.

The Murji'a consist of four groups: The Khārijite Murji'a, the Qadarite Murji'a, the Jabrite Murji'a and the pure Murji'a. Muḥammad b. Shabīb, al-Ṣāliḥī, and al-Khālidī belonged to the Qadarite Murji'a, as did also the Ghailānīya, the followers of Ghailān al-Dimashqī, who was the first to introduce the belief in *qadar* and postponement. We shall, however, deal only with the pure Murji'ites.

1 The Yūnusīya

The Yūnusīya are the followers of Yūnus b. 'Awn al-Numairī who maintained that īmān consists in knowledge of God and submission to him, in forsaking pride and having love of God in the heart. Whoever possesses these qualities is a *mu'min*. Acts of obedience other than these do not form part of *īmān*, and not to perform them does not injure the essence of *īmān*. A man will not be punished for this omission if his faith is pure and his conviction is true.

Yūnus held that Iblīs knew that God was one, but he became an unbeliever through his pride: 'He refused and waxed proud and so he became one of the unbelievers.'[2] He also said that the man, in whose heart submission to God and love of him are established with sincerity and conviction, will not rebel against God and disobey him; but if he does commit an act of disobedience, it will do him no harm because of his conviction and sincerity. A believer enters Paradise on account of his sincerity and love alone, not on account of his deeds and his obedience.

2 The 'Ubaidīya

The 'Ubaidīya are the followers of 'Ubaid al-Mukta'ib. It is related of him that he said that all sins other than polytheism will certainly be forgiven. When a man dies a monotheist, he said, no sin that he has committed or evil that he has done will harm him. Al-Yamān tells of 'Ubaid al-Mukta'ib and his followers that they held that God's knowledge was eternally nothing other than himself; likewise the religion revealed by him was certainly nothing other than himself. 'Ubaid maintained that God (High, indeed, be he exalted above that they say!) is in the likeness of man; and he applied to God the words of the Prophet: 'God created Adam in the image of the Most Merciful.'

3 The Ghassānīya

The Ghassānīya are the followers of Ghassān al-Kūfī who maintained that faith consists of knowledge of God and his Prophet, together with acknowledgment of what God has revealed and what the Prophet has brought: in general, however, and not in particular. He also held that faith increases but does not decrease. He said, too, that if any one says, 'I know that God has forbidden the eating of pork, but I do not know whether the pork forbidden by God is this goat or something else,' such a one would be a believer. If also he says, 'I know that God has enjoined pilgrimage to the Ka'ba but I do not know where the Ka'ba is, perhaps it is in India' – such a one would be a believer. What Ghassān means is that beliefs of this kind are matters outside faith; not that there is any real doubt about them, for it is impossible for an intelligent man to doubt in which direction the Ka'ba is; similarly, the difference between a pig and a goat is obvious.

Strangely enough Ghassān maintained that Abū Ḥanīfa held similar views and considered him a Murji'ite. Perhaps he has told an untruth about him. It is true, however, that Abū Ḥanīfa and his followers were called Sunnite Murji'a and many writers on sects have regarded Abū Ḥanīfa as a Murji'ite. Perhaps the reason for this is that when he said that faith is belief in the heart, and that it neither increases nor decreases, they thought that he looked upon deeds as secondary to faith. But how could this man who had been so engaged in the sphere of deeds favour disregarding deeds? There is another reason also [for his being called a Murji'ite], namely, that he used to oppose the Qadarites and the Mu'tazilites who arose in the early days of Islam. The Mu'tazilites were accustomed to call Murji'ites all those who opposed them on the question of *qadar*, as also did the Wa'īdīya among the Khārijites. It is not unlikely, therefore, that the name was given to him by these two sects. God, however, knows best.

4 The Thaubānīya

The Thaubānīya are the followers of Abū Thaubān the Murji'ite, who maintained that faith is knowledge and acceptance of God and his prophets, and of every thing that reason does not permit [not] to do, but whatever reason manifests as not obligatory is not part of faith. According to him all deeds are secondary to faith.

Those who followed the views of Abū Thaubān were: Abū Marwān Ghailān b. Marwān al-Dimashqī, Abū Shimr, Muwais b. 'Imrān, al-Faḍl al-Raqqāshī, Muḥammad b. Shabīb, al-'Attābī and Ṣāliḥ Qubba. Ghailān believed that the power, *qadar*, to do good and evil belongs to man. On the question of the imāmate he maintained that it could be validly held by other than the Quraish; that anyone who lives according to the Qur'ān and the *sunna* is fit for it; that it is determined by the consensus of the community alone. This is surprising, as the community has in fact agreed that the imāmate is not valid in other than the Quraish. It was for this reason that the Anṣār were persuaded to give up their demands when they said, 'Let there be an *amīr* from us and an *amīr* from you.'

Ghailān combined three different doctrines: free will, Murji'ism and Khārijism.

This Thaubānīya sect which we have included among the Murji'a, is unanimous in holding that if God forgave one sinner on the day of judgment he would forgive every believing sinner who was in the same position; again, if he brought one out of hell he would also bring out every other person in a similar position. It is surprising, however, that they were not sure whether believers among the people of Unity would necessarily come out of hell or not.

It is said of Muqātil b. Sulaimān that he held that sin does not harm a man who believes in God's unity and has faith, and that a believer will not enter hell. The truth, however, is that, according to him, a believer who is disobedient to his Lord will be punished on the day of judgment on the Bridge across hell; he will be subjected to the scorching heat and flame, and will suffer in proportion to his sin, but at last he will enter paradise. Muqātil compared this to grain in a frying pan over a fire.

It is reported of Bishr b. Ghiyāth al-Muraisī that he held that if those who commit grave sins enter hell they will come out of it after they have been punished for their sins; but that they should remain in hell eternally would be impossible and unjust.

It is said that the first person to believe in *irjā'* was al-Ḥasan b. Muḥammad b. 'Alī b. Abū Ṭālib, who wrote letters on this matter to the capital cities. He did not, however, make deeds secondary to faith, as did the Murji'ite sects of the Yūnusīya and the 'Ubaidīya. He maintained, nevertheless, that a man committing grave sins does not become an unbeliever, because committing acts of obedience and refraining from acts of disobedience are not essential to faith in the sense that faith would cease to exist in the absence of them.

5 The Taumanīya

The Taumanīya are the followers of Abū Mu'ādh al-Taumanī who maintained that faith is that which protects from unbelief. The word faith refers to certain qualities. If a person loses these he becomes an unbeliever; indeed, if he loses only one of these qualities he becomes an unbeliever. One of these qualities by itself, however, is not called faith, nor is it even part of faith. If a man commits an act of disobedience, either grave or venial, about which Muslims are not agreed that it is unbelief, he does not thereby become a *fāsiq*, though it can be said that he has transgressed and disobeyed. Those qualities [which constitute faith] are knowledge, belief, love, sincerity and acceptance of what has been revealed through the Prophet. Whoever omits prayer and fasting, considering it lawful to do so, becomes an unbeliever. If, however, someone omits them with the intention of doing them at another time, he does not become an unbeliever. Whoever kills a prophet or strikes him becomes an unbeliever, not on account of killing or striking him, but on account of contempt, hostility and hatred. To this view also Ibn al-Rāwandī and Bishr al-Muraisī are inclined; they assert that faith is confession in heart and tongue, whereas unbelief is a denial and rejection. To make obeisance to sun, moon and idols is not unbelief in itself, but a sign of unbelief.

6 The Ṣāliḥīya

The Ṣāliḥīya are the followers of Ṣāliḥ b. 'Umar al-Ṣāliḥī. Al-Ṣāliḥī, Muḥammad b. Shabīb, Abū Shimr and Ghailān all hold both free will and *irjā'*. Though we had committed ourselves to mentioning only the views of the pure Murji'ites, it has occurred to us to mention these also, because they differ from the Murji'a on a number of points.

Ṣāliḥī says that faith is knowledge of God in a general way, that is, to know that the universe has a creator and no more. Unbelief is simple ignorance of him. If someone said that God is 'One of Three', this itself is not unbelief, though it will be said only by those who are unbelievers. He maintains that knowledge of God is love of him and submission to him; this is possible with the proof, *ḥujja*, of the Prophet. It would be in accordance with reason to believe in God and not believe in his prophet; though the Prophet has said, 'Whoever does not believe in me does not believe in God.' Al-Ṣāliḥī also said that prayer, *ṣalāt*, is not worship of God, and that there is not worship of God except faith in him. Faith consists in the knowledge of God; it is an undivided quality which does not increase or decrease. Similarly, unbelief is an undivided quality which does not increase or decrease.

Abū Shimr, the Murji'ite Qadarite, says that until the proof of God's existence becomes known through the prophets, faith lies in the knowledge of God, love of him and submission to him in the heart, joined with a confession that he is one and that there is nothing like him. When, however, the proof of the prophets becomes known, to accept them and believe in them becomes part of faith and knowledge. But to accept what is revealed by God through them does not form part of basic faith. Again, not every quality of faith is itself faith, nor is it part of faith; but only when all the qualities of faith are found together do they constitute faith. Among the qualities of faith Abū Shimr included knowledge of justice, by which he understood that the power to do good and evil lies in man without any of it being ascribed to God.

Ghailān b. Marwān, a Qadarite-Murji'ite, says that faith is secondary knowledge, love of God, submission to him and acceptance of what the Prophet has made known and of whatever has come from God. Primary knowledge is natural and necessary. Knowledge, therefore, according to him, is of two kinds: (a) natural knowledge, which is a knowledge a man has that the universe has a maker and that he himself has a creator – but this knowledge is not called faith; (b) faith, which is secondary knowledge and is acquired.

Conclusion

The following is a supplementary list of reported Murji'ite leaders: al-Ḥasan b. Muḥammad b. 'Alī b. Abū Ṭālib, Sa'īd b. Jubair, Ṭalq b. Ḥabīb, 'Amr b. Murra, Muhārib b. Ziyād, Muqātil b. Sulaimān, Dharr, 'Amr b. Dharr, Ḥammād b. Abū Sulaimān, Abū Ḥanīfa, Abū Yūsuf, Muḥammad b. al-Ḥasan and Qudaid b. Ja'far. These are all authorities on Ḥadīth. They do not declare those who commit grave sins unbelievers on that account, nor do they maintain that they shall be eternally in hell; in this they differ from the Khārijites and the Qadarites.

Chapter 6

The Shī'ites

Introduction

The Shī'ites are those who follow 'Alī only. They hold that his caliphate and imāmate were based on designation and appointment, either open or hidden. They maintain also that the imāmate must remain in 'Alī's family; if it were ever to go outside of it, this would be either because of a wrong on the part of another, or because of dissimulation on the part of the rightful imām. According to them the imāmate is not a civil matter, validly settled by the will of the people appointing an imām of their own choosing: it is a fundamental matter and a basic element of religion. Messengers of God may not ignore and disregard it, nor leave it to the choice of the common people.

Common to the Shī'ites is the doctrine of the necessity of designation and appointment. They all hold that the prophets and imāms must be immune from grave and minor sins. They believe, too, in association and dissociation in word, deed and mind, except at the times of legitimate dissimulation. In this some of the Zaidīya differ. There is much dispute and controversy among them on the question of how the imāmate is transmitted from one imām to another; and, so, whenever the occasion arises for its transmission or non-transmission, various conflicting opinions and points of view are proposed.

The Shī'ites are divided into five different sects: the Kaisānīya, Zaidīya, Imāmīya, Ghulāt (the Extremists) and Ismā'īlīya. In questions of theology some of these sects lean to Mu'tazilism, some to Orthodoxy and others to Anthropomorphism.

1 The Kaisānīya

These are the followers of Kaisān, a *mawlā* of 'Alī b. Abū Ṭālib, Commander of the Faithful. Kaisān is said to have been a pupil of Muḥammad b. al-Ḥanafīya. His followers believed in him in a way that exceeded all bounds. Thus, for example, they held that his knowledge embraced all sciences; that from his two masters he had learned all secrets, including the power of allegorical interpretation and insight into the esoteric; that he had knowledge also of the heavens and of the souls of men.

Common to the Kaisānīya is the doctrine that religion consists of obedience to a man. Hence they interpreted the fundamental religious duties, as prayer, fasting, alms, pilgrimage and the rest in terms of [obedience to] certain persons. Some of them went so far as to abandon religious laws once they were able to render obedience to a certain man; the belief of others in the resurrection was weakened; others, again, were converted to a belief in metempsychosis, incarnation and a return from the dead. Some did not go beyond a particular man in their allegiance, believing that he would not die, and, indeed, that it was impossible for him to die till he returned from concealment. Others, however, transferred the imāmate in the true sense to another man, but were afterwards disturbed and confused about the matter. Some, though not descendants of 'Alī, actually claimed the authority of the imāmate. All are, indeed, confused and divided among themselves.

If one believes that religion consists in obedience to a man, and finds none, that one has no religion. May God protect us from this confusion and bewilderment! Lord, guide us in the right path.

(a) The Mukhtārīya

These are the followers of Mukhtār b. Abū 'Ubaid al-Thaqafī. Mukhtār was first a Khārijite, then a follower of Zubair and, finally, a Kaisānī Shī'ite. He believed in the imāmate of Muḥammad b. al-Ḥanafīya after that of 'Alī, Commander of the Faithful, though it is said that he held that Muḥammad was imām not after 'Alī himself, but after Ḥasan and Ḥusain. He propagated the cause of Muḥammad, proclaiming himself as one of his followers and emissaries. He gave out many ideas full of lies and errors which he attributed to Muḥammad. When Muḥammad came to know of this he dissociated himself from him, and told his followers that this man had spread these ideas among the people to serve his own purposes and gather support.

Mukhtār succeeded well for two reasons. One was that he attributed both his knowledge and his mission to Muḥammad b. Al-Ḥanafīya; the other that he took upon himself the cause of avenging Ḥusain b. 'Alī, devoting himself day and night to fighting against the tyrants who had conspired to kill him.

Mukhtār held the view that there can be change, *badā'*, in God. Now the word *badā'* may be understood in different ways. It may, firstly, be taken as a change in knowledge, in the sense that God may attain to a knowledge which is the opposite of his former knowledge (I do not think that any rational man would hold such an opinion); secondly, as an enlightenment with respect to will, that is, that God may discover that the opposite to what he had willed and decreed was right; thirdly, as a change in command, that is, that God should command something and afterwards command its contrary. Whoever does not allow abrogation would be of the opinion that different commands at different times [merely] succeeded each other.

Mukhtār was led to adopt the belief in *badā'* by his claim that he knew events which were about to take place, either because of a revelation he had received, or because of a message from the imām. Whenever he foretold an event to his followers, and the outcome was in accordance with what he had said, he would make use of it as proof of the genuineness of his mission. If, however, it turned out otherwise he would say that God had changed his mind. He made no distinction, therefore, between *naskh* (abrogation) and *badā'*, but simply said, 'If abrogation of commands is possible so also is change in the foretelling of future events.'

Muḥammad b. al-Ḥanafīya is said to have dissociated himself from Mukhtār when he heard that he was deceiving people, and making them believe that he was his supporter and emissary. He also dissociated himself from the errors and deceptions which Mukhtār had introduced, as his false interpretations and distorted fantasies. One of these fantasies concerned an old chair he had, covered with silk brocade and ornamented in a variety of ways, of which he said, 'This is one of the treasures of 'Alī, Commander of the Faithful; this is to us what the Ark was for the Israelites.' When, therefore, Mukhtār was about to go into battle against his enemies, he would put the chair in the midst of his soldiers as they were drawn up for battle, and say to them, 'Go into battle; success, triumph and victory are yours. This chair in your midst is like the ark to the Israelites. In it are reassurance and security; and angels from above will come down upon you to assist you.' The story is well known, also, of the white pigeons which appeared in the air after Mukhtār had announced to his soldiers that angels would come down in the form of white pigeons. Well known, too, are the skilful rhymes which he composed.

Mukhtār was induced to associate himself with Muḥammad b. al-Ḥanafīya because of the people's strong faith in him, and the love that filled their hearts for him. Muḥammad b. al-Ḥanafīya was, indeed, a man of great learning and profound knowledge, as well as an acute thinker, and possessed also of sound practical judgment. 'Alī, Commander of the Faithful, had told him of the forthcoming struggles of various kinds, and instructed him in the knowledge of the signposts along the Path. However he chose isolation and preferred obscurity to fame. Knowledge of the imāmate is said to have been entrusted to him to be given to one qualified; before he departed from this world he had deposited it where it belonged.

Al-Sayyid al-Ḥimyarī and the poet Kuthayyir 'Azza were among Muḥammad b. al-Ḥanafīya's followers. Kuthayyir composed the following lines about him:

> Behold, the imāms from the Quraish, possessors of the truth, of whom there are only four – 'Alī and his three sons. These three are the grandsons [of Muḥammad], about whom there is no obscurity. One grandson was a man of faith and righteousness; another is buried in Karbalā'; and the third shall not taste death till he advances at the head of his cavalry with his banner before him. He has gone into concealment at Raḍwā, where he lives on honey and water, and for a while he will not be seen amongst men.

Al-Ḥimayrī also believed that Muḥammad b. al-Ḥanafīya had not died, but that he was on the mount of Raḍwā, protected on either side by a lion and a leopard, with two springs nearby pouring out an abundance of water and honey, that he would return from his concealment, and fill the earth with justice as now it is full of injustice. This is the first appearance of the Shī'ite doctrine of concealment and return from concealment. It was a doctrine that continued to be held by some of the Shī'a, who at last came to look upon it as part of religion, and a pillar, indeed, of Shī'ism. After the death of Muḥammad b. al-Ḥanafīya the Kaisānīya became divided among themselves on the question of the course of the imāmate, and broke up into various schools.

(b) The Hāshimīya

These are the followers of Abū Hāshim b. Muḥammad b. al-Ḥanafīya. They hold that Muḥammad died and that the imāmate passed to his son

Abū Hāshim. Abū Hāshim had been instructed by his father in the secrets of the sciences. He had been taught the correspondence between the heavenly spheres and souls; how, too, to understand the meaning of revelation through allegorical interpretation, and to grasp the correlation between the exoteric and the esoteric. It is the belief of the Hāshimīya that beneath the exoteric, *ẓāhir*, there is the esoteric, *bāṭin*; that every individual has a spirit; that every revelation has an interpretation; that for every type in this world there is a prototype in the other world. All the wisdom and mysteries that are spread throughout the world are found gathered together in a human person. It is this knowledge which 'Alī appropriated for his son, Muḥammad b. al-Ḥanafīya, who in turn imparted the secret of it to his son Abū Hāshim. Whoever possesses this knowledge is truly the imām.

After Abū Hāshim his followers became divided into five groups. One group maintained that Abū Hāshim died in the Khārijite region on returning from Syria, having appointed as his successor Muḥammad b. 'Alī b. 'Abdullāh b. 'Abbās. The appointment was then transferred to the offspring of 'Abbās and in this way the caliphate passed to the 'Abbāsids. Moreover, the 'Abbāsids claimed that the caliphate belonged rightly to them because of their close blood relationship with the Prophet; for when the Prophet died his uncle 'Abbās was the nearest of kin, with right of succession. Another group held that, after the death of Abū Hāshim, the imāmate belonged to his brother's son, Ḥasan b. 'Alī b. Muḥammad b. al-Ḥanafīya. A third group, however, denied this. According to them Abū Hāshim appointed his brother, 'Alī b. Muḥammad, who in turn appointed his son Ḥasan; the imāmate, therefore, belonged to the offspring of al-Ḥanafīya and did not pass to others. Still another group said that Abū Hāshim appointed 'Abdullāh b. 'Amr b. Ḥarb al-Kindī, and, therefore, the imāmate was transferred from Abū Hāshim to 'Abdullah, into whom Abū Hāshim's spirit moved. This man, however, had neither learning nor piety; and some of his followers, realizing his dishonesty and deceitfulness, forsook him, and supported instead the imāmate of 'Abdullāh b. Mu'āwiya b. 'Abdullāh b. Ja'far b. Abū Ṭālib.

The following are some of the views of 'Abdullah [b. 'Amr. b. Ḥarb]. Spirits pass by transmigration from one bodily form to another and receive rewards or punishments through these forms, whether human or animal. God's spirit underwent a continuing process of transmigration, till it finally reached 'Abdullāh himself and became incarnate in him. 'Abdullāh, accordingly, claimed both divinity and prophethood, as well as a knowledge of the unseen. His foolish followers worshipped him, denied the resurrection and believed instead in transmigration in this world, with the bestowal of rewards and punishments through the forms taken in it. The words of God: 'No sin shall be imputed to those who believe and do good works for what they may have eaten, if they are mindful of their duty to God,'[1] 'Abdullāh interpreted in the sense that whosoever finds the imām and acknowledges him is free from guilt in whatever he eats, and reaches his fulfilment.

From 'Abdullāh arose the two sub-sects of the Khurramīya and the Mazdakīya in Iraq. When he died in Khurāsān his followers became divided among themselves. Some said that he had not died, but was alive and would return; others that he had died, and that his spirit had gone to Isḥāq b. Zaid b. al-Ḥārith al-Anṣāri. These latter are the Ḥārithīya who declare lawful that which is unlawful, and live their lives as though bound by no religious obligations. Between the followers of 'Abdullāh b. Mu'āwiya and those of Muḥammad b. 'Alī there is a strong difference of opinion in regard to the imāmate. Both claim that its leader was appointed by Abū Hāshim, without, however, being able to establish their claim on any sound basis.

(c) The Bayānīya

These are the followers of Bayān b. Sam'ān al-Tamīmī, to whom they claim the imāmate was transmitted on the death of Abū Hāshim. Bayān was an extremist who believed in the divinity of 'Alī, Commander of the Faithful. According to him a divine particle became incarnate in 'Alī and was embodied in him. By virtue of this divine particle 'Alī knew the unseen and hence when he foretold the outcome of battles, the event was as he had said. It was by virtue of the same divine particle that he fought the infidels and gained the victory over them. It was by this power, too, that he uprooted the gate of Khaibar. 'Alī was referring to it when he said, 'I uprooted the gate of Khaibar not with bodily power, nor with strength derived from food; but I uprooted it with heavenly power bestowed by God and shining with divine light.' This heavenly power which 'Alī possessed may be compared to a lamp in a niche, the divine light itself being the light of the lamp.

Bayān said that perhaps 'Alī would at some time appear again. The words of God: 'Do they wait that Allāh should come to them in the shadows of the clouds?'[2] he interpreted as referring to 'Alī. 'Alī is the one who comes in canopies of clouds with the thunder as his voice and the lightning as his smile. Bayān also claimed that this divine particle had passed to himself through metempsychosis, and for this reason he had a right to the imāmate and to the caliphate. It was because of this same particle, too, that Adam was worthy of the prostration of the angels.

Bayān also maintained that God is human in form, with limb corresponding to limb and part to part, adding that he would perish entirely except his face; as God himself has said, 'Everything will perish entirely except his face.'[3] In spite of this preposterous nonsense Bayān wrote to Muḥammad b. 'Alī b. al-Ḥusain al-Bāqir calling upon him to acknowledge him, adding: 'Accept Islam, and you will be saved. Whoever submits will be raised up, for you do not know to whom God may grant the prophethood.' The messenger was ordered by Bāqir to eat the paper he brought, and having done so, died immediately. The name of the messenger was 'Umar b. Abū 'Afīf.

A number of followers gathered around Bayān, who gave him allegiance and accepted his teachings. He was, however, put to death on account of his doctrines by Khālid b. 'Abdullāh al-Qasrī. He is said to have been burned together with al-Kūfī, who is known as Ma'rūf b. Sa'īd.

(d) The Rizāmīya

These are the followers of Rizām b. Razm. They hold that the imāmate passed from 'Alī to his son Muḥammad, from Muḥammad to his son Abū Hāshim, and then by designation from Abū Hāshim to 'Alī b. 'Abdullāh b. 'Abbās. After this it went to Muḥammad b. 'Alī who in turn appointed as imām his son Ibrāhīm, a friend of Abū Muslim, who supported his imāmate and propagated his cause.

The Rizāmīya arose in Khurāsān at the time of Abū Muslim. It is even said that Abū Muslim himself was a Rizāmite, because of the fact that the Rizāmīya bestowed the imāmate upon him, saying that he had a claim to it. They asserted, too, that God's spirit had become incarnate in him and had helped him against the Umayyads, enabling him to destroy them and put them all to death. They believed also in the transmigration of souls.

Al-Muqanna' (The Veiled One) who claimed divinity for himself on account of the extraordinary signs he performed, was at first a Rizāmite. The Mubayyida of Transoxiana, a section of the Khurramīya, became his followers. They believed in the renunciation of religious obligations, and held that religion consists only in acknowledgment of the imām. Some of them, however, said that religion consists of two things: acknowledgment of the imām, and fulfilment of the trust committed to one. Whoever attains to these two things attains to perfection, and is no longer subject to religious obligations.

Some Rizāmīya held that the imāmate passed by designation, and in no other way, from Abū Hāshim b. Muḥammad b. al-Ḥanafīya to Muḥammad b. 'Alī b. 'Abdullāh b. 'Abbās.

Abū Muslim, who established the ['Abbāsid] dynasty, belonged at first to the Kaisānīya sect, from whose missionaries he acquired the different kinds of learning which were peculiar to them. He learnt from them that they were only custodians of this knowledge, and so he looked for one in whom it had its permanent abode. He then sent a message to Ja'far b. Muḥammad al-Ṣādiq, saying, 'I have proclaimed a revolt, and have called on men to transfer their allegiance from the Umayyads to the descendants of the Prophet. If you are interested in the matter, you need do no more.' Ja'far al-Ṣādiq replied, saying, 'You are not a representative of mine; and, besides, the time is not yet opportune.' Abū Muslim then turned to Abu 'l-'Abbās 'Abdullāh b. Muḥammad al-Ṣaffāḥ and entrusted the caliphate to him.

2 The Zaidīya

These are the followers of Zaid b. 'Alī b. al-Ḥusain b. 'Alī b. Abū Ṭālib. They hold that the imāmate belongs to the offspring of Fāṭima, and cannot legitimately be held by others. However, they recognize as imām any Fāṭimid who is learned, pious, brave and generous, and who declares his imāmate: allegiance, they maintain, must be given to such a one whether he is a descendant of Ḥasan or a descendant of Ḥusain. Acting on this belief some of the Zaidīya recognize the imāmate of the imāms Muḥammad and Ibrāhīm, the sons of 'Abdullāh b. Ḥasan, who had revolted during the reign of Manṣūr, and were on that account put to death. They also admit the possibility of two imāms in different regions; provided they are both endowed with the above qualities, each has a right to allegiance.

While under the influence of these ideas Zaid b. 'Alī determined to learn the sciences of theology and law in order to become adorned with knowledge. In theological matters he became a pupil of Wāṣil b. 'Aṭā', the 'Weaver' and 'Stammerer', leader and chief of the Mu'tazilites, even though in Wāṣil's opinion, his grandfather, 'Alī b. Abụ Ṭālib, was not necessarily right in his battles with the People of the Camel, and in those against the Syrians. According to Wāṣil one of the parties was wrong, but he did not specify which. From Wāṣil, therefore, Zaid learned Mu'tazilism, and all his followers became Mu'tazilites.

One of Zaid's views was that it was possible for a man of lesser excellence, *al-mafḍūl*, to be imām, even though there was to be found a man of greater excellence, *al-afḍal*. He said:

> 'Alī b. Abū Ṭālib was the most excellent of the Companions, but the caliphate was entrusted to Abū Bakr partly for reasons of expediency, and partly from religious considerations. There was, for example, the need to extinguish the fire of civil war and set at rest the hearts of the people, whose experience of the wars which took place at the time of the Prophet was still recent; and the sword of 'Alī, Commander of the Faithful, was still moist with the blood of the Quraishite and other polytheists. Moreover, there was a lingering rancour in the hearts of men and a desire for vengeance. Men's hearts, therefore, were not fully disposed towards 'Alī, and they were not ready to give him wholehearted submission. Accordingly it was expedient that the man exercising the imāmate should be one known to them to be gentle, kind, of mature age, an early adherent of Islam and close to the Prophet.
>
> Do you not recall that during his last illness, when Abū Bakr proposed to confer the caliphate upon 'Umar b. al-Khattāb, Commander of the Faithful, the people cried out in protest, saying to him, 'You have placed over us one who is severe and harsh.' Thus they did not approve of the choice of 'Umar, Commander of the Faithful, because of his sternness and severity, his strict enforcement of religious laws and his harsh treatment of the enemy. Abū Bakr, however, reassured them by saying, 'If God were to call me to account I would answer that I appointed the best man among them and the best for them!' Accordingly it is permissible for a man of lesser excellence to be an imām, even though there may be found a man of greater excellence, one to whom may be referred matters of law and whose decisions may be followed.

When the Shī'ites of Kūfa heard that Zaid had expressed these views, and learnt that he did not dissociate himself from the two senior Companions, they rejected him for the rest of his life. It was for this reason that they were called Rāfiḍa (Rejectors).

Differences arose between Zaid b. 'Alī and his brother Muḥammad b. 'Alī al-Bāqir; not, however, on this issue, but rather on the question of Zaid being a disciple of Wāsil b. 'Aṭā, and of learning from a man who believed it possible that his grandfather was in error in fighting those who broke their allegiance; or those who deviated, or those who actively rebelled against him. They differed also in regard to Zaid's views on *qadar* which were contrary to those held by the descendants of the Prophet. A further point of disagreement was Zaid's opinion that an imām must rise up in revolt in order to be an imām. Finally. Bāqir one day said to him, 'It would follow from your views that your father was not an imām, for he did not at any time rise in revolt, nor did he show any sign of doing so.'

When Zaid b. 'Alī was slain and his body crucified, Yaḥyā b. Zaid assumed the imāmate. Yaḥyā went to Khurāsān where many rallied in support of him. A prophecy from Ja'far b. Muḥammad al-Ṣādiq was communicated to him that he would be put to death just as his father had been, and crucified as he was. This came about as was foretold. The imāmate then passed to the imāms, Muḥammad and Ibrāhīm, who rose up in Medīna. Ibrāhīm afterwards went to Baṣra where he gained support. Both of these men, however, were also killed. Ṣādiq had already foretold to them all that would happen to them, at the same time telling them that his predecessors had foretold it all to him. Ṣādiq also foretold that the Umayyads while conscious at the same time of the rancour of the descendants of the Prophet against them, would lift their heads so high above the people that if the mountains tried to rival them in height, they would raise their heads above them too. He also went on to say that it was not permissible for one of the descendants of the Prophet to rise up and proclaim himself until God permitted the collapse of their empire, – pointing to Abu 'l-'Abbās and Abū Ja'far, the sons of Muḥammad b. 'Alī b. 'Abdullāh b. 'Abbās. Then, pointing to Manṣūr, he said, 'We shall not pursue the affair of the caliphate until this man and his descendants have had their enjoyment of it.'

Zaid b. 'Alī was put to death in Kunāsa in the city of Kūfa by Hishām b. 'Abd al-Malik; Yaḥyā b. Zaid in Juzjān of Khurāsān by the governor; Muḥammad the Imām in Medīna by 'Īsā b. Hāmān, and Ibrāhīm the Imām in Baṣra – both of these latter by the order of Manṣūr. After that the Zaidīya remained disorganized till the appearance of their leader Nāṣir al-Aṭrūsh in Khurāsān. Nāṣir was sought after so that he might be put to death, but he abandoned his campaign and went into hiding. Later he went into the districts of Dailam and al-Jabal which had not yet embraced Islam. He accordingly summoned the people to Islam, as taught by the school of Zaid b. 'Alī. This they embraced and followed. The Zaidīya remained strong in that region and were ruled over by a succession of their imāms.

In certain matters of doctrine this group of the Zaidīya differs from their cousins, known as the Mūsawīya. In time most of the Zaidīya abandoned the belief in the imāmate of the one of lesser excellence.

They also criticised the Companions of the Prophet, as did the Imāmīya.

The Zaidīya are divided into three groups: the Jārūdīya, Sulaimānīya and Batrīya. The Ṣāliḥīya hold the same views as the Batrīya.

(a) The Jārūdīya

These are the followers of Abu 'l-Jārūd Ziyād b. Abū Ziyād. They hold that the Prophet appointed 'Alī, not by name but by description; and it is he who is the imām after the Prophet. Men failed in their duty in not recognizing the description, and in not seeking for the one described. They set up, instead, Abū Bakr of their own accord, and thus became unbelievers. In holding this doctrine Abu 'l-Jārūd was in opposition to his imām, Zaid b. 'Alī, who did not hold this belief.

The Jārūdīya differ among themselves as to the interruption of the imāmate and its continuation. According to some of them the imāmate continued in succession from 'Alī to Ḥasan, from Ḥasan to Ḥusain, from Ḥusain to 'Alī b. Ḥusain Zain al-'Ābidīn, from 'Alī b. Ḥusain to his son Zaid b. 'Alī, and, lastly, to the imām Muḥammad b. 'Abdullāh b. al-Ḥasan b. al-Ḥusain b. 'Alī b. Abū Ṭālib, in whose imāmate they believed. Abū Ḥanīfa gave allegiance to Muḥammad, and became one of his followers. When in due course the matter was brought to the notice of Manṣūr he imprisoned Abū Ḥanīfa and kept him in captivity till his death. It is said that it was during the reign of Manṣūr that Abū Ḥanīfa swore allegiance to the imām Muḥammad b. 'Abdullāh. When Muḥammad was killed in Medīna, Abū Ḥanīfa remained faithful to his oath of allegiance, in the conviction that allegiance should be given to the house of the Prophet. This matter was reported to Manṣūr, and there then took place what we have already described.

Those who believed in the imāmate of the imām Muḥammad b. 'Abdullāh, differed among themselves. Some said that he had not been killed, but was still alive and would rise up to fill the earth with justice. Others, however, accepted his death and transferred the imāmate to Muḥammad b. al-Qāsim b. 'Alī b. ['Umar b. 'Alī] b. Ḥusain b. 'Alī of Ṭālaqān. Muḥammad was taken prisoner during the reign of Mu'taṣim, and, when brought before the Caliph, confined to his house till his death. Others, again, believed in the imāmate of Yaḥyā b. 'Umar of Kūfa. When Yaḥyā rose in revolt and called upon the people to follow him, many rallied to him. He was killed during the reign of Musta'īn, and his head brought to Muḥammad b. 'Abdullāh b. Ṭāhir. One of the 'Alawīya said about this incident, 'You killed the most honourable of men who ride on horses, though I came pleading to you to be gentle. It is impossible for me to meet you without the edge of the sword between us.' Yaḥyā's full name was Yaḥyā b. 'Umar b. Yaḥyā b. Ḥusain b. Zaid b. 'Alī.

As for Abu 'l-Jārūd, he was called Surḥūb, a name given to him by Abū Ja'far Muḥammad b. 'Alī al-Bāqir, which, as he explains, is the name of a blind devil living in the sea. Among his followers were Fudail al-Rassān and Abū Khālid al-Wāsiṭī. His followers differ among themselves on questions of law and *sunna*. Some hold that the knowledge possessed by the descendants of Ḥasan and Ḥusain is like that of the Prophet; knowledge is thus bestowed upon them naturally and necessarily without study. Others, however, maintain that the knowledge they possess is one shared by others, and may be acquired either from them or from others.

(b) The Sulaimānīya

These are the followers of Sulaimān b. Jarīr, who held that the imāmate is a matter to be decided by the deliberation of the community, and may even be determined by the agreement of two of the best Muslims. He further said that the imāmate may validly exist in a man of lesser excellence even though one of greater excellence does exist. Sulaimān also upheld the legitimacy of the imāmate of Abū Bakr and 'Umar by the choice of the community, a legitimacy arising from *ijtihād* [a judgment based on reason]. He used sometimes to say, nevertheless, that the community was in error in giving allegiance to them while 'Alī was present, though the error did not actually amount to a sin, *fisq*; it was an error of judgment, *khaṭa' ijtihādī*. 'Uthmān, however, he attacked for the innovations which he had introduced, and declared him an unbeliever because of them. He also branded 'Ā'isha, Zubair and Ṭalḥa as unbelievers because they embarked on a war against 'Alī.

The Rāfiḍa, too, were attacked by Sulaimān. According to him the Rāfiḍite leaders had laid down two doctrines for their followers, as a consequence of which no one could ever prevail against them. One of these was their doctrine of *badā'* (change). Whenever they foretold that they would have power, might and victory, but what they had foretold did not come about, they would say, 'There was a change in what seemed fit to God.' The other is *taqīya* (dissimulation). Whatever they had a mind to say they said; but when it was pointed out to them that it was not true, and its falsehood was laid open before them, they would say, 'Whatever we said or did was dissimulation.'

Some of the Mu'tazila follow Sulaimān in his doctrine that the imāmate of one of lesser excellence is lawful even though one of greater excellence is living. Among them were Ja'far b. Mubashshir, Ja'far b. Ḥarb and Kathīr al-Nawā, who is a Traditionalist. They held that the imāmate was that aspect of religion which promotes the public welfare; it is not required for the knowledge of God and his unity, because this knowledge is obtained through reasoning. The imāmate is needed, however, for the administration of divine law, for purposes of adjudication between disputing parties, for the care of orphans and widows, for the defence of the faith, for the proclamation of the word, and for the fight against the enemies of religion. Moreover, by the imāmate Muslims form a united body, and there is no anarchy in the community. It is not necessary, therefore, for the imām to be the most learned man of the community, nor the most senior and most wise, for the needs of the community can be supplied by one of inferior qualities, though there may be found a man well endowed with the required qualities or even excelling in them.

Most Sunnites also are inclined to this view, and even say that the imām need not be one capable of exercising personal judgment in matters of law, *mujtahid*; nor need he be acquainted with the areas of *ijtihād* [independent judgment based on reason]. He must, however, have the service of someone who is capable of *ijtihad*, whom he can consult in matters of law, and whose opinion he can ask as to what is lawful or unlawful. Nevertheless he must, in general, be a man of sound judgment and deep insight into contemporary affairs.

(c) The Ṣāliḥīya and the Batrīya

The Ṣāliḥīya are the followers of Ḥasan b. Ṣāliḥ b. Ḥayy, and the Batrīya the followers of Kathīr al-Nawā al-Abtar. Both hold the same views. Their doctrine of the imāmate is the same as that of the Sulaimānīya, except that they do not commit themselves on the question as to whether 'Uthmān is a believer or an unbeliever. They say:

> When we hear traditions in 'Uthmān's favour and hear that he is one of the ten to whom Paradise is promised, we admit that we must acknowledge the soundness of his *islām* and his faith, and that he is one of those who will go to Paradise; but when we look at his deeds, such as his negligence in failing to discipline the Umayyads and the Banū Marwān, or his autocratic behaviour contrary to the ways of the Companions, we feel obliged to say, 'We must declare him an unbeliever.' We are, therefore, uncertain about him; so we suspend judgment, and refer the matter to 'the best of Judges.'

As for 'Alī they say that he was, after the Prophet, the most excellent of men and the one most eligible for the imāmate; but of his own accord he handed it over to others, and submitted to them, willingly giving up his own rights. We are content with what he was content, and approve what he approved; we cannot do otherwise. If 'Alī had not consented Abū Bakr would have perished.

The Ṣāliḥīya also recognize the legitimacy of the imāmate of one of inferior qualities, and of deferring the claim of one well endowed with the required qualities, or even one excelling in them, provided the better is agreeable. They claim that whatever descendant of Ḥasan and Ḥusain unsheathes his sword, and is at the same time learned, pious and brave, he is an imām. Some of them also lay down the condition that he should be cheerful of countenance. They are greatly confused if two imāms arise at the same time, both of whom possess the necessary qualities, and both of whom unsheathe their swords. If both are equal in these respects, they look for the one who is more excellent and more pious. If both are still equal, they look for the one who is sounder in judgment and more resolute in action. If these two are again equal, they disqualify one another and, as far as they are concerned, the matter is ended. The quest begins all over again: the imām will be led and the ruler ruled. If the claimants belong to two different regions, each will become the only imām in his region, and his people will be obliged to render him obedience. If one of them pronounces a legal opinion different from that of the other, each will be right, even though the pronouncement means that the blood of the other imām is forfeit.

In our time most of the Ṣāliḥīya observe blind obedience, *taqlīd*, without any recourse to their own opinion, *ra'y*, or personal judgment, *ijtihād*. In theological questions they follow closely the teaching of the Mu'tazilites: indeed, they venerate the Mu'tazila leaders more than they do the imāms who are descendants of the Prophet. In matters of law they follow the school of Abū Ḥanīfa, except in some questions, in which they agree with al-Shāfi'ī and the Shī'ites.

Leaders among the Zaidīya

The following are the chief figures among the Zaidīya: Abu 'l-Jārūd, Ziyād b. Mundhir al-'Abdī, who was anathematized by Ja'far b. Muḥammad al-Ṣādiq; Ḥasan b. Ṣāliḥ b. Ḥayy; Muqātil b. Sulaimān; the *dā'ī* Nāṣir al-Ḥaqq Ḥasan b. 'Alī b. Ḥasan b. Zaid b. 'Umar b. Ḥusain b. 'Alī; the other *dā'ī* of Ṭabaristān, Ḥusain b. Zaid b. Muḥammad b. Ismā'īl b. Ḥasan b. Zaid; Muḥammad b. Naṣr.

3 The Imāmīya

The Imāmīya are those who believe that after the Prophet, the imāmate belonged to 'Alī on the grounds of clear designation and unambiguous appointment – an appointment made, not by referring to him through a description, but by indicating him in person. They say that in religion, and in Islam, there was nothing of greater importance than the appointment of an imām, which enabled the Prophet to leave this world with his mind at peace with regard to the community. The Prophet was raised up to settle disputes and establish harmony. He could not, therefore, depart from the community and leave it untended, allowing each man to think for himself and go his own way with no one else in agreement with him. On the contrary, it was necessary for him to appoint someone to whom the people could turn, and designate someone in whom they could place their confidence and trust. The Prophet had in fact appointed 'Alī, at times by allusion and at other times by open declaration.

Some examples of the Prophet's allusions to 'Alī may be given. On one occasion he sent Abū Bakr to recite the sūra of *al-Barā'a* to the people in the assembly, and afterwards sent 'Alī to be their reader as well as his emissary to them. The Prophet then said, 'Gabriel appeared to me, saying, 'One of your men shall impart it'' (or, perhaps, the words were 'One of your people'), thus indicating his preference for 'Alī over Abū Bakr. Again, the Prophet was in the habit of appointing other Companions over Abū Bakr and 'Umar as heads of delegations; thus he appointed 'Amr b. al-'Āṣ over them in one delegation, and Usāma b. Zaid in another. However he never appointed anyone over 'Alī.

As regards open declarations, what happened at the beginning of Islam may be taken as an example. When the Prophet asked, 'Who will swear allegiance to me at the price of his property?' a number of people did so. He next asked, 'Who will swear allegiance to me with his life's breath? The one who does so shall be my successor, and take over this charge after me.' No one responded to this, until at last 'Alī, Commander of the Faithful, stretched forth his hand to him, and swore allegiance to him with his life's breath, an oath to which he always remained faithful. After this incident the Quraish used to taunt Abū Ṭālib with the words: 'Muḥammad has appointed your son over you.'

Another example may be given of an incident that occurred when Islam had reached its perfection and order was established. The word of God came down, saying: 'O Apostle! Proclaim the message which has been sent to you from your Lord. If you do not, you will not have delivered his message. God will protect you from men.'[4] When the Prophet reached the pool of Khumm, he asked for the land between the tall trees to be cleared. The call then went out that the prayer was about to begin. While the Prophet was still in the saddle, he said:

> Of whomsoever I am the master, 'Alī is the master. May God befriend those who befriend him, and be an enemy to those who are enemies to him; may he assist those who assist him, and forsake those who forsake him. May the truth be with him wherever he goes. So, I have delivered [the message].

This he said three times.

> According to the Imāmīya this was a clear appointment. [They say]: We call to mind those of whom the Prophet was the master, and the sense in which he was the master, then we apply it to 'Alī. The Companions understood *tawliya* (appointment) as we understand it. Even 'Umar when he met 'Alī said to him: 'Blessed are you, 'Alī. You have now become the master of every believer, both man and woman!'

According to the Imāmīya, also, the words of the Prophet: 'The best judge among you is 'Alī, is an open declaration of his imāmate; for there is no meaning to the imāmate unless the imām is the chief judge in every case, and the adjudicator between disputants in every dispute. This is the meaning of God's words: 'Obey God, and obey also his messenger and those charged with authority among you.'[5] They explain that 'those charged with authority among you' are those to whom judgment and government have been entrusted. When the Immigrants and the Helpers were disputing about the caliphate, the judge in the matter was 'Alī, Commander of the Faithful, and no other. Again, when the Prophet spoke of the characteristic qualities of his followers, he said, 'In the matter of religious obligations Zaid excels, in the recitation of the Qur'ān Ubayy, and in the knowledge of what is lawful and unlawful Mu'ādh.' When, however, he spoke of 'Alī's characteristic qualities, he said, "Alī excels among you as a judge.' Judgment is something requiring every kind of knowledge, but not every kind of knowledge demands the quality of judgment.

The Imāmīya go even further than this to the point of slandering the leading Companions and declaring them unbelievers, or at least accusing them of injustice and hostility. The text of the Qur'ān, on the other hand, bears witness to their justice, and expresses God's approval of them all, as in the words: 'God was pleased with believers when they swore allegiance to you under the tree.'[6] On this occasion the Companions numbered one thousand four hundred. God also said in praise of the Immigrants and Helpers, and those who followed them in sincerity of spirit, 'The first and foremost of those who left their homes, *al-Muhājirūn*, and of those who helped them, *al-Anṣār*, and those who followed them in a true spirit, God is well pleased with them and they with him.'[7] God also said, 'God turned with favour to the Prophet and to Immigrants and Helpers, who followed him in the time of trial.'[8] Again, 'God has promised to those among you who believe and do good deeds that he will surely grant them an inheritance in the land, as he granted it to those before them.'[9] This shows how great is their standing in the eyes of God, as well as the esteem and honour in which they were held by the Prophet. It is a matter of wonder to me how the adherents of a religion can allow themselves to slander them, and ascribe unbelief to them, seeing that the Prophet said, 'Ten of my Companions are in Paradise: Abū Bakr, 'Umar, 'Uthmān, 'Alī, Ṭalḥa, Zubair, Sa'd b. Abū Waqqāṣ, Sa'īd b. Zaid, 'Abd al-Raḥmān b. 'Awf and Abū 'Ubaidah b. al-Jarrāḥ.' Moreover, other traditions exist in favour of each one individually. If there are unfavourable reports about some of them, these reports must be treated with circumspection, because the Rāfiḍites have been found guilty of many lies and fabrications.

The Imāmīya do not agree as to who the imāms actually are after Ḥasan, Ḥusain and 'Alī b. Ḥusain. Their differences, indeed, are more numerous than those of all other sects put together. Some of them go so far as to say that the seventy or more sects mentioned in the Prophetic tradition refer to the Shī'ites alone; as to the other sects they do not belong to the Community. All the sects of the Imāmīya agree on the imāmate itself, and its transmission down to Ja'far b. Muḥammad al-Ṣādiq, but they disagree as to which one of his children was appointed after him; for Ja'far had five, some say six, sons: Muḥammad, Isḥāq, 'Abdullāh, Mūsā and Ismā'īl. Some of the sons died without offspring, but others left descendants. Some of the Imāmīya believe in stopping [at a particular imām] and waiting for him in the belief that he will return, whereas others believe in the continual transmission of the imāmate from one imām to another. The differences between them will be discussed more fully in our treatment of the various sub-sects.

At first the Imāmīya followed their imāms in doctrinal matters. When after a long time a number of conflicting traditions appeared purporting to come from their imāms, each sub-sect went its own way. Thus some of the Imāmīya became Mu'tazilites: either Wa'īdīya or Tafḍīlīya. Others, again, became Traditionalists, following either the Mushabbiha or the Orthodox. Others, finally, lost their way and went astray. Even God did not seem to care in what wadi he destroyed them.

(a) The 'Wāqifa' of the Bāqirīya and Ja'farīya

These are the followers of Muḥammad al-Bāqir b. 'Alī Zain al-'Ābidīn and his son Ja'far al-Ṣādiq in whose imāmate they believed, and in that also of Bāqir's father Zain al-'Ābidīn. Some of them, however, do not go any further than either Bāqir or Ṣādiq, and therefore do not recognize the transmission of the imāmate to their descendants, whereas others do. We have chosen this group as a distinct sect in our treatment of the Shī'ites, because among the Shī'ites there are some sects which go no further than Bāqir and believe in his return, just as there are others who believe in the imāmate of Abū 'Abdullāh Ja'far b. Muḥammad al-Ṣādiq, and go no further.

Sādiq was a man of profound learning in religious matters and one who had arrived at the fullness of wisdom. He had renounced the allurement of worldly things and lived a life of complete detachment from all earthly pleasures. For some time he stayed in Medīna where he instructed those of the Shī'a who were his adherents, passing on to them the secrets of knowledge. He then went to Iraq and remained there for some time. Never at any time did he seek the imāmate nor contend with anyone for the caliphate. Whoever is immersed in the ocean of knowledge has no desire for shallow waters, and whoever climbs to the heights of truth has no fear of falling. It has been said: 'Whoever becomes a friend of God seeks to be apart from other men; and whoever seeks friendship in any other than God will be seized by the devil.'

On his father's side Ṣādiq belonged to the family of the Prophet, and on his mother's side was descended from Abū Bakr al-Ṣiddīq. He dissociated himself from the things attributed to him by some of the Extremists; moreover, he dissociated himself also from these people themselves and anathematized them. He also dissociated himself from the views peculiar to the Rāfiḍa and from their follies, such as belief in concealment and return, change or mind in God, metempsychosis, incarnation and anthropomorphsim. The Shī'a, however, differed among themselves after his death. Each sect had its own views which it sought to spread amongst its followers, while attributing them to him and connecting them with him. The master himself, however, was free from all this, as he was also from Mu'tazilism and belief in free will.

Ṣādiq's doctrine on [God's] will is as follows. God has willed something for us and something from us. What he has willed for us he has kept secret from us; what he has willed from us he has made known to us. Why then should we be anxious about what he has willed for us and neglect what he has willed from us? Of *qadar* he said, '*Qadar* is a medium between two extremes; it is neither absolute determinism nor absolute freedom.' In his prayer he used to say, 'O God, if I obey you, the thanks are yours; if I disobey you, the fault is mine. Neither I nor anyone else can claim merit for whatever good we do, nor have we an excuse in the evil that we do.'

We shall now give an account of the groups which differ among themselves concerning this man: not because they provide a detailed expression of the views of his followers, but because these groups claim to belong to his family and to the descendants of his children. This must be remembered.

(b) The Nāwūsīya

These are the followers of a man called Nāwūs, though according to some accounts they belonged to the village of Nāwūsā. They believe that Ṣādiq is still alive, and that he will not die till he reappears, and at his reappearance he will be triumphant. Ṣādiq is the *qā'im* and the *mahdī*. According to them, he said, 'If you should see my head rolling down to you from a mountain, do not believe what you see, for your master is the man of the sword.' Abū Ḥāmid al-Zauzānī said that the Nāwūsīya declared that 'Alī was still alive; that before the day of judgment the earth would open up and give him forth, and that he would then fill the earth with justice.

(c) The Afṭaḥīya

The Afṭaḥīya believe in the transmission of the imāmate from Ṣādiq to his son 'Abdullāh al-Afṭaḥ, the full brother of Ismā'īl. Their mother was Fāṭima, daughter of Ḥusain b. Ḥasan b. 'Alī, and he himself was the eldest son of Ṣādiq.

According to the Afṭaḥīya Ṣādiq said, 'The imāmate should belong to the eldest son of the imām.' Again, 'The imām is he who sits in my seat.' Now it was 'Abdullāh who sat in his seat. He also said, 'No one washes the imām, no one prays at the funeral service for him, and no one removes his seal or buries him except the imām'; and it was 'Abdullāh who did all these things. Ṣādiq entrusted something to one of his followers with instructions to give it to the one who should claim it and to acknowledge him as imām. No one asked for it except 'Abdullāh. Yet 'Abdullāh lived only seventy days after his father, and died leaving no male issue.

(d) The Shumaiṭīya

These are the followers of Yaḥyā b. Abū Shumaiṭ. They maintain that Ja'far said, 'The name of your [next] master is the same as that of your Prophet.' They also assert that Ja'far's father had said to him, 'If a son is born to you and you give him my name, he shall be the imām.' Accordingly the imām in succession to him was his son Muḥammad.

(e) The Ismā'īlīya al-Wāqifa

These hold that Ismā'īl was the designated imām after Ja'far, as the sons of Ja'far also agreed. They differ among themselves, however, as to whether or not he died during the lifetime of his father. Some of them say that he did not die, but that his father had declared that he had died to save him from the 'Abbāsid caliphs; and that he had held a funeral assembly to which Manṣūr's governor in Medina was made a witness.

Some, on the other hand, say that he really did die. Designation, however, cannot be withdrawn, and has the advantage that the imāmate remains in the descendants of the person designated, to the exclusion of others. Therefore the imām after Ismā'īl is Muḥammad b. Ismā'īl. This sect is known as the Mubārakīya. Some of them go no further than Muḥammad b. Ismā'īl, and believe in his return after his concealment. Others transfer the imāmate to their hidden imāms, and after them to those imāms who are publicly known and *qā'ims*. These are the Bāṭinīya whose views we shall consider separately. The group, however, which we are now considering, holds that the imāmate comes to an end with either Ismā'īl b. Ja'far or Muḥammad b. Ismā'īl. The best known Ismā'īl-ite sect is the Bāṭinīya Ta'līmīya to whom we shall devote a separate chapter.

(f) The Mūsawīya and Mufaḍḍalīya

The Mūsawīya and the Mufaḍḍalīya form one group. They believe in the imāmate of Mūsā b. Ja'far who had been designated by name when Ṣādiq said, 'Your seventh imām is your *qā'im*. (Or he may have said; 'Your master is your *qā'im*'). He is the namesake of the one who received the Torah.'

When the Shī'a became aware that the lives of the sons of Ṣādiq followed different courses (one died in the lifetime of his father without leaving issue; about the death of another there was a difference of opinion;

one lived only a short time after his father's death, and another died without leaving any issue), and that it was Mūsā alone who took charge of affairs and assumed responsibility after his father's death, they turned to him and rallied in support of him. Among those who did so were Mufaḍḍal b. ʻUmar, Zurāra b. Aʻyun and ʻAmmār al-Sābāṭī.

The Mūsawīya tell of Ṣādiq that he said to one of his followers, 'Count the days.' So he counted them from Sunday till Saturday. Then Ṣādiq asked him, 'How many did you count?' He replied, 'Seven.' Jaʻfar then said, pointing to his son Mūsā al-Kāẓim, 'Sabbath of the Sabbaths, sun of all ages and light of the months, one who does not trifle and dally – this *qā'im* of yours is your seventh [imām].' Jaʻfar also said of Mūsā that he bore a resemblance to Jesus.

When Mūsā came out in revolt and declared his imāmate, Hārūn al-Rashīd had him brought from Medīna and kept in confinement at the house of ʻĪsā b. Jaʻfar. Afterwards he was sent to Baghdad where he was confined in the house of Sindī b. Shāhik. It is said that, while he was still in prison, Yaḥyā b. Khālid b. Barmak gave him poisoned dates and thus caused his death; he was then taken out of the house and buried in the cemetery of Quraish at Baghdad.

After Mūsā's death the Shīʻites differed among themselves about him. Some were uncertain about his death, saying, 'We do not know whether he has died or not.' These are known as the Mamṭūra, the name given to them by ʻAlī b. Ismāʻīl, who said to them, 'You are nothing but rain-drenched dogs.' Others, however, firmly held that Mūsā had died. These are known as the Qaṭʻīya. Others went no further than Mūsā, declaring that he did not die, but would come out again after his concealment. These are called the Wāqifa.

(g) The Twelvers

The Twelvers are those who are firmly of the opinion that Mūsā al-Kāẓim b. Jaʻfar al-Ṣādiq had died. They are also known as the Qaṭʻīya. They transmit the imāmate after Mūsā to his descendants. According to them the imām following Mūsā was his son, ʻAlī al-Riḍā, who is buried in Ṭūs. After him came Muḥammad al-Taqī al-Jawād, who is buried in the cemetery of the Quraish at Baghdad. Taqī was followed by ʻAlī b. Muḥammad al-Naqī who is buried at Qumm. Next came Ḥasan al-ʻAskarī al-Zakī, followed by his son Muḥammad the *qā'im*, the Awaited One, who [disappeared] at Samarra. Muḥammad was the twelfth imām.

This completes the list of the imāms according to the Twelvers of our time. In order that nothing may be left unrecorded, we must mention the controversies which arose about each of these imāms; also the disputes occurring between them and their brothers, as well as those between them and their cousins.

Of these Shī'a there were those who believed in the imāmate of Aḥmad b. Mūsā b. Ja'far instead of his brother 'Alī al-Riḍa. Those who followed 'Alī al-Riḍa doubted at first of the imāmate of his son Muḥammad, for when 'Alī died Muḥammad was still young, unfit to be an imām and unschooled in the ways of the imāmate. A number of people, however, held to his imāmate, but at his death differed among themselves, some believing in the imāmate of his son Mūsā and others of his son 'Alī. It was said that 'Alī was the one known as al-'Askarī. These again had differences of opinion at 'Alī's death, some believing in the imāmate of his son Ja'far and others of his son Ḥasan. Amongst these factions there was a leader named 'Alī b. Fulān al-Ṭāḥin, a theologian who supported the claim of Ja'far b. 'Alī, and won the people over to him. In this he had the support of Fāris b. Hātim b. Māhawaih. Their argument was as follows: 'When 'Alī died and was succeeded by Ḥasan al-'Askarī, we examined him and found him wanting in knowledge.' For this reason they nicknamed all those who believed in the imāmate of Ḥasan the Ḥimārīya. After Ḥasan's death they consolidated Ja'far's claim by contending that as Ḥasan died without leaving a successor, his imāmate was null and void: Ḥasan died without issue, and an imām does not die without leaving issue to succeed him.

Ja'far gained possession of the heritage of Ḥasan after making certain accusations against him, namely, that he had made pregnant his father's, or someone else's, concubines. This became generally known to the Sultan and to his subjects, both those in high circles and those amongst the common people. It caused serious discord among those believing in the imāmate of Ḥasan, and they split up into various groups. It also confirmed the others in the belief in the imāmate of Ja'far; and many of these, too, who had supported the imāmate of Ḥasan joined them. Amongst these latter was Ḥasan b. 'Alī b. Fuḍāl, one of their most distinguished men and a leading jurist, who had a profound knowledge of *fiqh* and Ḥadīth.

After the imāmate of Ja'far these Shī'ites believe in that of 'Alī b. Ja'far and Fāṭima, daughter of 'Alī and sister of Ja'far, though there are some who support that of 'Alī b. Ja'far without Fāṭima. On the deaths of 'Alī and Fāṭima many differences of opinion arose among them. On the question of the imāmate some of them went to extremes, as, for example, Abu 'l-Khaṭṭāb al-Asdī.

Those who believed in the imāmate of Ḥasan broke up into eleven groups after his death. These groups have no names by which they are distinguished, but we shall give some account of them. One group says that Ḥasan did not die, but is the *qā'im*. As it is clear that he had no son, it is impossible, they maintain, that he should have died, for the world cannot be without an imām. It is our belief, they say, that the *qā'im* may have two concealments. This is one of the two. He shall appear again, however, and be known; after this he shall disappear once more.

Another group holds that Ḥasan died, but is, nevertheless, living, and is the *qā'im*. They say, 'We believe that the meaning of *al-qā'im* is a resurrection after death. Accordingly we assert that there is no doubt at all that Ḥasan has died, but, since he has no son, he must live after death.'

A third group maintains that Ḥasan did, indeed, die, but having designated his brother Ja'far as imām; the imāmate, therefore, reverted to Ja'far.

According to the fourth group Ḥasan has really died and the imām is Ja'far. We were mistaken, they say, in believing in the imāmate of Ḥasan, for he was not an imām. When he died and left no issue, it became clear to us that Ja'far's claim was right and Ḥasan's wrong.

The fifth group also believes that Ḥasan died. However, they say:

> We were mistaken in believing in Ḥasan's imāmate, for the true imām was Muḥammad b. 'Alī, brother of Ḥasan and Ja'far. When we came to learn of Ja'far's moral depravity, which was openly manifested, and learnt, too, that Ḥasan was equally dissolute, except that he kept his depravity hidden, we were convinced that they were not imāms; so we turned to Muḥammad, and finding that he had issue, acknowledged him as the imām rather than his brothers.

The sixth group says that Ḥasan had a son. It is not true, as is commonly held, that he died without issue. He did, in fact, have a son who was born two years before his father's death. However, this son went into concealment out of fear of Ja'far and his other enemies. His name is Muḥammad. He is the imām, the *qā'im*, the *ḥujja* (the 'proof').

According to the seventh group Ḥasan had a son, but he was not born till eight months after his death. It is a mistake, therefore, to say that when he died Ḥasan had a son, for if that were so it would not have remained unknown. It is only obstinacy to deny what is evident.

The eighth group holds that it is certain that Ḥasan died and had no son. It is not true, as is claimed, that his concubine was pregnant. It is beyond doubt, therefore, that after Ḥasan there is no imām. It is quite conceivable, however, that God may remove the *ḥujja* from amongst men on the earth because of their sins. This, therefore, would be an interruption and constitute a period of time in which there was no imām. The earth today is without a *ḥujja* [and therefore, in a period of interruption], just as there was also an interruption before the coming of the Prophet.

According to the ninth group Ḥasan died; and, indeed, the fact of his death is beyond any doubt. They say:

> Why people have so much differed on this point, we cannot understand. We have no doubt that a son was born to Ḥasan, but whether before or after his death we do not know. We know, however, with certainty that the world cannot be without a *ḥujja*, who is the hidden successor. We shall acknowledge him, and hold fast to his name until he appears in person.

The tenth group says:

> We believe that Ḥasan died, but it is absolutely necessary for men to have an imām in order that the world may not be without a *ḥujja*. We do not know, however, whether this *ḥujja* is one of Ḥasan's descendants or the descendant of another.

The last group abstains from committing itself in this confusing matter. They simply say:

> We do not know for certain the true state of affairs, though we have no doubt about Riḍā and believe in his imāmate. The Shī'ites have disagreed on every point, and so we refrain from committing ourselves in this matter till God manifests the *ḥujja* and he appears in person. Whoever beholds him will have no doubt about his imāmate, nor will he need a miracle or a sign; his miracle will be that all manner of men will follow him without any dispute or resistance.

These are the eleven groups for each one of which the imāmate ends at one or other imām. Thus all the series have a termination. The strange thing is that they say that the concealment has now lasted for two hundred and fifty years and more. But they also say that if the *qā'im* appears and he is over forty years old, then he is not the imām; though, indeed, [Shahrastānī comments], we do not know how two hundred and fifty and more years can pass away in forty years.

When it was objected that it was difficult to imagine so long a concealment, the Twelvers replied, 'Are not Enoch and Elijah still alive on earth after thousands of years, and without need of food and drink?

Then why should not that be possible for one of the descendants of the Prophet?' Another objection was:

> With all this difference of opinion among you how can you validate your claim to a hidden imām? Moreover, Enoch is not entrusted with the care of the people; whereas the imām according to you is charged with their guidance and the administration of justice, just as the people on their part are obliged to obey and follow the example of his *sunna*. If one cannot be seen, how can he be followed?

Because of this the Imāmīya follow closely the Mu'tazila in matters of doctrine, but on the question of attributes they follow the Mushabbiha, though remaining all the time confused and bewildered. There is continual strife between their traditionalists and their rational theologians who charge one another with unbelief. The same conflict and mutual accusations are found between the Tafḍiilīya and the Wa'īdīya. May God preserve us from this confusion!

The strange thing is that those who believe in the imāmate of the Awaited One, in spite of all the divisions of which I have spoken, do not hesitate to claim divine prerogatives for that imām. They also interpret the words of God, 'Say, 'Do righteousness and soon your work will be observed by God, his apostle and the believers; soon you will be brought back to him who knows the hidden and the open",[10] by saying that this one is the awaited imām, the one to whom knowledge of the hour will be granted. They further maintain that he is never absent from us, and that he will reveal our lives to us when he makes a reckoning with mankind. They also put forward other foolish opinions and senseless claims.

[Shahrastānī adds the verse]: 'I have wandered around all these places and looked closely at them, but I have seen only a bewildered occupant, with his chin in his hands or ruefully clicking his teeth.'

The names of the twelve imāms according to the Imāmīya are as follows: al-Murtaḍā, al-Mujtabā, al-Shahīd, al-Sajjād, al-Bāqir, al-Ṣādiq, al-Kāẓim, al-Riḍā, al-Taqī, al-Naqī, al-Zakī, and lastly, the *ḥujja*, the *qā'im*, the Awaited One.

4 The Ghālīya

The Ghālīya (the 'Extremists') are those who went to extremes regarding their imāms, whom they excluded from the limitations of creatures and upon whom they bestowed divine qualities. Sometimes they likened an imām to God, at other times they likened God to man. Thus they fell into two extremes. These erroneous ideas of the Ghālīya have their origin in the doctrines held by those believing in incarnation and transmigration of souls, or in the beliefs of Jews and Christians, since the Jews liken God to man and the Christians liken man to God. These ideas so deeply influenced the minds of the extreme Shī'ites that they attributed divine qualities to some of their imāms.

Anthropomorphism first arose among the Shī'ites and was only later found among some of the Sunnites. The Shī'ites, however, came under the influence of Mu'tazilism which they saw was more rational and further removed from anthropomorphism and belief in incarnation.

The innovations of the Ghālīya may be reduced to four: anthropomorphism, *badā'* (change of mind in God), return of the imām and metempsychosis. The Ghālīya are known by different names in different places. Thus in Isfahān they are called al-Khurramīya and al-Kūdhīya, in Rayy al-Mazdakīya and al-Sanbādhīya, in Ādharbaijān they are known as al-Duqūlīya, in another place as al-Muḥammira, and in Transoxiana as al-Mubayyiḍa.

The Ghālīya are divided into the following eleven groups.

(a) The Saba'īya

These are the followers of 'Abdullāh b. Saba', the one who said to 'Alī, 'Thou art Thou', that is, 'Thou art God'. 'Alī, thereupon, banished him to Tsesiphon. 'Abdullāh is said to have been a Jew who was converted to Islam. While still a Jew he used to say that Joshua b. Nūn was the legatee, *waṣī*, of Moses. He also said the same later of 'Alī whose appointment as imām he was the first to uphold. From him all kinds of extremists arose.

'Abdullāh held that 'Alī was still living and had not died. There was in him a divine element, and so it is impossible for him to be overcome by death. 'Alī it is who comes in the clouds; his voice is the thunder and the lightning his smile. He will finally come down to earth and fill it with justice, as now it is filled with injustice.

Ibn Saba' expressed these views only after the death of 'Alī. A number of people gathered around him, who formed the first group to believe in stopping at an imām, *tawaqquf*, in his concealment and return. They held likewise that after 'Alī the divine element was transmitted from one imām to the other. Ibn Saba' further said that this fact was known to the Companions, though they did not act according to it. For example, when 'Alī had gouged out someone's eye in the sanctuary as a punishment, and this was reported to 'Umar, he said, 'What shall I say of God's hand which gouged out an eye in God's sanctuary?' Thus 'Umar used the name of the divinity for 'Alī because he knew of the divine element in him.

(b) The Kāmilīya

These are the followers of Abū Kāmil who declared that all the Companions were unbelievers for not swearing allegiance to 'Alī. At the same time he censured 'Alī for not asserting his claim, and found his inactivity inexcusable. He said 'Alī ought to have come out openly and made known the truth. Abū Kāmil, nevertheless, went to extremes in favour of 'Alī.

Abū Kāmil used to say that the imāmate is a light which passes from one person to another. In one man that light becomes prophethood and in another imāmate. Again, by metempsychosis the imāmate may sometimes become prophethood. Abū Kāmil believed also in the transmigration of souls at death. Though divided into different groups the Ghālīya share in common this belief in transmigration and incarnation. Transmigration has, indeed, been held by one sect or another in every religious community; it has been derived by them either from Mazdakite Magians, Indain Brahmins, philosophers or Sabeans.

The Kāmilīya believe that God is present in every place, that he speaks through every tongue, and that he manifests himself in each and every individual. This takes place by incarnation. Incarnation, however, may be either partial or total. Partial incarnation is like the sun shining in an alcove or on a piece of crystal. Total incarnation, on the other hand, is similar to the appearance of an angel in human form, or that of a devil in the form of an animal.

Transmigration is of four kinds, namely: *naskh, maskh, faskh* and *raskh*. These will be fully explained in our account of their Magian exponents. The highest stage of transmigration is that of the angels and the prophets, while the lowest is that of the devils and the jinn. Abū Kāmil believed in transmigration in a general way without going into any details.

(c) The 'Albā'īya

These are the followers of al-'Albā' b. Dhirā' al-Dawsī, called by some al-Asdī. Al-Dawsī gave precedence to 'Alī over the Prophet, and said that it was 'Alī who had sent out Muḥammad, and 'Alī he called God.

He maintained, too, that Muḥammad was blameworthy, because, as he said, Muḥammad was sent to call the people to 'Alī but called them to himself. Those who hold this opinion are called the Dhimmīya. Some of the 'Albā'īya believe in the divinity of both 'Alī and Muḥammad, but give precedence to 'Alī in divine prerogatives. These are called the 'Ainīya. Others, however, who also believe in the divinity of both but give superiority to Muḥammad in divinity, are called the Mīmīya. Some believe also in the divinity of all those 'under the mantle', *aṣḥāb al-kisā'*: Muḥammad, 'Alī, Fāṭima, Ḥasan and Ḥusain. They say these five are one and the Spirit is equally present in them all; none, therefore, has precedence over the others. They also dislike saying 'Fāṭimah' in the feminine form, and say 'Fāṭim' without the 'hā'. Thus one of their poets said, 'In religion I follow God, and after God these five: the Prophet, his two grandsons, the Shaikh ['Alī] and Fāṭim.'

(d) The Mughīrīya

These are the followers of Mughīra b. Sa'īd al-'Ijlī. Mughīra claimed that after Muḥammad b. 'Alī b. Ḥusain the imāmate belonged to Muḥammad al-Nafs al-Zakīya, the 'pure soul', son of 'Abdullāh b. Ḥasan b. Ḥasan, who rose in revolt in Medīna. He believed that Muḥammad was still alive and had not died. Mughīra was *mawlā* of Khālid b. 'Abdullāh al-Qasrī. After Imām Muḥammad he claimed for himself first the imāmate, then the prophethood. He also considered forbidden things lawful. Regarding 'Alī he went to extremes beyond the credibility of any sane person.

Mughīra also believed in anthropomorphism. He said that God has a form and a body, having parts as letters of the alphabet do. His form is that of a man made of light upon whose head is a crown of light, and from whose heart wisdom springs forth. He maintained, too, that when God willed to create the world he uttered his Great Name, which flew down upon his head in the form of a crown. This, he said, is the meaning of God's words: 'Glorify the Great Name of your Lord who created and gave proportion.'[11]

After this God looked upon the deeds of men which he had written on his palm; he was angered at the sight of their sins and broke out into a sweat. From his sweat two oceans formed, one salty and the other fresh; the salty one was dark but the fresh one was luminous. God now looked into the luminous ocean and saw his shadow. He took out the eye of his shadow and from it created the sun and the moon. The rest of the shadow he destroyed, saying, 'There shall be no other God with

Me.' God now created all things from the two oceans, the believers from the luminous ocean and the unbelievers from the dark ocean. First he created the shadows of men, creating the shadows of Muḥammad and 'Alī before those of the rest of men.

God then proposed to heaven, earth and the mountains that they take upon themselves 'the trust',[12] namely, of protecting 'Alī from [those seeking to do him injustice in regard to][13] the imāmate but they refused. God next proposed the trust to men. 'Umar asked Abū Bakr to undertake it and promised to help him in the betrayal of 'Alī, provided he appointed him to the caliphate as his successor. This he agreed to do, and in outward appearance they both set out to protect 'Alī. This is what God has said, 'Man undertook it; he indeed was unjust and foolish.'[14] Muhgīra held that the following verse was revealed about 'Umar: 'Like Satan when he said to man, 'Deny your God', but when he did deny him, he said, 'I am free of you.''[15]

When Mughīra was killed his followers differed among themselves. Some believed that they should wait for his return, whereas others believed in waiting for the imāmate of Muḥammad just as he himself had done. Mughīra had believed in the imāmate of Abū Ja'far Muḥammad b. 'Alī, but went to extremes regarding him and believed in his divinity. As a result Bāqir dissociated himself from him and anathematized him.

Mughīra had said to his followers, 'Wait for him (Abū Ja'far). He will come back, and Gabriel and Michael will swear allegiance to him between the *rukn* (the corner of the Ka'ba) and the *maqām* (the standing place of Abraham).' He also declared that Abū Ja'far would bring back the dead to life.

(e) The Manṣūrīya

These are the followers of Abū Manṣūr al-'Ijlī, who at first claimed to be a follower of Abū Ja'far Muḥammad b. 'Alī al-Bāqir. But when Bāqir dissociated himself from him and rejected him, he claimed that he himself was the imām, and called upon people to follow him. When Bāqir died, he declared, 'The imāmate has passed to me', and made a public proclamation of this claim.

A group of his followers made their appearance amongst the Banū Kinda in Kūfa. When, however, Yūsuf b. 'Umar al-Thaqafī, the governor of Iraq during the reign of Hishām, came to hear of his claim and his wicked propaganda, he seized him and had him crucified.

Abū Manṣūr also maintained that 'Alī was the 'piece falling from heaven';[16] or, perhaps, what he said was, 'The piece falling from heaven is God himself.' When he claimed the imāmate for himself he maintained that he had been taken up to heaven and seen God who had stroked his head with his hand, saying to him, 'O my son, go down and make my message known.' He then sent him down to earth; he, therefore, is the piece fallen from heaven.

Abū Manṣūr further maintained that there would never cease to be apostles, and that apostleship would never come to an end. He also said that Paradise is a man with whom we are bidden to associate: he is the imām of the age. Hell, too, is a man whom we are ordered to oppose: this man is the enemy of the imām. All forbidden things he interpreted in terms of certain men whom God has commanded us to oppose, and all matters of obligation in terms of certain men with whom God has commanded us to associate. His followers considered it lawful to kill their opponents, take their property and possess their women.

The Manṣūrīya are a section of the Khurramīya. Their purpose in interpreting obligations and prohibitions in terms of certain men is, that whoever is successful in discovering such a man and recognizing him is free henceforth from obligation, and is no more the subject of command; for he has already reached Paradise and attained to perfection. One of the innovations of al-'Ijlī was that he said the first object of God's creation was Jesus, son of Mary, and then after him 'Alī b. Abū Ṭālib.

(f) The Khaṭṭābīya

These are the followers of Abu 'l-Khaṭṭāb Muḥammad b. Abū Zainab al-Asdī al-Ajda' ('the Mutilated One'), a *mawlā* of Banū Asd, who claimed to be an adherent of Abū 'Abdullāh Ja'far b. Muḥammad al-Ṣādiq. When, however, Ṣādiq heard of his false and extravagant views about him, he not only dissociated himself from him and anathematized him, but also called upon his followers to dissociate themselves from him. He was very insistent on this, and went to great lengths in dissociating himself from Abu 'l-Khaṭṭāb and in anathematizing him.

When Abu 'l-Khaṭṭāb seceded from Ṣādiq, he claimed the imāmate for himself. He said that imāms are prophets firstly, and then divine beings. He believed in the divinity of Ja'far b. Muḥammad and that of his forefathers. They are all, according to him, sons of God and beloved of him. Divinity is a light in the prophethood, and prophethood is a light in the imāmate; it is impossible for the world to be without such signs and lights. He asserted that at this time Ja'far was the divinity. God, indeed, was not the sensible form which is seen by men; but when he came down to this world he took this form, and in this form he was seen by men.

When 'Īsā b. Mūsā, Manṣūr's general, heard of Abu 'l-Khaṭṭāb's evil propaganda he had him put to death in the salt marshes of Kūfa. After his death the Khaṭṭābīya became divided into different sub-sects. One of these held that after Abu 'l-Khaṭṭāb the imām was a man called Mu'ammar, to whom they gave allegiance as they had done to Abu l'Khaṭṭāb. They believed that the present world would not come to an end, and that the Paradise enjoyed by men consists of pleasant things, luxuries and general well-being. Hell, on the other hand, consists of unpleasant things, hardship and suffering endured by men. They looked upon alcohol, fornication and all other forbidden things as lawful. They believed also in discarding prayer and other religious obligations. This group is called the Mu'ammarīya.

Another group maintained that after Abu 'l-Khaṭṭāb the imām was Bazīgh. This man held that Ja'far was God, in the sense that God had appeared to men in the form of Ja'far. He also held that every believer receives revelation from God, and he interpreted the words of God: 'No one can believe except by the will of God',[17] as meaning by revelation from God. In a like manner he interpreted the other words of God, 'Your Lord revealed to the bee.'[18] He maintained, too, that some of his followers were superior to Gabriel and Michael, and held that of a man who had reached perfection it should not be said that he died; rather, of the one who reached perfection it should be said that he returned to the heavenly world. All of his followers claim to see their dead ones in the morning and in the evening. The group is called the Bazīghīya.

Another group held that after Abu 'l-Khaṭṭāb the imām was 'Umair b. Bayān al-'Ijlī. Their beliefs are the same as those of the first group though they admit that they do die. They set up a tent in Kunāsa at Kūfa where they all gathered to worship Ṣādiq. A report on them was brought to Yazīd b. 'Umar b. Hubaira who took 'Umair prisoner and crucified him in Kunāsa at Kūfa. This group is called the 'Ijlīya, or also the 'Umairīya.

Another group held that after Abu 'l-Khaṭṭāb the imām was Mufaḍḍal al-Ṣairafī. The members of this sect believed in the Lordship of Ja'far, but not in his prophethood and apostleship. They are known as the Mufaḍḍalīya.

Ja'far b. Muḥammad al-Ṣādiq dissociated himself from all of these sects, rejected them and anathematized them. All of them are confused, misguided and ignorant about the true character of their imāms, and utterly lost.

(g) The Kayyālīya

These are the followers of Aḥmad b. al-Kayyāl, a *dā'ī* (missionary) of one of the descendants of the Prophet after Ja'far b. Muḥammad al-Ṣādiq, who, I suppose, was one of the hidden imāms.

Al-Kayyāl seems to have picked up a number of learned expressions which he blended with erroneous views and empty speculations. He introduced innovations in every field of knowledge, based neither on tradition nor reason. At times he even denied what is manifested by sense experience. When they [members of the family] learnt of his innovations they dissociated themselves from him and anathematized him. They also ordered their followers to reject him and dissociate themselves from him. When al-Kayyāl heard of this he called people to himself, at first claiming the imāmate and then declaring that he was the *qā'im*.

One of al-Kayyāl's views was that whoever can establish the correspondence between souls and the heavenly world, and is able also to explain the manner of operation of both worlds (that is, the world of the heavens or the upper world, and the world of souls or the lower world), that man is the imām. Again, whoever embraces all things in himself, and is able to manifest all universals in his own particular person, that man is the *qā'im*. He held that at no time did anyone attain this except [himself] Aḥmad al-Kayyāl, and, therefore, he is the *qā'im*.

Al-Kayyāl was killed by a man who had at first followed him in his heresy that he was the imām, and subsequently the *qā'im*. There are still extant many writings in Arabic and Persian expounding his views about the universe. They are full of empty rhetoric, and repugnant both to the *sharī'a* and to reason.

Al-Kayyāl said that there are three realms: the highest, the lowest and the human realms. In the highest realm there are five places. The first is 'the place of places': it is an empty space in which nothing is found, nor is it directed by a spiritual being. This place encloses all things. It is to this place that the 'Throne' in the Qur'an refers. Below it is the place of the highest soul, and below this the place of the rational soul, *al-nafs al-nāṭiqa*. Below this again is the place of the animal soul, and, finally, below that is the place of the human soul.

According to al-Kayyāl the human soul wanted to mount to the abode of the highest soul. It began the ascent and passed through two places, namely, those in which dwelt the animal and rational souls. When, however, it came near the dwelling place of the highest soul, it became tired and exhausted, stopping helpless, and began to decay and disintegrate. It was then flung down to the lowest world, and whilst in that stage of decay and disintegration it passed through many different states. The highest soul then looked upon it with compassion and bestowed upon it a part of its light. The resultant effect was that from it the various things of the world were composed: the heavens, the earth, and other composite things as minerals, vegetables, animals and human beings. In the turmoil of this composition, there was sometimes gladness, sometimes grief, sometimes joy, sometimes sorrow, sometimes health and well-being, sometimes trial and tribulation. At last the *qā'im* appeared and restored everything to a state of perfection: all things composite were dissolved, all contraries annihilated and the spiritual overcame the material. This *qā'im* was none other than Aḥmad al-Kayyāl. That he was the *qā'im* he attempted to show by one of the weakest and most unconvincing of arguments conceivable. His proof was that his name of Ahmad symbolized the four worlds. Thus the *alif* in his name stood for the highest soul, the *ḥā* for the rational soul, the *mīm* for the animal soul and the *dāl* for the human soul.

Al-Kayyāl maintained that the four worlds are the fundamental elements. As to 'the place of places' nothing whatever exists in it. Corresponding to the highest realm there is the lower corporeal world. The firmament is empty and corresponds to the 'place of places'; below that is fire, below the fire is air, below the air is earth and below the earth is water. These four correspond to the four worlds. He goes on to say that man corresponds to fire, birds to air, animals to earth, fish and other like creatures to water. To water he assigned the lowest place and among composite things he assigned to fish the lowest rank.

Al-Kayyāl then compared the human realm, which is one of the three realms and is itself the realm of souls, with the two realms already mentioned, namely, the spiritual and the corporeal. Thus man, he said, has five senses: (1) hearing, which corresponds to 'the place of places' because it is empty, and also to the firmament; (2) sight, which corresponds to the highest soul of the spiritual world, and by reason of the pupil of the eye, *insān al-'ain*, to the fire of the corporeal world, because fire alone has a pupil; (3) smell, which corresponds to the rational soul of the spiritual world and to air of the corporeal world, because smelling takes place through air, by which man is revived and refreshed; (4) taste, which corresponds to the animal soul of the spiritual world and to earth of the corporeal world, as an animal belongs to earth and taste to animal; (5) touch, which corresponds to the human soul of the spiritual world and to water of the bodily world, since fish are found exclusively in water and touch is a special characteristic of fish; sometimes in writing, 'fish' is used to express touch.

Al-Kayyāl also said that the name Aḥmad, which is composed of *alif, ḥā, mīm* and *dāl*, corresponds to the two worlds. Of its correspondence with the higher spiritual world we have already spoken. With regard to its correspondence with the lowest corporeal world he said that *alif* signifies man, *ḥā* animal, *mīm* bird, and *dāl* fish. *Alif* signifies man because it is upright in figure like a man; *ḥā* signifies animal because it is bent like an animal, and also because *ḥā* is the letter with which the name of animal begins; *mīm* resembles the head of a bird and *dāl* the tail of a fish. He added that God created man in the form of the name *Aḥmad*; his stature is like *alif*, his hands like *ḥā*, his stomach like *mīm* and his two long legs like *dāl*.

Al-Kayyāl also made the astonishing statement that prophets are leaders of those who follow unquestioningly, and those who follow unquestioningly are blind. The *qā'im*, however, is a leader of those who have insight, and those with insight are men of intelligence. This insight is acquired through establishing correspondence between the world of the heavens and the world of souls. Al-Kayyāl's views on correspondence, as they have been explained to you, are so ridiculous and baseless that no intelligent man would ever pay attention to them, let alone believe them.

Stranger even than all this are his perverse interpretations [of the Scripture], and the comparisons he makes between the obligations of the *sharī'a* and religious precepts with the things of the two worlds, namely, the world of the heavens and the world of souls, together with his claim that he alone knows them. How can this be true? Many a learned man has established the same correspondence before him, though not in the spurious way in which he has done it. Not less strange are his understanding of the Scale as meaning the two worlds, the Path as meaning himself, Paradise as meaning the attaining [by men] to his insight into things, and Hell as meaning the attaining to the contrary of his insight. As these are the basic principles of his thought, you may easily understand what its various branches are like.

(h) The Hishāmīya

These are the followers of two different Hishāms, Hishām b. al-Ḥakam, known for his anthropomorphic views, and Hishām b. Sālim al-Jawālīqī, who followed these views. Hishām b. al-Ḥakam was a Shī'ite theologian. He had a number of disputes with Abu 'l-Hudhail on theological matters, among them being questions of anthropomorphism and God's knowledge of things.

Ibn Rāwandī relates of Hishām that he said that there is some kind of resemblance between God and corporeal things, otherwise these could not lead to a knowledge of him. According to Ka'bī, however, he said that God is a body having parts and some form of mass, but he does not resemble any creature nor does any creature resemble him. It is also said of him that he believed that God is seven spans high, in the measure, however, of his own span, that he is in a special place and locality; that he moves, but that his movement is his activity and not movement from one place to another. He said, too, that in himself God is a finite being, but, nevertheless, he is not finite in his power. According to Abū 'Īsā al-Warrāq he also said that God is in contact with his throne in such a way that no part of him overlaps it, nor does any part of the throne extend beyond him.

Hishām's views are as follows. God eternally knows himself, but things other than himself he knows after they have come to be, with a knowledge which cannot be said to be either created or eternal. The reason is that knowledge is an attribute, and an attribute cannot be further described. Nor can it be said that God's knowledge is he or other than he, or that it is part of him.

Hishām's doctrine about God's power and life differs from that on his knowledge, though he does not hold that they are created. God, he said, wills things and his will is a form of movement. His will, again, is not himself nor other than himself. With regard to God's word he held that it was an attribute of God, and cannot be said to be either created or uncreated.

Hishām held that accidents are not capable of leading us to a knowledge of God, because some of them require a proof of their own existence. What leads to the knowledge of God must be something whose existence is immediately evident, and not something known by inference. He said also that capacity is anything without which an act cannot be, as for example, instruments, limbs, time and place.

Hishām b. Sālim said that God is in the form of a man. His upper part is hollow and lower part solid. He is a bright radiant light, and besides five senses, he has hands, feet, nose, ears, eyes, mouth and black hair, which is black light. He is not, however, flesh and blood.

Hishām also said that capacity is part of the one who is capable. It is further reported of him that he maintained that it was possible for prophets to commit sins, though he believed in the sinlessness of the imāms. He distinguished between the two by saying that a prophet receives a revelation in which he is warned of his sin, and repents; the imām, however, does not receive a revelation, and so he must be sinless.

Hishām b. al-Ḥakam went to extremes with regard to 'Alī and said that he was God to whom obedience must be rendered. This Hishām b. al-Ḥakam, a theologian of one-eyed vision, should not have forgotten his own criticism of the Mu'tazila. Indeed he commits a greater error than that of which he accuses his opponents and falls into a worse form of anthropomorphism, for he had criticized al-'Allāf by saying:

> You say that God knows with knowledge but his knowledge is his essence. God would, therefore, be like created beings in that he would know with knowledge, but unlike them in that his knowledge would be his essence; thus he would know but not like other beings which know. Why then do you not say that God is a body but unlike other bodies? That he has a form but unlike other forms? A mass but unlike that of other things?

And so on.

Zurāra b. A'yun agreed with Hishām that God's knowledge is created. He further added that his power, life and other attributes are also created; that before the creation of these attributes God was not knowing, powerful, living, hearing, seeing, willing and speaking. He supported the imāmate of 'Abdullāh b. Ja'far, but when he consulted him on some questions and found him not well informed, he went back to Mūsā b. Ja'far. According to some reports he did not believe in 'Abdullāh's imāmate, but simply pointed to the Qur'ān, saying, 'This is my imām; it had become somewhat too difficult for 'Abdullāh b. Ja'far.'

The Zurārīya are reported to have held that the knowledge possessed by an imām is a necessary knowledge, and it is impossible for him to be ignorant. The reason is that all his knowledge is natural and necessary. What is known to others through reasoning is to the imāms primary and necessary knowledge, and what is natural to them cannot be attained by others.

(i) The Nu'mānīya

These are the followers of Muḥammad b. al-Nu'mān Abū Ja'far, 'the Crosseyed', known as Shaitān of al-Ṭāq; they are also called the Shaiṭānīya. The Shī'a call Muḥammad b. al-Nu'mān 'Mu'min of al-Ṭāq'. He was a pupil of Muḥammad b. 'Alī b. Ḥusain al-Bāqir who had handed on to him the secrets both about himself and about his learning. The report that he was an anthropomorphist is not true. He is said to have agreed with Hishām b. al-Ḥakam that God does not know a thing till it comes into existence. He held that God by essence is one who knows, and not one who does not know. But he knows things only when he decrees and wills them. Before this it is impossible for him to know them, not because he is not a knower, but because a thing is not a thing till he decrees it and creates it by his decree. This decree, according to him, is God's will, and God's will is identical with his action.

Muḥammad b. al-Nu'mān said that God is light in the form of a divine man. He denied that he had a body, but said, 'It is related in tradition that God created man in his image, or in the image of the Most Merciful. This must be accepted.' A similar view about the form of God is reported of Muqātil b. Sulaimān. It is also related of Dawūd al-Jawāribī, Na'īm b. Ḥammād al-Miṣrī and other Traditionalists that they believed God to have a form and limbs. Dawūd is further reported to have said, 'Do not ask me whether he has a pudendum or a beard, but you may ask me about other things because these are proved from traditions.'

Muḥammad b. al-Nu'mān composed many works for the Shī'a, among them being, *Do (it). Why did you do (it)?* and *Do (it). Do not do (it).* He mentioned in these that there are four principal groups. The first according to him are the Qadarites, the second the Khārijites, the third the masses of the people, and the fourth the Shī'ites. He held that of these only the Shī'ites would find salvation in the next world.

It is related of Hishām b. Sālim and Muḥammad b. al-Nu'mān that they refrained from any discussion of God. They reported the saying of one whose words they believed must be accepted, and who being asked about God's word: 'Your Lord is your final end',[19] said, 'Discussion must end when it turns on God.' Therefore they refrained from saying anything of God or even speculating about him till their death. This is the report of the copyist.

Included also among the Shī'a are the following sects:

(j) The Yūnusīya

These are the followers of Yūnus b. 'Abd al-Raḥmān al-Qummī, *mawlā* of the family of Yaqṭīn. Yūnus maintained that angels bear the Throne and that the Throne bears the Lord; for according to tradition the angels groan under the weight of the magnitude of God on the Throne. Yūnus was one of the Shī'a anthropomorphists and wrote several books for them on the subject.

(k) The Nūsairīya and the Isḥāqīya

These are extremist Shī'ite sects, with a number of adherents who support their doctrine and defend the chief exponents of their views. There are differences amongst them as to how the name of the divinity is to be used for the imāms of the Prophet's family. They believe that a spiritual substance may assume a bodily form – something which reason cannot deny. In the good category one may consider the example of the appearance of Gabriel either in the form of some particular person, or of a bedouin or in any other human form. In the evil category one may consider the appearance of the devil in human form in order to commit evil in that form, or the appearance of jinn in human form in order to speak human language. Similarly, we say, God has appeared in the form of men. After the Prophet there was no one better than 'Alī, and after 'Alī no one better than his chosen sons who were the best of men; God, therefore, appeared in their form, spoke through their tongue and used their hands. It is in this sense that we have used the word divine for them. We have claimed this privilege for 'Alī and none other, because he was especially chosen and supported by God to be the recipient of the innermost secrets of things. The Prophet said, 'I judge things as they appear but God knows what is hidden.' It was on this account that the fight against the infidels was the responsibility of the Prophet, but the fight against the hypocrites was the responsibility of 'Alī. It was on this acount, too, that the Prophet compared 'Alī with Jesus, son of Mary, when he said, 'Were it not that people might say of you what they said of Jesus, son of Mary, there is something I would have said about you.'

Sometimes these sects maintained that 'Alī had a share in the apostleship, since the Prophet said, 'There is one of you who will fight in defence of its [Qur'ān's] interpretation, as I have fought in defence of its revelation: this man is 'the mender of sandals'.' So knowledge of interpretation, fighting against the hypocrites, conversing with jinn and tearing down the portals of Khaibar (a thing not done by physical power): all these things are the best proofs that there is in 'Alī a divine element and a supernatural power. Therefore he is the one in whose form God appeared, by whose hand God created, and through whose tongue God commanded. Hence they say that 'Alī existed before the creation of the heavens and earth. ['Alī] said, 'We [the imāms] were shadows on the right hand of the throne: we glorified God and the angels glorified him together with us.' These shadows, and these forms which manifest these shadows, are 'Alī's essence and they shine unceasingly with God's light, both in this world and in that other world. For this reason 'Alī said, 'Aḥmad and I are like one light to another': that is, there is no difference between the two lights, except that one comes first and the other follows. According to these Shī'ites this manifests a form of participation.

The Nuṣairīya are more inclined to insist on the divine element, whereas the Isḥāqīya tend to stress the co-sharing in the prophethood. There are also many other differences between them which, however, we shall not mention.

We have now treated all of the Islamic sects except the Bāṭinīya, who by some authors in their doctrinal treatises are included among the sects and by others treated separately. On the whole they are a group different from all the seventy-two sects.

Conclusion

The Shī'ite leaders and writers among the Traditionalists.

Amongst the Zaidīya the following are Jārūdīya: Abū Khālid al-Wāsiṭī, Manṣūr b. al-Aswad and Hārūn b. Sa'd al-'Ijlī. The following are Batrīya: Wakī' b. al-Jarrāḥ, Yaḥyā b. Ādam, 'Ubaidullāh b. Mūsā, 'Alī b. Ṣāliḥ, al-Faḍl b. Dakīn, and Abū Ḥanīfa.

Muḥammad b. 'Ajlān rose in support of Muḥammad, the imām. The following rose in support of Ibrāhīm the imām: Ibrāhīm b. Sa'īd, 'Abbad b. 'Awwām, Yazīd b. Hārūn, al-'Alā' b. Rāshid, Hashīm b. Bashīr, al-'Awwam b. Ḥawshab, and Mustalim b. Sa'īd.

Amongst the Imāmīya and the other Shī'ite groups were the following: Sālim b. Abu 'l-Ja'd, Sālim b. Abū Ḥafṣa, Salama b. Kuhail, Thuwair b. Abū Fākhita, Ḥabīb b. Abū Thābit, Abu 'l-Miqdām, Shu'ba, al-A'mash, Jābir al-Ja'fī, Abū 'Abdullāh al-Jadalī, Abū Isḥaq al-Sabī'ī, al-Mughīra, Ṭāwūs, al-Sha'bī, 'Alqama, Hubaira b. Biryam, Ḥabba al-'Irnī, and al-Ḥārith al-A'war.

Among the writers were the following: Hishām b. al-Ḥakam, 'Alī b. Manṣur, Yūnus b. 'Abd al-Raḥmān, al-Shakkāl, al-Faḍl b. Shādhān, al-Ḥusain b. Ishkāb, Muḥammad b. 'Abd al-Raḥmān, Ibn Qibba, Abū Sahl al-Naubakhtī, and Aḥmad b. Yaḥyā al-Rāwandī. Among the later ones was Abū Ja'far al-Ṭūsī.

5 The Ismā'īlīya

We have earlier mentioned that the Ismā'īlīya differ from the Mūsawīya and the Twelvers in believing in the imāmate of Ismā'īl, the eldest son of Ja'far, and the first to be designated for the imāmate. They hold that Ṣādiq did not take another wife during his marriage to Ismā'īl's mother, nor did he have a concubine. In this he followed the example of the Prophet in regard to Khadīja and of 'Alī in regard to Fāṭima.

We have already spoken of the disagreements among the Ismā'īlīya as to whether or not Ismā'īl died during the life of his father. Some maintained that he did in fact die, and the only advantage accruing from his designation was that the imāmate passed after him to his sons exclusively. In the same way Moses appointed Aaron who, too, died during the life of his brother, and the only advantage of his designation was that the imāmate passed to his sons, as designation cannot be retracted. It is impossible, moreover, to believe in a change of mind, *badā'*. Again an imām does not appoint one of his sons without the counsel of his predecessor; appointment is not valid where there are uncertainty and ignorance.

Some, on the other hand, say that Ismā'īl did not die, but he was reported to have died for the purpose of concealment, and to be out of reach of those who might seek to kill him. Several reasons are given for believing this. One is that Muḥammad who was young, and was Ismā'īl's brother on his mother's side, went to the bed on which Ismā'īl was lying, and having removed the sheet saw that his eyes were open. He ran back terrified to his father, crying out to him, 'My brother is alive . . . My brother is alive.' His father replied, 'The descendants of the Prophet appear like this in death.' Another reason given is the motive for having his death witnessed and the testimony of those present recorded, for it was unknown for a person's death to be recorded. This motive was manifested when the news was brought to Manṣūr that Ismā'īl b. Ja'far had been seen in Basra, and passing by an invalid person had prayed for him, and that this person with God's permission had recovered. Manṣūr sent a message to Ṣādiq that Ismā'īl b. Ja'far was alive and had been seen in Baṣra; whereupon Ṣādiq sent the record of his death, bearing on it the signature of the governor of Medīna.

The Ismā'īlīya say that following upon Ismā'īl the cycle of seven imāms is completed with Muḥammad. Then begins the era of the hidden imāms, who went about secretly but sent out emissaries, who appeared openly on their behalf. They hold that the world can never be without an imām who is alive and a *qā'im*, either visible and manifest, or hidden and concealed. When the imām is manifest it is possible for his *ḥujja* (proof) to be hidden, but if the imām is hidden it is necessary for his *ḥujja* and emissaries to be manifest. According to them the imāms are always in series of seven, like the days of the week, or the seven heavens, or the seven planets, but the *Nuqabā'* (chiefs) are always in series of twelves. In this matter the Imāmīya, who believe in a definite number of imāms, fell into confusion and determined the number of imāms in accordance with the number of *nuqabā'*. At the end of the series of hidden imāms, al-Mahdī manifested himself, followed by al-Qā'im, followed in turn by their descendants who designated one another in succession to the imāmate. One of the beliefs of the Ismā'īlīya is that whoever dies in ignorance of the imām of his time dies a pagan; so also does anyone who dies without allegiance to an imām.

The message of the Ismā'īlīya differed from one age to another, and their doctrine varied from person to person. We shall first mention their early doctrines, and afterwards those of the one who propounded a New Message.

The Ismā'īlīya are most commonly known as the Bāṭinīya. This name was given to them because of their belief that for every 'exoteric' there is an 'esoteric', and for every revelation an interpretation. They are known by many other names amongst different people. In Iraq they are called the Bāṭinīya, the Carmathians, or the Mazdakites; in Khurāsān they are known as the Ta'līmites and heretics. They themselves say, 'We are Ismā'īlīya, because we differ from other Shī'ite sects by this name and on account of this person [from whom the name is derived].'

The early Bāṭinīya have combined theories of their own with those derived from the philosophers, and in this way composed their works. Of God, therefore, they say:

> We shall not say either that he exists or does not exist, that he is knowing or not knowing, that he is powerful or not powerful, and so on with all the other attributes. To assert the reality of such attributes requires that there be something common to God and other existing things in the aspect in which the word is used of him; this would be anthropomorphism. It is not possible, therefore, to assert anything absolutely of him or deny anything absolutely of him; but rather we must say that he is the God of opposites, Creator of contradictories and Judge of contraries.

On this matter they quote a saying of Muḥammad b. 'Alī al-Bāqir:

> As God gives knowledge to those who know, we say of him that he is knowing, and as he gives power to those who have power we say of him that he is powerful; therefore, he is knowing and powerful in the sense that he gives knowledge and power, not in the sense that knowledge and power subsist in him, or that knowledge and power are qualities he possesses.

It is, therefore, said of the early Bāṭinīya that they deny the reality of attributes, and strip God of them all. They further say:

> We hold the same thing about eternity: God himself is neither eternal nor temporal. His command and his word, however, are eternal, though his creative activity is temporal. By his command he created the First Intelligence, which is fully in act. Through the mediation of this First Intelligence he next created the Soul, which is not fully in act. The relationship between the Soul and the Intelligence is like that of sperm to the fully developed creature; or like that of an egg to a bird, or that of a child to its parents, or that of the product to the producer, or that of female to male, or finally, like that of one spouse to another.

The Ismā'īlīya also maintain that when the Soul longed for the state of perfection enjoyed by the Intelligence it needed to move from imperfection to perfection. The movement itself required an instrument of movement. The heavenly bodies then came into being and moved in a circular motion under the direction of the Soul. Next the simple elements came into being, moving in a straight line under the direction of the Soul. Thus composite things came into being, as minerals, vegetables, animals and men; and individual souls were united with bodies. Mankind is distinguished from all other things in having a special capacity to receive these illuminations; the world of man stands parallel to the rest of the universe.

In the celestial world there is an Intelligence and a Universal Soul. There must be therefore in this world a personalized intelligence which is also universal, *kull*. This intelligence is the perfect person, the one who has reached the fullness of perfection. He is known as the *nāṭiq* (the revealer), and is the prophet. There must be also a personalized soul which, too, is universal. This soul is like a child still imperfect but advancing towards perfection, or like sperm on the way to its full development, or like a female uniting with a male. This soul is called *asās* (first principle) and is the *waṣī* (the legatee).

Just as the heavenly bodies and elements move by motion received from the Soul and the Intelligence, so, too, souls and individuals are moved by religious laws under an impulse received from the Prophet and the *waṣī* of every age. These are always in a series of sevens till the last phase is reached and the time of the resurrection has come, when obligations shall cease and *sunna* and laws disappear. These movements of the heavens and religious laws are intended as a means for the Soul to reach its state of perfection, which lies in its reaching the level of Intelligence, becoming one with it and attaining the same actuality. This is the Great Resurrection. The moment the whole firmament is destroyed, all the elements and other things composite will be dissolved. Heaven will be split asunder; the planets will be scattered; the earth will be transformed and the sky shall be rolled up just as a scroll is rolled for the written book. On that day men will be called to their account, the good will be separated from the evil, the obedient from the disobedient; particular manifestations of evil will be united with the Devil, the seducer and liar. From the moment of movement up to the moment of rest is the beginning; from the moment of rest to infinity is perfection.

The Ismā'īlīya also say that divine ordinances, the *sunna* and provisions of the *sharī'a*, such as those relating to buying and selling, hiring, gifts, marriage, divorce, injury, retribution and blood money: all these have their corresponding elements in the universe, number corresponding to number and law corresponding to law. Religious codes are a world of sacred ordinances, and the universe on its part is a religious code, physical and created. Similarly letters and words in their structure are like forms and bodies in their composition. The relationship of single letters to words is like that of pure elements to composite bodies. Every letter has its counterpart in the world, with its own individual nature through which it influences minds. It is in this way that knowledge acquired from words of instruction becomes food for the mind, just as food obtained from created things becomes nourishment for the body. God has decreed that every existing thing should have its food from that out of which it was created. On the analogy of this theory of correspondence they go on to speak of the number of words and verses [of the Qur'ān]. They say that the formula of consecration, *tasmiya*, is composed of seven letters [in the first half] and twelve [in the second], and that the formula of the profession of faith consists of four words in the first part of the testimony and three in the second; there are seven syllables in the first part and six in the second, twelve letters in the first part and twelve in the second.

In the same manner they were able to show a correspondence in every verse in a way that no rational person would attempt without acknowledging his inability, fearing he might make correspondence with the contrary. This search for correspondence was a procedure adopted by their predecessors, who had composed a number of books about it. They summon people in every age to an imām who knows correspondences in this field, and finds the ways of these patterns and conventions.

The leaders of the New Message, however, abandoned this method when Ḥasan b. Muḥammad b.al-Ṣabbāḥ proclaimed his mission and confined himself to presenting compelling arguments to his opponents.

He obtained support, and secured himself in fortresses. He first went up to the fortress of Alamūt in the month of Sha'bān in the year AH 483, after first having gone to the region where the imām dwelt, and learning from him how to preach the message to his contemporaries. On his return he began calling upon people to designate for every age an imām who is a true imām and *qā'im*; and to distinguish the sect which will obtain salvation by this mark, namely, that it has an imām while the others do not. This is the substance of what he has said, with much repetition, in Arabic and Persian.

We shall reproduce in Arabic what al-Ṣabbāḥ has written in Persian, but the translator must not be censured. The one who succeeds is the one who follows truth and avoids falsehood, and it is God who gives success and help. We shall begin with the four chapters with which al-Ṣabbāḥ introduced his message. They are written in Persian and I have translated them into Arabic.

In the first chapter al-Ṣabbāḥ says that whoever expresses an opinion about the knowledge of God must say one of two things. He must either say: I know God only from reason and reflection without the need of instruction from a teacher; or, the knowledge of God is not attained by reasoning and reflection but rather by instruction from a teacher. Whoever says the former may not reject another's reason and reflection; if he does so, he has himself become a teacher, because in his very rejection he is teaching, as well as pointing out that the one whose reasoning and reflection are rejected is in need of another. These two divisions are therefore necessary, because when a man expounds a view or holds an opinion he does so either of his own accord, or on another's authority. This is the substance of the first chapter, which is a refutation of those who uphold independent judgment and reasoning.

In the second chapter he says that, as the need for a teacher has been shown, the question arises would any teacher at all be suitable, or whether there would be need of a truthful teacher? He replies that whoever holds that any teacher will do may not reject his opponent's teacher. If he does so he has shown the need for a truthful and reliable teacher. It is said that this is in refutation of the Traditionalists.

In the third chapter he asks:

> If the need for a truthful teacher is established, does it not become necessary first to know who the teacher is, then to find him, and, finally, to learn from him? Or is it possible to learn from any teacher without determining one in particular and ascertaining his truthfulness?

The second case, he says, goes back to the first. Whoever cannot walk along a path without a guide and companion, then [for him] the finding of the companion has priority over the path. This is a refutation of the Shī'ites.

In the fourth chapter he says that there are two classes of people. The first consists of those who say that in order to know God we stand in need of a truthful teacher who must first of all be known as such and specified; after that we must learn from him. The other class learns about everything from anyone whether he is a teacher or not. The preceding arguments have shown that the truth lies with the first group; their leader must, therefore, be regarded as the chief exponent of the truth. Similarly, he shows that falsehood lies with the second group, and so their chiefs must be the chief exponents of falsehood. He says:

> This is how through the truth we come to know the exponent of the truth in a general way; after this through the exponent of the truth we come to know the truth in a detailed way. Thus a vicious circle is avoided.

By the truth al-Ṣabbāḥ meant our need, and by the one making known the truth the one who is needed. He further said that through our need we come to know the imām, and through the imām we come to know the extent of our need. In the same way it is through the possible that we come to know the necessary, that is, the Necessary Being, and through the Necessary Being we come to know the degrees of possibility in possible beings. He added that in exactly the same way we come to the knowledge of the Unity.

To this al-Ṣabbāḥ added several more chapters of exposition, either developing his arguments or refuting those of others. The greater part, however, is in the form of refutation either by the use of an *argumentum ad hominem*, or by showing that disunity is a proof of falsehood and unity is a proof of truth. Among these are chapters on truth and falsehood, 'minor' and 'major'. Truth and falsehood, he says, are found in the world. The sign of truth is unity and the sign of falsehood is disunity. Unity is a fruit of the Teaching, and disunity of personal opinion. The Teaching is possessed by the group which follows the imām, but personal opinion is found in the diverse groups who follow their chiefs.

Truth and falsehood according to Ḥasan Sabbāḥ resemble one another in some respects and differ from one another in others; they are also diametrically opposed to one another, but within each there are grades: this was his criterion of judgment in all his statements. He said, 'I have derived this criterion from the words of the Testimony, *shahāda*, which is composed of denial and assertion, or of denial and exception: whatever merits denial is false; whatever merits assertion is true.' He applied this criterion to good and evil, truth and falsehood and all other contraries. His aim in every written and spoken word was to show that there was a teacher. He sought also to show that the unity of God implies both the unity and the prophethood in order that there may be unity; and that prophethood implies both the prophethood and the imāmate in order that there may be prophethood. This was the sole aim of his theology.

Al-Ṣabbāḥ did not permit the common people to go deeply into knowledge. In the same way he did not allow those more advanced to study ancient works, unless they knew the nature of these books and the authority of their authors in their respective fields of knowledge. In the matter of metaphysics he and his followers did not go beyond saying, 'Our God is the God of Muḥammad.' He said [to his opponents], 'You say, 'Our God is the God of reason, that is, one to whom any intelligent person can attain." However, if one of his followers was asked, 'What do you say of God? Is he one or many? Knowing or not? Powerful or not?' he would only say: 'My God is the God of Muḥammad. 'It is he who has sent his Apostle with guidance and religion of truth, that it may prevail over all religion even though the idolators detest it.'[20] The Apostle is the one who leads to God.'

[Shahrastānī says] I have had many a debate with these people about the aforementioned premises, but they only say, 'Do we need you? Shall we take any notice of what you say? Must we learn from you?' I have sometimes granted the need for an imām, and asked them:

> Where is the needed one? What would he decide for me in metaphysics? What would he lay down for me in matters intellectual? For a teacher is not sought for his own sake but in order to teach. You have in reality closed the gate of knowledge and opened the door of unquestioning submission and blind obedience.

No rational person would accept a doctrine without understanding it, or follow a path unless it has been clearly proven to be the right one. Nevertheless, it is true that in dispute one should begin by recourse to a judge and end by accepting his judgment: 'No, by thy Lord! They cannot be true believers until they make thee a judge in their disputes, and feel in themselves no resistance to your decisions, but submit to them whole-heartedly.'[21]

Notes

Introduction

1 Also Abu 'l-Fatḥ b. Aḥmad al-Shahrastānī.
2 Cf. Ibn Khallikān, *Wafayāt al-a'yān*, ed. Iḥsān 'Abbās.
3 *Ibid.*, p. 273. Cf. also Ṣalāh al-Dīn Khalīl b. Aibak al-Ṣafadī, *Kitāb al-Wāfī bi 'l-Wafayāt*, Bibliotheca Islamica, vol. 3, p. 278.
4 The list of Shahrastānī's works given by Badran in his introduction to the *Milal* is as follows:
(1) *Kitāb al-Milal wa 'l-Niḥal*; (2) *Kitāb Nihāyat al-Iqdām*; (3) *Al-Irshād ilā 'aqā'id al-'ibād*; (4) *Al-Aqṭār fi 'l-uṣūl*; (5) *Tārīkh al-ḥukamā*; (6) *Talhkīṣ al-aqsām li-madhāhib al-anām*; (7) *Daqā'iq al-awhām*; (8) *Sharḥ sūra Yūsuf*; (9) *Al-'Uyūn wa 'l-anhār*; (10) *Ghāyat al-marām fī 'ilm al-kalām*; (11) *Qiṣṣat Mūsā wa 'l-Khiḍr*; (12) *Al-Mabda' wa 'l-Ma'ād*; (13) *Majālis maktūba*; (14) *Muṣāra'at al-falāsifa*; (15) *Al-Manāhij wa 'l-āyāt*; (16) *Shubhāt Aristatālīs wa Ibn Sīna wa naqḍuhā*; (17) *Nihāyat al-awhām*;
Badrān also includes the disputed *Mafātīḥ al-asrār.* Cf. Kitāb al-Milal wa 'l-Niḥal, ed. Muḥammad b. Fatḥullāh Badrān, Cairo, 1956, p. 8 f.
5 Cf. 'Alī b. Zaid Zāhīr al-Din Al-Baihaqī, *Tārīkh ḥukamā' al-Islām*, ed. Muḥammad Kurd 'Alī, Damascus, 1946, p. 141.
6 *Ibid.*
7 Al-Shahrastānī, *Kitāb Nihāyat al-Iqdām fī 'ilmi 'l-kalām*, ed. Alfred Guillaume, Oxford University Press, London, 1934, p. x.
8 *Ibid.*, p. ix.
9 'Abd al-Wahhāb b. 'Alī Al-Subkī, *Ṭabaqāt al-Shāfi'īya al-kubrā*, ed. Maḥmūd Muḥammad al-Tanaḥī & 'Abd al-Fattāḥ Muḥammad al-Ḥulw, Cairo, 1964, vol. 6, pp. 128–130.
10 *Al-Wāfī*, vol. 3, p. 278 f.
11 Cf. p. 11, passim.
12 Thus he quotes with approval the following tradition. The Prophet

also said: 'My community will be divided into seventy-three sects but only one of these will be saved, the others will perish.' When asked which was the one that would attain salvation, he replied, 'Those who follow the *sunna* and the congregation.' He was further asked, 'What is the *sunna* and the congregation?' He replied, 'That which I and my companions practise.' Cf. below, p. 10; cf. also p. 12 and the opening remarks on the Ṣifātīya (pp. 79f) and the Anthropomorphists (pp. 88f).

13 Cf. below, p. 167.

14 Cf. below, p. 168.

15 Cf. below, p. 170.

16 Cf. MS. 78/8086; *al-Milal* p. 19.

17 *Al-Milal wa 'l-Niḥal*, translated by Dr Sayyid Moḥammad Riḍa Jalālī Nā'īnī Iqbāl AH 1350, p. 42 f. Professor Pājūh of Tehran University also expressed oral agreement with this opinion.

18 *Essays and Studies* presented to Stanley Arthur Cook, ed. J. Winston Thomas, London, 1950, ch. XI.

19 Aḥmad b. Yaḥyā al-Murtaḍā, *Kitạb Ṭabaqāt al-Mu'tazila*, Catholic Press, Beirut, 1961, p. 1.

20 Cf. Albert N. Nader, *Le système philosophique des Mu'tazila*, Beyrouth, 1956, p. 44.

21 Abu 'l-Ḥasan 'Alī b. Ismā'īl al-Ash'arī, *Maqālāt al-Islāmīyīn*, ed., H. Ritter, Istanbul, 1929, Leipzig, 1933.

22 Cf. below, p. 149.

23 Cf. Abu 'l-Ḥasan 'Alī b. Ismā'īl al-Ash'arī, *Maqālāt al-Islāmīyīn*, ed. Muḥammad Muḥyi al-Din 'Abd al-Ḥamīd, Cairo, 1954, vol. 1, p. 78.

24 Cf. below, p. 155.

25 Cf. below, p. 50; also 'Abd al-Raḥīm al-Khayyāṭ, *Kitāb al-intiṣār wa 'l-radd 'ala Ibn al-Rāwandī al-Mulḥid*, ed. H. S. Nyberg, Cairo, 1925, p. 44.

26 The statement is to the effect that all men are infidels; cf. below, p. 60, and *Kitāb al-Intiṣār*, p. 54 f.

27 Shāfhūr b. Ṭāhir al-Isfarā'īnī, *Al-Tabṣīr fi 'l-dīn wa tamyīz al-firqa al-nājiya 'an al-firaq al-hālikīn*, Cairo, 1940, p. 41 f; cf. also *al-Milal*, p. 53.

28 Cf. 'Abd al-Qāhir b. Ṭāhir al-Baghdādī, *al-Farq bain al-firaq*, Cairo, p. 14.

29 Cf. below, p. 17.

30 Cf. *Al-Farq bain al-firaq*, p. 277 f.

31 Cf. below, p. 50.

32 *Ibid.*

33 *Ibid.*, p. 57.

34 *Ibid.*, pp. 46f.

35 *Ṭabaqāt*, p. 128.

36 Al-Shahrastānī, *Kitāb al-Milal wa 'l-Niḥal*, ed. Muḥammad b. Fatḥullāh Badrān, Cairo, 1951.

General Introduction

1 Qur'ān, 7, 181.
2 *Ibid.*, 15, 36.
3 *Ibid.*, 64, 6.
4 *Ibid.*, 17, 61.
5 *Ibid.*, 17, 94.
6 *Ibid.*, 7, 12.
7 *Ibid.*, 43, 52.
8 *Ibid.*, 2, 118.
9 *Ibid.*, 15, 33.
10 *Ibid.*, 2, 268.
11 *Ibid.*, 3, 154.
12 *Ibid.*, 3, 156.
13 *Ibid.*, 16, 35.
14 *Ibid.*, 36, 47.
15 *Ibid.*, 13, 13.
16 *Ibid.*, 3, 144.

Prelude

1 Qur'ān, 43, 86.
2 *Ibid.*, 4, 83.

Part I

Introduction

1 Qur'ān, 3, 19.
2 *Ibid.*, 30, 30.
3 *Ibid.*, 5, 3.
4 *Ibid.*, 5, 48.
5 *Ibid.*, 22, 78.
6 *Ibid.*, 42, 13.
7 *Ibid.*, 5, 3.
8 *Ibid.*, 22, 78.

Section I Muslims

Introduction

1 Qur'ān, 49, 14.
2 *Ibid*., 2, 112.
3 *Ibid*., 5, 3.
4 *Ibid*., 3, 19.
5 *Ibid*., 2, 113.
6 *Ibid*., 2, 132.

Chapter 1 The Mu'tazilites

1 Qur'ān, 8, 42.
2 *Ibid*., 42, 7.
3 *Ibid*., 111, 3.
4 *Ibid*., 5, 110.
5 *Ibid*., 89, 22.
6 *Ibid*., 6, 158.
7 *Ibid*., 7, 34.
8 *Ibid*., 6, 38.
9 *Ibid*., 35, 24.
10 *Ibid*., 8, 63.
11 *Ibid*., 49, 7.
12 *Ibid*., 2, 7.
13 *Ibid*., 4, 155.
14 *Ibid*., 36, 9.
15 The full name as given by al-Murtaḍā is Abu 'l-Qāsim 'Abdullāh b. Maḥmūd al-Ka'bī. See above p. V.
16 Cf. A. S. Tritton, *Muslim Theology*, pp. 148-9:

His doctrine of the Qur'ān was very like that of Abu 'l-Hudhail, that it is an accident and can be in many places at once. He differed from the rest of the Mu'tazila by holding that the word of God endures. When a man reads the Qur'ān, God creates a word for himself along with the spoken words, and this word is heard, letter by letter, with every recitation. Al-Juwainī adds further details. The 'word' is words which accompany the sounds but are not those sounds; they are in the written book also but are not the visible letters and lines; they are heard though they are not sounds. In every recitation are the sounds, the reading (sense), and the word of God. During the recitation the word inheres in one who is not God; when the reader stops, the word ceases to be in him. If many recite a verse together, the word of God is in each one yet it is still one. Both God and man need a special constitution to produce those sounds which are speech.

Chapter 2 The Jabrīya

1 Qur'ān, 11, 107.
2 *Ibid.*

Chapter 3 The Ṣifātīya

1 Qur'ān, 20, 5.
2 *Ibid.*, 38, 75.
3 *Ibid.*, 89, 22.
4 *Ibid.*, 75, 22.
5 *Ibid.*, 17, 15.
6 *Ibid.*, 21, 23.
7 *Ibid.*, 38, 75.
8 *Ibid.*, 3, 7.
9 *Ibid.*, 36, 58.
10 *Ibid.*, 28, 30.
11 *Ibid.*, 4, 164.
12 *Ibid.*, 7, 144.
13 *Ibid.*, 7, 145.
14 *Ibid.*, 9, 6.
15 *Ibid.*, 56, 77 ff.
16 *Ibid.*, 80, 13 ff.
17 *Ibid.*, 97, 1.
18 *Ibid.*, 2, 185.
19 *Ibid.*, 16, 40.
20 *Ibid.*, 36, 82.

Chapter 4 The Khārijites

1 Qur'ān, 2, 204.
2 *Ibid.*, 2, 207.
3 *Ibid.*, 4, 77.
4 *Ibid.*, 5, 54.
5 *Ibid.*, 3, 28.
6 *Ibid.*, 40, 28.
7 *Ibid.*, 4, 95.
8 *Ibid.*, 9, 90.
9 *Ibid.*, 6, 145.
10 *Ibid.*, 6, 96.

Chapter 5 The Murji'ites

1 Qur'ān, 7, 111.
2 *Ibid.*, 2, 34.

Chapter 6 The Shi'ites

1 Qur'ān, 5, 93.
2 *Ibid.*, 2, 210.
3 *Ibid.*, 28, 88.
4 *Ibid.*, 5, 67.
5 *Ibid.*, 4, 59.
6 *Ibid.*, 48, 18.
7 *Ibid.*, 9, 100.
8 *Ibid.*, 9, 117.
9 *Ibid.*, 24, 55.
10 *Ibid.*, 9, 105.
11 *Ibid.*, 87, 1 f.
12 *Ibid.*, 33, 72.
13 The text as stands suggests that 'the trust' offered was to prevent 'Alī from obtaining the imāmate, whereas it is clear from the sources especially Baghdādī, that 'the trust' is one of protection of 'Alī from those seeking to do him injustice. The context itself also favours protection. We have, therefore, added the words of Baghdādī to give this sense; cf. *al-Farq bain al-Firaq*, Cairo, p. 240.
14 Qur'ān, 33, 72.
15 *Ibid.*, 59, 16.
16 *Ibid.*, 34, 5.
17 *Ibid.*, 10, 100.
18 *Ibid.*, 16, 68.
19 *Ibid.*, 53, 42.
20 *Ibid.*, 9, 33.
21 *Ibid.*, 4, 65.

Bibliography

Ash'arī, Abu 'l-Ḥasan 'Alī b. Ismā'īl, *Maqālāt al-Islāmīyīn*, ed. H. Ritter, Istanbul, 1929 Leipzig, 1933/Muḥammad Muḥyī al-Dīn 'Abd al-Ḥamīd, Cairo, 1954.

Baghdādī, 'Abd al-Qāhir, *al-Farq bain al-Firaq*, ed. Muḥammad Muḥyī al-Dīn 'Abd al-Ḥamīd, Cairo, n.d.

Al-Baihaqī, 'Alī b. Zaid Zāhir al-Dīn, *Tārīkh ḥukamā' al-Islām*, ed. Muḥammad Kurd 'Alī, Damascus, 1946.

Ibn al-Athīr, *al-Kāmil*, Beirut, 1965.

Ibn Khallikān, *Wafayāt al-A'yān*, ed. Iḥsān Abbās, Beirut, 1972.

Isfarā'īnī, Shāhfūr b. Tāhir, *Al-Tabṣīr fi 'l-Dīn wa Tamyīz al-Firqa al-Nājiya 'an al-Firaq al-Hālikīn*, Cairo, 1940.

Al-Khayyāṭ, 'Abd al-Raḥīm Muḥammad, *Kitāb al-Intiṣār wa 'l-radd 'alā Ibn al-Rāwandī al-Mulḥid*, ed. H. S. Nyberg, Cairo, 1925.

Al-Murtaḍa, Aḥmad b. Yaḥyā, *Kitāb Ṭabaqāt al-Mu'tazila*, Beirut, 1961.

Nader, Albert N., *Le système philosophique des Mu'tazila*, Beyrouth, Les Lettres Orientales, 1956.

Al-Ṣafadī, Ṣalāh al-Dīn Khalīl b. Aibak, *Kitāb al-Wāfī bi 'l-Wafayāt*, Istanbul, Bibliotheca Islamica, Damascus, 1931.

Al-Sharastānī, Muḥammad b. 'Abd al-Karīm, *Kitāb al-Milal wa 'l-Niḥal*, ed. Muḥammad b. Fatḥullāh Badrān, Cairo, 1951, 1956. Translated into Persian by Afẓal al-Dīn Ṣadr Turkah-i Isfahānī, ed. Dr Sayyid Muḥammad Riḍā Jalālī Nā'īnī, Tehran, n.d.

Al-Shahrastānī, Muḥammad b. 'Abd al-Karīm, *Kitāb Nihāyat al-Iqdām fī 'Ilm al-Kalām*, ed. Alfred Guillaume, London, OUP, 1934.

Al-Subkī, 'Abd al-Wahhāb b. 'Alī, *Ṭabaqāt al-Shāfi'īya al-Kubrā*, ed. Maḥmūd Muḥammad al-Tanaḥi 'Abd al-Fattaḥ Muḥammad al-Ḥulw, Cairo, 1964.

Essays and Studies presented to Stanley Arthur Cook, ed. Thomas J. Winston, London, 1950.

Tritton, A. S., *Muslim Theology*, London, Luzac, 1947.

Watt, W. M., *The Formative Period of Islamic Thought*, Edinburgh, Edinburgh University Press, 1973.

Glossary

badā' derived from *badā* meaning to appear or seem. *Badā'* in God means change in opinion and knowledge.

fāsiq a sinful person; a person not meeting the legal requirements of righteousness (Hans Wehr); according to Mu'tazila, a grave sinner who ceases to be a *mu'min*, but is not an unbeliever, *kāfir*.

ḥujja proof or argument. According to Shī'a the person of the prophet or imam is himself the 'proof', *ḥujja*, through whom God is known.

ijtihād exercise by a jurist of his personal opinion in a matter of Islamic Law.

imām ordinarily used for one who leads in the congregational prayer. Also used as a synonym for a caliph. With Shī'a it acquired a connotation of spiritual leadership.

īmān faith and belief.

irjā' giving of hope to a sinner or postponement of judgment regarding such a person.

jabr determination of man's act by God.

kasb acquisition: the term is used by Ash'arī to define human responsibility in one's acts. Acts are created by God, but acquired by man.

luṭf divine grace.

muwāfāt the state of faith in man at the time of his death.

nāṭiq revealer – a term used by Shī'a.

qadar determination of good and evil by God or by man. If by God, often called predetermination; if by man, often known as free will.

qā'im one who rises after death; resurrector. In the Ismā'īlīya the word is used for the seventh imām before the beginning of the new cycle.

shubha doubt, or calling into question.
taqīya a doctrine held by many Shī'a and some Khārijite sects allowing members to live in a state of dissimulation, i.e., hiding one's belief and sectarian identity.
taqlīd blind obedience in matters of Islamic Law.
ta'ṭīl and *tanzīh* holding God's attributes as non-entities.
tawallud coming into being of secondary or associated affects.
waṣī a legatee.

Index of personal names

Aaron, 164
'Abbād b. 'Awwām, 63, 163
'Abbās b. 'Abd al-Muṭṭalib, 103
'Abd al-Karīm b. 'Ajrad, 105, 108, 111
'Abd al-Malik b. Marwān, 43, 44, 105
'Abd Rabbihī, the elder, 102
'Abd Rabbihī, the younger, 102
'Abd al-Raḥmān b. 'Awf, 141
'Abd al-Raḥmān b. Muljim, 103
'Abdullāh b. 'Abbās, 18, 99
'Abdullāh b. 'Āmir, 21, 52
'Abdullāh b. 'Amr b. Ḥarb al-Kindī, 22, 129
'Abdullāh b. al-Ḥārith b. Naufal al-Naufalī, 102
'Abdullāh b. Ḥasan b. Ḥasan, 23, 132
'Abdullāh b. Ibāḍ, 114
'Abdullāh b. Ja'far, 23, 141, 143, 160
'Abdullāh b. al-Kawwā', 99, 101
'Abdullāh b. Mākhūn, 102
'Abdullāh b. Mas'ūd, 52, 76
'Abdullāh b. Mu'āwiya b. 'Abdullāh b. Ja'far b. Abū Ṭālib, 22, 129, 130
'Abdullāh b. Muḥammad b. 'Aṭīya, 114
'Abdullāh b. Saba', 21, 150
'Abdullāh b. Sa'd b. Abū Sarḥ, 21
'Abdullāh b. al-Sadiwarī, 110
'Abdullāh b. Sa'īd al-Kullābi, 26, 78
'Abdullāh b. 'Umar, 118
'Abdullāh b. Wahb al-Rāsibī, 99, 101
'Abdullāh b. Yaḥyā al-Ibāḍī, 114
'Abdullāh b. Yazīd, 117
'Abdullāh b. al-Zubair, 102, 105
Abraham, 8, 13, 34, 153
Abū 'Abdullāh al-Jadalī, 163
Abū 'Adbullāh b. Maslama, 117
Abū 'Abdullāh Muḥammad b. Ismā'īl al-Bukhārī, 18
Abū 'Abdullāh Muḥammad b. al-Karrām, 26, 27, 92, 95, 118
Abū 'Abd al-Raḥmān b. Maslama, 117
Abū Baihas al-Haiṣam b. Jābir, 106, 107, 108
Abū Bakr (al-Ṣiddīq), 19, 20, 51, 87, 101, 133, 135, 136, 138, 139, 141, 142
Abū Bakr al-Aṣamm, 25, 62, 64
Abū Bakr b. Fūrak, 26
Abū Bakr Muḥammad b. 'Abdullāh b. Shabīb al-Basrī, 117
Abū Dharr, 21, 52
Abū Fudaik, 104, 105
Abū Ḥāmid al-Zauzānī, 143
Abū Ḥanīfa, 76, 121, 135, 138, 163

Abū Hārūn al-ʻAbdī, 117
Abū Hāshim ʻAbd al-Salām, 65
Abū Hāshim b. Abū ʻAlī Jubbā'ī, 26, 43, 46, 66, 67, 68, 69, 70, 80
Abū Hāshim b. Muḥammad b. al-Ḥanafīya, 22, 46, 129, 130, 131, 132
Abu 'l-Hudhail Hamdān b. al-Hudhail al-ʻAllāf, 25, 46, 47, 48, 115, 158
Abu 'l-Ḥusain ʻAlī b. Zaid al-Ibāḍī, 117
Abu'l-Ḥusain al-Baṣrı, 26, 43 68, 70
Abu'l-Ḥusain Kulthūm b. Ḥabıb al-Muhallabī, 117
Abu'l-Ḥusain Muḥammad b. Muslim al-Ṣāliḥī, 117
Abū ʻĪsa al-Warrāq, 159
Abū Isḥāq al-Sabīʻī, 163
Abū Jaʻfar al-Ṭūsī, 163
Abu'l-Jārūd Ziyād b. Abū Ziyād (Surḥūb), 135, 136, 139
Abū Kāmil, 151
Abū Khālid al-Wāsiṭī, 136, 163
Abu 'l-Khaṭṭāb Muḥammad b. Abū Zainab al-Asdī al-Ajdaʻ, 146, 154, 155
Abū Lahab, 52
Abū Manṣūr al-ʻIjlī, 153, 154, 155
Abū Marwān Ghailān b. Muslim, 117
Abu'l-Miqdām, 163
Abū Muʻādh al-Taumanī, 122
Abū Muḥammad ʻAbdullāh b. Muḥammad al-Ḥasan al-Khālidı, 117
Abū Mujālid, 5
Abū Mūsā al-Ashʻarī, 78, 79, 99
Abu Musa al-Murdār, ʻĪsā b. Ṣubaiḥ, 25, 59, 60
Abū Muslim, 113, 131, 132
Abū Rāshid Nāfiʻ b. al-Azraq, 102
Abū Shla Naubakhtī, 163
Abu'l-Shaʻthā', 117
Abū Shimr, 25, 53, 121, 123
Abū Sufyān, 19
Abū Ṭālib, 139
Abū Thaubān (the Murji'ite), 121
Abū ʻUbaidah b. al-Jarrāḥ, 141
Abū Yaʻqūb al-Shaḥḥām, 25, 48
Abū Yūsuf, 124
Abū Zakarīyā Yaḥyā b. Aṣfaḥ, 117
Abū Zufar, 25, 60
Adam, 12, 13, 14, 16, 29, 50, 53, 90, 91, 96, 103, 131
al-Ādamī, 25, 48
Aḥmad b. ʻAlī al-Shaṭawī, 25
Aḥmad b. Ayyūb, 54
Aḥmad b. Ḥanbal, 78, 88
Aḥmad al-Hujaimī, 89
Aḥmad b. al-Kayyāl, 156, 157, 158, 162
Aḥmad b. Khābiṭ, 25, 53, 54, 55
Aḥmad b. Mūsā b. Jaʻfar, 146
Aḥnaf, 101
ʻĀ'isha, 21, 88, 103, 136
Akhnas b. Qais, 112
ʻAlā' b. Rāshid, 163
ʻAlbā' b. Dhirāʻ al-Dawsī, 151
ʻAlī (b. Abū Ṭālib), 19, 45, 51, 52, 62, 78, 88, 97, 98, 99, 100, 101, 102, 103, 118, 119, 125, 126, 127, 128, 130, 131, 132, 133, 135, 136, 138, 139, 140, 141, 143, 149, 150, 151, 152, 153, 154, 160, 162, 163
ʻAlī b. ʻAbdullāh b. ʻAbbās, 22, 131
ʻAlī b. Fulān al-Ṭāḥin, 146
ʻAlī b. Harmala, 117
ʻAlī b. al-Ḥusain, Zain al-ʻĀbidīn, 23, 135, 141, 142, 145, 149
ʻAlī b. Ismāʻīl, 145
ʻAlī b. Jaʻfar al-Ṣādiq, 23
ʻAlī b. al-Kirmānī, 113
ʻAlī b. Manṣūr, 163
ʻAlī b. Muḥammad b. ʻAlī al-Riḍā, 24, 145, 146
ʻAlī b. Muḥammad b. al-Ḥanafīya, 129

'Alī al-Riḍā, 23, 146, 149
'Alī b. Ṣāliḥ, 163
'Allāf *see* Abu 'l-Hudhail
'Alqama, 163
A'mash, 163
'Ammār al-Sābāṭī, 145
'Amr b. al-'Ās, 21, 79, 88, 139
'Amr b. Dharr, 124
'Amr b. Murra, 124
Amr b. 'Ubaid, 24, 45
Asfahānī, Dawūd b. 'Alī, 78, 88
Ash'arī, Abu'l-Ḥasan, 26, 63, 68, 75, 78, 79, 80, 81, 82, 84, 85, 86, 87, 88, 89, 96, 109
Ash'ath b. Qais, 21, 98, 101
Ashtar, 99
'Aṭīya b. al-Aswad al-Ḥanafī, 102, 104, 105
'Aṭīya al-Jurjānī, 113
'Attāb b. al-A'war, 99
'Attābī, 121
'Awwām b. Ḥawshab, 163

Baihasī, 117
Bāqillānī, Qāḍī Abū Bakr, 80, 82, 83
Bāqir, Muḥammad *see* Muḥammad b. 'Alī . . .
Bayān b. Sam'ān, 22, 130, 131
Bazīgh, 155
Bishr b. Ghiyāth al-Muraisī, 75, 122, 123
Bishr b. Marwān, 108
Bishr b. al-Mu'tamir, 25, 56, 59

Ḍaḥḥāk b. Qais, 117
Dawūd al-Jawāribī, 89, 161
Dharr, 124
Ḍirār b. 'Amr, 26, 76, 85
Dhu'l-Khuwaiṣira al-Tamīmī, 100
Dhu'l-Thudayya *see* Ḥurqūṣ b. Zubair

Elijah, 148
Enoch, 148, 149

Faḍl b. Dakīn, 163
Faḍl al-Ḥadathī, 25, 53, 55
Faḍl b. 'Isā al-Raqqāshī, 117, 121
Faḍl b. Shādhān, 163
Fāris b. Ḥātim b. Māhawaih, 146
Fāṭima, 19, 51, 132, 143, 152, 163
Fāṭima, daughter of 'Alī b. Mūsā al-Kāẓim, 146
Fāṭima, daughter of Ḥusain b. Ḥasan b. 'Alī, 143
Fuḍail al-Rassān, 136

Gabriel, 37, 92, 139, 152, 155, 162
Ghailān al-Dimashqī, 24, 43, 119, 121, 123
Ghālib b. Shādhak, 110
Ghassān al-Kūfī, 120, 121

Ḥabba al-'Irnī, 163
Ḥabīb b. Abū Thābit, 163
Ḥabīb b. Murra, 117
Ḥafṣ b. Abu'l-Miqdām, 116
Ḥafṣ al-Fard, 26, 76
Ḥajjāj, 102, 106, 108
Ḥakam b. Umayya, 51
Ḥammād b. Abū Sulaimān, 124
Ḥamza b. Adrak, 110
Ḥārith al-A'war, 163
Ḥārith al-Ibāḍī, 116
Ḥārith b. 'Umaira, 108
Hāritha b. Badr al-'Itābī, 102
Hārūn al-Rashīd, 26, 145
Hārūn b. Sa'd al-'Ijlī, 163
Ḥasan b. 'Alī, 22, 23, 51, 126, 132, 135, 136, 138, 141, 149, 152
Ḥasan b. 'Alī b. Fuḍāl, 146
Ḥasan b. 'Alī b. Muḥammad b. 'Alī al-Riḍa, 24, 146, 148
Ḥasan b. 'Alī b. Muḥammad b. al-Ḥanafīya, 129
Ḥasan b. 'Alī, Nāṣir al-Ḥaqq, 138
Ḥasan al-'Askarī al-Zakī, 24, 145, 146, 147
Ḥasan al-Baṣrī, 24, 43, 44, 45, 46
Ḥasan b. al-Ḥasan, 23
Ḥasan b. Muḥammad b. 'Alī b. Abū Ṭālib, 122, 124

Ḥasan al-Ṣabbāḥ, 167, 168, 169, 170
Ḥasan b. Ṣāliḥ b. Hayy, 137
Hāshim b. Bashīr, 163
Ḥāzim b. 'Alī, 111
Hishām b. 'Abd al-Malik, 43, 134, 153
Hishām b. 'Amr al-Fuwaṭī, 25, 62, 63
Hishām b. al-Ḥakam, 25, 50, 71, 73, 158, 159, 160, 163
Hishām b. Sālim al-Jawāliqī, 158, 159, 161
Hubaira b. Biryam, 163
Hūd, 15
Ḥurqūṣ b. Zuhair al-Bajalī, 99, 100
Ḥusain b. 'Alī, 22, 23, 51, 126, 127, 132, 135, 136, 138, 141, 143, 149, 152
Ḥusain b. Ishkāb, 163
Ḥusain al-Karābīsī, 109
Ḥusain b. Muḥammad al-Najjār, 26, 74, 75
Ḥusain b. al-Raqqād, 100
Ḥusain b. Zaid b. Muḥammad b. Ismā'īl b. Ḥasan b. Zaid, 138

Iblīs, 103, 120
Ibn Jarmūz, 21
Ibn Qibba, 163
Ibn al-Rāwandī, 53, 61, 64, 123, 159
Ibrāhīm, 106
Ibrāhīm b. 'Adbullāh b. Ḥasan b. Ḥasan, 23, 132, 134, 163
Ibrāhīm b. Sa'īd, 163
Ibrāhīm b. al-Sindī, 60
Idrīs b. 'Abdullāh al-Ḥasanī, 43
'Ijlī, Mukram b. 'Abdullāh, 113
'Ikrima, 117
'Imrān b. Ḥiṭṭān, 103, 117
'Īsā b. al-Haitham, 25, 60
'Īsā b. Hāmān, 134
'Īsā b. Ja'far, 145
'Īsā b. Mūsā, 155
'Īsā al-Ṣūfī, 25
Isfarā'īnī, 26, 84
Isḥāq b. Ja'far al-Ṣādiq, 141
Isḥaq b. Zaid b. al-Ḥārith al-Anṣārī, 130
Iskāfī, 25, 52, 60, 63
Ismā'īl b. Ja'far al-Ṣādiq, 23, 141, 144, 163, 164
Ismā'īl b. Sumai', 117

Jābir al-Ja'fī, 163
Ja'far (al-Ṣādiq), 23, 132, 134, 138, 141, 142, 143, 144, 145, 149, 154, 155, 156
Ja'far b. 'Alī, 24, 146, 147
Ja'far b. Ḥarb, 25, 53, 59, 60, 137
Ja'far b. Mubashshir, 25, 53, 60, 137
Jāḥiẓ, 26, 63, 64
Jahm b. Ṣafwạn, 26, 72, 73, 74, 113, 117
Jesus (son of Mary), 15, 145, 154, 162
John, 12
Joshua b. Nūn, 150
Jubbā'ī, 26, 43, 65, 66, 67, 68
Juwainī, 83, 84

Ka'bī, 48, 49, 50, 53, 56, 58, 60, 64, 65, 75, 89, 105, 109, 115, 159
Kaisān, 126
Kathīr al-Nawā al-Abtar, 137
Khadīja, 163
Khalaf al-Khārijī, 110
Khālid b. 'Adbullāh al-Qasrī, 131, 152
Khālidī, 119
al-Khayyāṭ, Abu 'l-Ḥusain, 25, 64, 65
Kuhmus, 89
Kulthūm b. Ḥabīb, 118
Kuthayyir, 128

Lot, 15
Luke, 12

Ma'bad b. 'Abd al-Raḥmān, 112
Ma'bad al-Juhanī, 24, 43
al-Mahdī, 165
Maḥmūd b. Subuktigin, 27

Maimūn b. Khālid, 106, 109, 110
Mālik b. Anas, 78, 88
Ma'mūn, 24, 26, 61
Manṣūr, Abū Ja'far, 24, 43, 132, 134, 135, 144, 164
Manṣūr b. al-Aswad, 163
Mark, 12
Ma'rūf b. Sa'īd al-Kūfī, 131
Marwān b. al-Ḥakam, 21, 52
Marwān b. Muḥammad, 114
Mary, 92
Matthew, 12
Messiah, 53, 54
Michael, 153, 155
Mis'ar b. Fadakī al-Tamīmī, 21, 98
Moses, 15, 90, 91, 150, 164
Mu'ādh b. Jabal, 140
Mu'ammar b. 'Abbād al-Sulamī, 25, 57, 58, 59
Mu'āwiya b. Abū Sufyān, 21, 22, 52, 88, 97, 101, 102
Muḍar, 89
Mufaḍḍal al-Sairafī, 155
Mufaḍḍal b. 'Umar, 145
Mughīra b. Sa'īd al-'Ijlī, 152, 153, 163
al-Muhallab b. Abū Ṣufra, 102
Muḥammad (the Prophet), 8, 10, 17, 18, 19, 20, 21, 37, 45, 51, 52, 54, 64, 75, 76, 86, 87, 88, 89, 91, 92, 99, 100, 103, 106, 113, 115, 116, 117, 118, 120, 122, 123, 124, 126, 129, 132, 133, 134, 135, 136, 138, 139, 140, 141, 144, 148, 151, 152, 153, 156, 163, 164, 166, 170
Muḥammad b. 'Abd al-Raḥmān, 163
Muḥammad b. 'Abdullāh b. Ḥasan b. Ḥasan, 23, 132, 134, 152, 163
Muḥammad b. 'Adbullāh b. Ḥasan b. Ḥusain, 135
Muḥammad b. 'Abdullāh b. Ṭāhir, 135
Muḥammad b. 'Ajlān, 163
Muḥammad b. 'Alī b. 'Abdullāh b. 'Abbās, 129, 132
Muḥammad b. 'Alī al-Riḍā, 23, 24, 130, 131, 145, 146, 147
Muḥammad al-Bāqir, 23, 131, 133, 134, 136, 142, 149, 152, 153, 160, 165
Muḥammad b. al-Haiṣam, 27, 92, 94, 95, 96
Muḥammad b. al-Ḥanafīya, 22, 126, 127, 128, 129
Muḥammad b. Ḥarb, 117
Muḥammad b. Ḥasan, 124
Muḥammad b. Ḥasan (the awaited one), 24, 145, 149
Muḥammad b. Ḥasan b. 'Alī . . . , 24
Muḥammad b. Ḥasan al-'Askarī, 145
Muḥammad b. 'Īsā, 89
Muḥammad b. 'Īsā Barghūth, 75, 117
Muḥammad b. Ismā'īl b. Ja'far al-Ṣādiq, 144, 164
Muḥammad b. Ja'far b. Muḥammad al-Ṣādiq, 23, 141
Muḥammad b. Maslama al-Anṣārī, 118
Muḥammad b. Naṣr, 138
Muḥammad b. al-Nu'mān (Abu Ja'far), 160, 161
Muḥammad b. al-Qāsim b. 'Alī b. Ḥusain b. 'Alī, 135
Muḥammad b. Rizq, 110
Muḥammad b. Ṣadaqa, 117
Muḥammad b. Shabīb, 25, 53, 119, 121, 123
Muḥammad b. Suwaid, 25, 60
Muḥammad al-Taqī al-Jawād, *see* Muḥammad b. 'Alī al-Riḍā
Muḥammad b. Yaḥyā b. Abū Shumait
Muḥārib b. Ziyād, 124
Muḥāsibı, Ḥārith b. Asad, 26, 78
Muḥriz b. Hilāl, 102
Mukhtār b. Abū 'Ubaid al-Thaqafī, 126, 127, 128
Muqanna', 131

Muqātil b. Sulaimān, 88, 122, 124, 161
Mūsā b. 'Imrān, 25, 53
Mūsā al-Kāẓim, 23, 141, 144, 145, 149, 160
Muslim b. 'Ubais b. Karīz b. Ḥabīb, 102
Mustalim b. Sa'īd, 163
Mu'taṣim, 26, 63, 135
al-Mutawakkil, 26, 48, 63
Muwais b. 'Imrān al-Baṣrī, 117, 121

Nāfi', 102, 103, 104, 106
Na'īm b. Ḥammād al-Miṣrī, 161
Najda b. 'Āmir al-Ḥanafī, 104, 105, 106
Nāsir al-Aṭrūsh, 134
Naṣr b. al-Ḥajjāj, 51
Naṣr b. Sayyār, 26, 113
Nāwūs, 143
Naẓẓām, 25, 48, 49, 50, 51, 52, 53, 54
Noah, 13, 90

Qādī 'Abd al-Jabbār, 26, 70
al-Qā'im, 165
Qais b. Abū Ḥāzim, 118
al-Qalānisī, Abu 'l-'Abbās, 26, 78
Qatarī b. al-Fujā'a al-Māzinī, 102
Qudaid b. Ja'far, 124

Rāwandī, Aḥmad b. Yaḥya, 163
Rizām b. Razm, 131
Rushaid al-Ṭūsī, 112

Sa'd b. Abū Waqqāṣ, 21, 118, 141
Sa'd b. 'Ubāda al-Ansārī, 19
Sa'd b. Zaid, 141
al-Ṣādiq *see* Ja'far
Saffāḥ, Abu'l-'Abbās, 132, 134
Ṣāḥib b. 'Abbād, 26, 59
Sa'īd b. al-'Ās, 21
Sa'īd b. Jubair, 124
Sa'īd b. Zaid, 101

Ṣakhr b. Ḥabīb al-Tamīmī, 102
Ṣāliḥ (prophet), 15
Ṣāliḥ b. Mikhraq al-'Abdī, 102
Ṣāliḥ b. Musarriḥ, 108
Ṣāliḥ Qubba b. Ṣubaiḥ b. 'Amr, 117, 121
Ṣāliḥ b. 'Umar al-Ṣāliḥī, 119, 123
Sālim b. Abū Hafṣa, 163
Sālim b. Abu'l-Ja'd, 163
Sālim b. Ahwāz al-Māzinī, 26, 73
Salama b. Kuhail, 163
al-Ṣalt b. Abu'l-Ṣalt, 109
al-Sayyid al-Ḥimyarī, 128
al-Sha'bī, 163
Shabīb b. Yazid b. Nu'aim al-Shaibānī, 108
al-Shāfi'ī, 138
Shahrastānī, 66, 68, 84, 148, 149, 170
Shaibān b. Salama, 112
al-Shakkāl, 163
Shīth, 34
Shu'aib (prophet), 15
Shu'aib b. Muḥammad, 110, 111
Shu'ba, 163
Sindī b. Shāhik, 145
Sufyān al-Thaurī, 78
Sulaimān b. Jarīr, 136

Ṭalḥa, 21, 45, 88, 103, 136, 141
Ṭalq b. Ḥabīb, 124
Tāwūs, 163
Tha'laba b. 'Āmir, 111
Tha'labī, 117
Thumāma b. Ashras al-Numairī, 25, 61, 63
Thuwair b. Abū Fakhita, 163

'Ubāda al-Anṣārī, 19
'Ubaid al-Mukta'ib, 120
'Ubaida b. al-Hilāl al-Yashkarī, 102
'Ubaidullāh b. Mūsā, 163
Ubayy b. Ka'b, 76, 140
'Umair b. Bayān al-'Ijlī, 155
'Umar b. Abū 'Afif, 131
'Umar b. al-Khaṭṭāb, 18, 19, 20, 51, 87, 101, 133, 136, 139, 140, 151, 153

'Umar b. 'Ubaidullāh b. Mu'ammar al-Tamīmī, 105
'Urwa b. Jarīr, 99, 101
'Urwa b. Udhaina, 101
Usāma b. Zaid, 18, 118, 139
'Uthmān b. 'Abdullāh b. Mu'ammar al-Tamīmī, 102
'Uthmān b. Abu'l-Ṣalt, 109
'Uthmān b. 'Affān, 20, 21, 45, 51, 52, 87, 97, 99, 100, 101, 102, 103, 136, 137, 141
'Uthmān b. Hayyān al-Muzanī, 106
'Uthmān b. Khālid al-Ṭawīl, 46
'Uthmān b. Mākhūn, 102

Wakī' b. al-Jarrāḥ, 163
al-Walīd, 106
al-Walīd b. 'Uqba, 21, 52
Waṣil b. 'Aṭā', 24, 43, 44, 45, 46, 132, 133
Wāthiq, 26

Yaḥyā b. Abū Shumait, 144
Yaḥyā b. Ādam, 163
Yaḥyā b. Aṣdam, 114
Yaḥyā b. Kāmil, 117
Yaḥyā b. Khālid b. Barmak, 145
Yaḥyā b. 'Umar, 135, 136
Yaḥyā b. Zaid b. 'Alī, 134
al-Yamān, 108, 117, 120
Yazīd b. 'Āṣim al-Muḥāribī, 99, 101
Yazīd al-Nāqiṣ, 24
Yazīd b. 'Umar b. Hubaira, 155
Yazīd b. Unaisa, 116
Yūnus (prophet), 120
Yūnus b. 'Abd al-Raḥmān al-Qummī, 161, 163
Yūnus al-Aswārī, 24, 25, 52
Yūnus b. 'Awn al-Numairī, 119
Yūsuf b. 'Umar al-Thaqafī, 153

Zaid b. 'Alī b. Ḥusain b. 'Alī b. Abū Ṭālib, 23, 132, 133, 134, 135, 140, 141
Zaid b. Ḥuṣain al-Ṭā'ī, 21, 98, 101
Zaid b. Thābit, 140
Zain al-'Ābidīn *see* 'Alī b. Ḥusain
Ziyād b. 'Abd al-Raḥmān al-Shaibānī (Abū Khālid), 112, 113
Ziyād b. Abīhi, 101, 102
Ziyād b. al-Aṣfar, 116, 117
Ziyād b. Mundhir al-'Abdī, 138
Zubair, 21, 45, 88, 126, 136, 141
Zubair b. Mākhūn, 102
Zurāra b. A'yun, 145, 160

Index of sects

'Ābidīya, 92
'Adlīya, 41
Afṭaḥīya, 143
'Ainīya, 152
'Ajārida, 99, 108, 111, 115
Akhnasīya, 112
'Alawīya, 135
'Albā'īya, 151, 152
'Ammārīya, 23
Ash'arites, 72, 78, 91
Aṭrāfīya, 110
'Aṭwīya, 105
'Awnīya, 107, 108
Azāriqa, 99, 102, 103, 104, 116

Bahshamīya, 65
Baihasīya, 99, 106, 107, 108
Barghūthīya, 74
Bātinīya, 144, 163, 165
Batrīya, 135, 137, 163
Bayānīya, 130
Bazīghīya, 155
Bid'īya, 114
Bishrīya, 56

Carmathians, 165

Dhimmīya, 152
Ḍirārīya, 72, 76
Duqūlīya, 150

Fudaikīya, 105

Ghailānīya, 119
Ghālīya, 125, 149–51
Ghassanīya, 120

Ḥadathīya, 53, 54
Ḥafṣīya, 116
Haiṣamīya, 92
Ḥamzīya, 110
Ḥārithīya, 116, 130
Hāshimīya, 128, 129
Ḥashwīya, 72, 81, 89
Ḥāzimīya, 111, 114
Ḥimārīya, 146
Hishāmīya, 62, 81, 89, 158
Hudhailīya, 46

Ibāḍīya, 99, 114, 115, 116, 117
'Ijlīya, 155
Imāmīya, 125, 135, 139, 140, 141, 149
Incarnationists, 15
Isḥāqīya, 92, 161, 163
Iskāfiya, 23, 25
Ismā'īlīya, 125, 163–7

Jabrīya, 11,15, 40, 72, 119
Ja'farīya, 25
Jāḥiẓīya, 63
Jahmīya, 72
Jārūdīya, 135, 163
Jubbā'īya, 65

Ka'bīya, 64
Kaisānīya, 125, 126, 128, 132
Kāmilīya, 151
Karrāmīya, 11, 27, 78, 92, 93, 94, 95, 96, 97
Kayyālīya, 156
Khābiṭīya, 53, 54
Khalafīya, 110
Khaṭṭābīya, 154, 155
Khawārij, 11, 12, 16, 21, 22, 24, 40, 44, 70, 98, 99, 101, 102, 103, 105, 108, 109, 110, 111, 112, 117, 119, 121, 124, 126, 129, 161
Khayyāṭīya, 64
Khurramīya, 130, 131, 150, 154
Kūdhīya, 150
Kullābīya, 72

Ma'badīya, 112
Maimūnīya, 109, 110
Majhūlīya, 114
Ma'lūmīya, 114
Mamṭūra, 23, 145
Manṣūrīya, 153, 154
Mazdakīya, 130, 150, 165
Mīmīya, 152
Mu'ammarīya, 57, 155
Mubārakīya, 23, 144
Mubayyiḍa, 131, 150
Mufaḍḍalīya, 144, 155
Muḥakkima, 99, 100, 101, 116; *see also* Khawarij
Muḥammadīya, 110
Mughīrīya, 152
Mujassima, 11, 15, 96
Mukhtārīya, 126
Mukramīya, 113, 114
Murdārīya, 59, 98
Murji'a, 11, 40, 44, 108, 119, 121, 122, 123, 124
Mūsawīya, 134, 144, 163
Mushabbiha (anthropomorphists), 78, 88, 90, 96, 141, 149
Mustadrika, 74
Mu'tazila, 11, 15, 26, 39, 40, 41, 43, 44, 45, 46, 48, 49, 54, 56, 57, 60, 61, 62, 63, 64, 65, 66, 69, 70, 71, 72, 73, 74, 75, 76, 77, 78, 81, 82, 83, 85, 88, 91, 97, 116, 121, 125, 132, 136, 138, 141, 142, 149, 150, 160

Najdāt al-'Ādhirīya, 99, 104, 105, 108, 116
Najjārīya, 11, 72, 74
Nāwūsīya, 143
Naẓẓāmīya, 48
Nu'mānīya, 160
Nuṣairīya, 161, 163

Orthodox, 10, 26, 39, 44, 70, 78, 88, 92, 125, 141

Qadarites, 11, 12, 15, 16, 41, 44, 46, 57, 107, 110, 119, 123, 124, 142, 161
Qarāmiṭa, *see* Carmathians
Qaṭ'iya, 23, 145

Rafiḍites, 16, 51, 70
Rizāmīya, 131, 132
Rushaidīya, 112

Saba'īya, 150
Ṣāliḥīya, 123, 135, 137, 138
Ṣaltīya, 109
Shabībiya, 108
Shaibānīya, 112, 113
Shī'a, 11, 12, 40, 78, 89, 119, 126, 128, 133, 141, 142, 144, 145, 146, 148, 150, 160, 161, 162, 163, 165, 169
Shu'aibīya, 110
Shumaiṭīya, 144
Ṣifātīya, 12, 39, 40, 41, 72, 74, 77, 78, 82, 92
Sinbādhīya, 150
Ṣufrīya Ziyādīya, 99, 116
Sulaimānīya, 135, 136, 137

Tafḍīlīya, 141, 149
Ta'līmīya, 144, 165
Taumanīya, 122
Tha'āliba, 99, 107, 111, 112, 113, 115
Thaubānīya, 121, 122
Thumāmīya, 61
Transmigrationists, 15

Tūnīya, 92
Twelvers, 145, 148, 163; *see also* Imamīya

'Ubaidīya, 120, 122
'Umairīya, 155
'Ushrīya, 112

Wāḥidīya, 92
Wa'īdīya, 11, 40, 44, 98, 119, 121, 141, 149

Wāqifa (Bāqirīya, Ja'farīya), 142
Wāqifīya, 106, 107
Wāṣilīya, 43

Yazīdīya, 116
Yūnusīya, 119, 161, 122

Za'farānīya, 74, 75
Zaidīya, 125, 132, 134
Zarīnīya, 92
Zurārīya, 160

Index of subjects

abrogation, 127
accident(s), 47, 50, 64, 65, 66, 70, 76, 82, 93
acquisition, 72, 75, 76, 82, 96, 111, 115
act(s), deed(s) of man: created by God, 46, 47, 73, 75, 76, 110, 111, 114, 115; created by man, 66, 109, 114; as movements, 49; as willed by God, 49
agreement of community, 51
analogy, 38, 51, 100
animal communities, 55
anthropomorphism, 78, 88, 89. 90, 92, 93, 95, 120, 150, 152, 158, 160, 165
apostle(s), apostleship, 5, 11
arithmetical principles and procedures, reason for use of, 27, 28, 29
asās, 166
association and dissociation, 99, 107, 108, 109, 111, 112, 116, 117, 125
attributes of God: (those) applicable to God, 73; aspects of essence, 43, 46, 79; authority of Qur'ān for, 43; as causal in meaning only, 165; continued to be manifested, 48; created, 160; denial of, 8, 16, 41, 42, 64, 73, 74, 76, 77, 88, 165; as entities subsisting in essence, 26, 80; eternity of, 77, 80; identity with essence, 25, 41, 42, 46, 67; kinds of, 77; known from acts, 79; like those of creatures, 26, 77; metaphorical, 42; as modes, 43, 46, 67, 68, 70; as negative in meaning, 76; reduction of, 43, 70; revealed attributes, meaning of, 77, 78, 85, 88, 89, 90, 96; as subsisting in essence, 79, 80, 96
authority, authoritative in religious law, 48, 53, 76

badā', 127, 136, 150, 164
Battles of Camel and Ṣiffīn: both, 45, 98, 100; Camel, 132; Ṣiffın, 99
belief, believer, 63, 74, 78, 85, 87, 88, 97, 114, 115, 116, 120, 122, 123

capacity, incapacity, 47, 49, 56, 61, 66, 75, 76, 79, 109, 114, 115, 116, 159
child, children: of believers and unbelievers till they decide, 108, 109, 111; of polytheists, 103, 108, 111, 115
compensation, 70
correspondence(s), 156, 157, 167
creation, origination, 59

creation, origination and annihilation, 93, 94

day of judgment, 60, 122
death, appointed time of, 48
designation, 144, 164
determinism, predetermination, 26, 44, 72, 73, 79, 113
din, 33
dissimulation, 103, 104, 105, 112, 117, 136
divine, divinity, 152, 153, 154, 159, 162, 163
divisions of mankind, 8, 9

exoteric and esoteric, 62, 129, 165

faith: qualities of, 74, 85, 107, 111, 120, 121, 122, 123; *see also imān*; at time of death, 62, 111, 114; *see also* final acts; faith and deeds, 45, 119, 121; faith and polytheism, 116
fāsiq, 52, 53, 66, 122
final state/act, 62, 116
first questioning, doubt, error and later manifestations: in Muslim community, 8, 16–27; in universe, 8, 12–16
forbidden and obligatory, 106, 107
forgiveness, 108, 120, 122
free will, 56, 88, 121, 123; *see also* man, power of
furū', furī, 38

God: appearances in human form, 155, 162, *see also* incarnation; attributes of, *see* attribures of God; change in, 127, *see also badā'*; cognition(s), *see* knowledge; commanding and forbidding, 58, 80, 81, 86, 115, 154, 166; as creator, 48, 50, 59, 61, 63, 82, 83, 84, 93, 94, 111, 115, 152, 153, 154, 166; discussion of, 151; doing good or best for man, 42, 49, 57, 67, 96; eternity of, 41, 42, 59, 68, 166; favour, 42, 69, 86; as finite, 159; form of, 131, 152, 159, 161, *see also* anthropomorphism; grace, 42, 56, 67, 69, 86, 97; hearing, 48, 65, 68, 69, 85, 94; help and abandonment, 87; justice of, 39, 42, 43, 44, 69, 79, 86, 110; knowledge of, 25, 59, 62, 67, 73, 76, 79, 80, 96, 113, 120, 158, 159, 160; in likeness of man, 120, *see also* anthropomorphism; manifestation of characteristics continued, 49; most proper, special, characteristic, 41, 42, 68, 84; obligations of, 57, 70, 86, 115; omnipresence, 75, 151; power of, 25, 49, 52, 56, 60, 67, 69, 76, 80, 93, 109; proof of existence, 62, 79, 84, 85; *qadīm*, *see* eternity of; quiddity, 76, 85; seeing, 48, 65, 69, 85, 94; speech (word) of, speaker, 39, 42, 58, 63, 75, 80, 90, 91, 92, 166; as substrate of accidents, 93, 95; on the throne, 78, 92, 93, 95, 159, 161; unity of, 39, 42, 92, 115, 169; will, willing, 46, 48, 49, 56, 58, 63, 65, 66, 74, 76, 81, 94, 109, 111, 142, 159, 161; word, 75, 80, 159, 166
good and evil: attributes apart from existence, 83; decreed by God, 90, *see also qadar*; known by reason, 52; nature of, 26, 49
Great Resurrection, 166

heaven (paradise) and hell, 46–7, 54–5, 60, 62, 64, 74, 122, 154, 155, 158
holy war, 106
ḥujja, 123, 147–9, 164
hypocrite(s), 97, 115

ignorance, 104, 105, 107, 110, 114, 165

iḥsān, 37–8
ijmā', *see* agreement of community
ijtihād, 104, 136, 137
imām(s), imāmate: concealment and return, 23, 126, 128, 141, 150; conferring of, succession to, 22, 25, 43, 51, 62, 70, 83, 97, 121, 125, 136, 143, 146, 163, *see also* designation; divine prerogatives, 149, 150–1, 152, 154–5; hidden, 144, 149, 156, 164; identity of rightful, 129, 132, 143, 144, 156; as judge, 140; knowledge, 129, 136, 149, 160; of man of lesser excellence, 133, 134, 136, 137, 138; necessity of, 100, 105, 125, 137, 139, 147, 148, 154, 164, 170; and prophethood, 151, 152, 154, 159, 170; qualifications for an, 23, 76, 100, 121, 125, 132, 134, 138, 147, 156; rebellion against, 99, 100, 109; return after death, 23, 126; in series of seven, 164; sinlessness of, 125, 159; transmission of, 125, 142, 163; two at same time, 97, 110, 132, 138
īmān, 37, 38, 45, 66, 75, 85, 89, 97, 120
incarnation, 91, 126, 129, 130, 131, 150, 151
intermediate position, 24, 44–5, 52, 61
irjā', 119, 122, 123
Islām, 34, 37
islām, 37–8
Islamic sects, principles on which numbered, 8, 10–11
istiṭā'a, *see* capacity
'iwaḍ, *see* compensation

jabr, 44, 72
jamā'a, 33
judgment: as belonging to God, 16, 99–100; suspension/reservation of, 107, 111–12, 119

kalām, origin of name, 24
kasb, *see* acquisition
knowledge of God, man's, 57, 61, 63, 76, 79, 114, 123–4, 137, 159, 168–70

the lawful and unlawful, forbidden, 107, 112, 114–15, 130, 152, 154
lufṭ, *see* God, grace of

al-Mahdī, 165; mahdī, 143
man: act(s), deed(s), *see* act(s), deed(s) of man; knowledge, 61, 63, 64; knowledge of God, *see* knowledge of God, man's; nature of, 50, 58; obligations towards God, *see* obligation(s); power of, 24, 42, 44, 46, 49, 52, 64, 72, 73, 81–3, 109, 110, 111, 124; *see also qadar*; responsibility, 107–8, 110; will, 58–9, 61, 63
mankind, beliefs of, 31
marriage(s), 99, 109, 112, 114, 117
Messiah, 53; as creator, 53; prerogatives of, 53
metampsychosis, 126, 130, 150, 151; *see also* transmigration of souls
milla, 33–4
minhāj, 33
miracle(s), 87–8, 115
movement: theory of 'leaps', 50; and rest, 46–7, 167
mujtahid, 104
mu'min, 45, 66, 120
muslim, 64, 106, 107
Muslim community, first and its manifestations, 16–27, 53
muwāfāt, *see* final state

names and judgments, 85
naskh, 127; *see also* abrogation
nāṭiq, 166
New Message, 165, 167
non-existent and thing, 25, 63, 65, 68, 70
nuqabā', 164

obedience (and disobedience), 87, 115, 116, 119, 120, 122
obedience, blind, 3, 138
obligation(s): as acts of grace, 42, 67; freedom from, ceasing, 154, 166; ignorance excusing from, 104, 105, 110; made known by reason, 42, 47, 52, 60, 61, 66, 74, 110; made known by revelation, 39, 76, 86

Path, 158
perfection, 155, 166
polytheist(s), polytheism, 64, 104, 112, 116, 117, 120
postponement, *see irjā'*
prayer, 123, 155
promise and warning, 39, 42, 52, 53, 85
proof, establishment of, 48
proof of prophet(s), 123
prophet(s), prophethood, prophecy, 34, 63, 70, 86, 103, 122, 125, 154, 158, 159, 162, 166, 170

qadar: belongs to God, 37, 41, 44, 46; belong to man, 24, 43, 46, 49, 62, 66, 107, 121, *see also* man, power of; belongs to both God and man, 41; as medium, 142–3
qā'im, 23, 24, 143, 144, 145, 147, 148, 149, 156, 157, 158, 164, 168
qiyās, *see* analogy
Qur'ān: as body, 65; as created, 60, 74, 75, 88; miraculours nature of, 25, 52, 60, 87; as uncreated, eternal, 75; versions of, 76; *see also* God, word of

reason: knowledge able to acquire, 52, 53, 56, 61, 66, 86, 97, 137; obligations of, 42, 47, 52, 60, 61, 74, 75, 76, 97
religion, 120; in what consists, 22, 38, 104, 126, 131
religious and religious communities, 33
religious beliefs, 8
repentance, 57, 75, 86, 105, 113
revelation: given to all believers, 155; literal truth of, 87
revelation and reason, 39, 42, 47, 52, 75, 76, 85, 86, 97
reward, 69
reward(s) and punishment(s), 42, 44, 45, 57, 60, 75, 76, 83, 86, 96, 104, 108, 111, 120, 122

ṣalāt, *see* prayer
salvation, 10, 161, 168
Scale, 158
secondary effects, 25, 56, 60, 61, 156
sharı'a, 22, 34, 66, 76, 105, 110, 116, 156, 158, 167
shir'a, 33
sin(s), sinner(s), grave, 44, 53, 66, 75, 85, 98, 99, 103, 109, 112, 115, 117, 119, 122, 124
substance(s), body(ies), 50, 57, 64, 65, 66, 67, 76, 82, 84, 162
substance(s), body(ies) and accidents, 50, 57, 64, 65, 82
suffering, 69
sunna, 10, 33, 88, 117, 136, 149, 166
sustenance, 47–8

taqīya, *see* dissimulation
taqlīd, *see* obedience
ta'ṭīl, *see* attributes of God, denial of
tawallud, *see* secondary effects
tawaqquf, 150; *see also* imām, imāmate, concealment and return
Throne, 156; *see also* God, on the throne
transmigration of souls, 54, 55, 129, 131, 151
truth and falsehood, 10, 169
'the trust', 153

unbelief, 106, 107, 117, 123
unbeliever(s), infidel(s), 60, 61, 63, 64, 74, 75, 104, 106, 107, 113, 114, 116–17, 120, 122, 123, 135; *see also* intermediate position
uṣūl, *uṣūlī*, 38

vision of God, beatific vision, 42, 55, 66, 74, 75, 76, 85

waṣī, 150, 166
world(s), realm(s), universe, 167; creation, formation of, 53, 61, 166; end of, 115, 155, 157; kinds of, 54, 156–8

zakāt, 111, 112
ẓāhir and *bāṭin*, *see* exoteric and esoteric